EQUALITY AND UNIVERSALITY

EQUALITY AND UNIVERSALITY
Essays in Social and Political Theory

André Béteille

OXFORD
UNIVERSITY PRESS

OXFORD
UNIVERSITY PRESS

YMCA Library Building, Jai Singh Road, New Delhi 110 001

Oxford University Press is a department of the University of Oxford. It furthers the
University's objective of excellence in research, scholarship, and education
by publishing worldwide in

Oxford   New York

Athens Auckland Bangkok Bogota Buenos Aires Cape Town
Chennai Dar es Salaam Delhi Florence Hong Kong Istanbul Karachi
Kolkata Kuala Lumpur Madrid Melbourne Mexico City Mumbai Nairobi
Paris São Paulo Shanghai Taipei Tokyo Toronto Warsaw

Oxford is a registered trade mark of Oxford University Press
in the UK and in certain other countries

Published in India
By Oxford University Press, New Delhi

©Oxford University Press 2002

ISBN 019 566260 1

Typeset by Jojy Philip in Adobe Garamond
Printed in India at Roopak Printers, New Delhi 110 032
Published by Manzar Khan, Oxford University Press
YMCA Library Building, Jai Singh Road, New Delhi 110 001

Dedicated
to the memory of

SURAJIT CHANDRA SINHA

Footfalls echo in the memory
Down the passage which we did not take
Towards the door we never opened
Into the rose-garden.

Contents

Acknowledgements

I have incurred many debts in the writing of this book, and I would like to thank the following persons in particular: Abhijit Dasgupta, Vinay Srivastava and Virginius Xaxa in the University of Delhi; David Lockwood, Alan Macfarlane and Jonathan Parry in England; Dipankar Gupta in the Jawaharlal Nehru University; and Ramachandra Guha whose exact location is often a matter of doubt.

The chapters of the book are based on papers published earlier. Several of them have been revised, rewritten and expanded to meet the requirements of the book, and in some cases the title has been altered to meet the same requirement. A few of the pieces, though published earlier, were written after the book was conceived and with its subject matter in mind. Appendix I was published before the volume was conceived but Appendix II was written after it had acquired a certain shape and for inclusion in it; both are republished without change.

Chapter 1 is a revised version, with a change of title, of an article first published in Tim Ingold (ed.), *Companion Encyclopedia of Anthropology*, Routledge, pp. 1010–39, 1994. Chapter 2 is a revised and substantially expanded version with a change of title, of 'The Mismatch between Class and Status', *Brit. Jnl. of Sociology*, 43(3): 513–26, 1996; it was written originally as a tribute to David Lockwood of whose work I reconfirm my admiration. Chapter 3 is reproduced from *Sociological Bulletin*, 45(1): 15–27, 1996; I acknowledge my gratitude to Professor Yogendra Singh for inviting me to deliver the special lecture at Bhopal on which it is based. Chapter 4 is reproduced from C. J. Fuller (ed.), *Caste Today*, Delhi: Oxford University Press, pp. 150–79, 1996. Chapter 5 was written for a conference in Delhi, organized by the Konrad Adenauer Stiftung to which I express my thanks for consent to publish it here; it was written specifically for inclusion in this volume.

Chapter 6 is reproduced from my book, *The Backward Classes in Contemporary India*, Delhi: Oxford University Press, pp. 45–69, 1992. It is based on the V. T. Krishnamachari Memorial Lecture delivered at the Institute of Economic Growth on 12 November 1990 at the height of the agitations that brought down the V. P. Singh Government. Chapter 7 is reproduced from *Contributions to Indian Sociology*, 25(1): 3–28, 1991. Chapter 8 is reproduced with some modifications from *Granthana* VII (1&2): 21–38, 1999; it is based on the Raja Rammohun Roy Memorial Lecture delivered in Calcutta on 22 May 1999. Chapter 9 is based on the inaugural M. N. Srinivas Memorial Lecture delivered at Amritsar on 27 December 2001 and although it was written for inclusion in this volume, it has been published also in *Sociological Bulletin*, 51(1): 3–27, 2002; I am grateful to Professor B. S. Baviskar, then President of the Indian Sociological Society and Professor Aneeta A. Minocha, then its Secretary, for making the occasion of the lecture a memorable one for me. Chapter 10 is a revised and substantially expanded version of a note first published under the same title in *Cambridge Anthropology*, 17(1): 1–12, 1994; the note was written in response to an article by Alan Macfarlane to whom I record my thanks once again. The two Appendices were both published earlier in *Economic and Political Weekly*, Appendix I in vol. xxviii, no. 16, pp. 753–6, 1993, and Appendix II in vol. xxxvi, no. 45, pp. 4271–5, 2001.

The book is dedicated to the memory of Surajit Sinha whom I came to know during the difficult transition from being a student, to entering a professional career. He lit up my life when I thought I had lost my way. He gave me free access to his time, his books, and his enchanting company, and made me feel that from then onwards I could go my own way. I have rarely known a more vivid and memorable person.

A.B.

Introduction

This book is an outcome of a continuing effort to understand a number of interrelated problems that arise from the presence of large inequalities in democratic societies. The field in which these problems have their setting is vast and uneven, and without clear boundaries or signposts. So much has been written on the subject that it is difficult to add something that will both be new and receive general assent. At the same time, when viewed over a sufficiently long stretch of time, perceptions of the subject do appear to have undergone some shifts. For one thing, economists and sociologists now have a much wider array of facts on which to build their arguments about inequality and stratification.

The availability of more facts does not necessarily lead to agreed conclusions. Where basic political and moral commitments are at issue, facts tend to be used to support conclusions reached in advance of their investigation and analysis. In India when people are opposed to an economic policy, they say within months of its adoption that it is leading to a clear increase of social inequality. This is done even by social scientists who ought to know that it takes years or even decades for an economic policy to have a visible effect on society as a whole.

An important reason for disagreement is that inequality takes many different forms and equality has more than one meaning. People often talk at cross purposes because they do not always have in mind the same aspects of inequality or the same standards of equality.

The sociological approach to inequality which is the one adopted in this work is, as against the common sense approach, a differentiated one. There are inequalities among individuals and disparities between groups; inequalities of caste and of class; inequalities of income, esteem and authority; and so on. These inequalities do not all run along the same lines; they sometimes reinforce and at other times cut across each other. Where simple judgements about increase or decrease of inequality are made without taking into account the multiplicity of dimensions, the judgements tend to be defective.

There are not only different dimensions or aspects of inequality, there are also different conceptions of equality. Democratic regimes have a very different attitude towards hierarchy from the attitudes that prevailed in most political regimes of the past. Yet, though they are all opposed to hierarchy, they are not all governed by a single or uniform conception of equality. The pursuit of equality as an ideal and a value is a characteristic feature of the modern world although that pursuit is constrained by both external and internal contradictions. Some forms of inequality are constitutive of collective life and the advance of equality must contend with these. Further, this advance itself reveals that the idea of equality is made up of diverse components that are not always in harmony with each other. As a consequence, there is a wide and sometimes an increasing gap between principle and practice in social life.

This book examines the different forms of inequality as well as the limits to the pursuit of equality. Although the focus is on contemporary India, the approach is general and comparative. We learn about ourselves through comparisons with others, and in the comparisons we make, the differences are no less revealing than the similarities. Moreover, general concepts such as status, power, and class are indispensable for a deeper understanding of the structure of society and the changes taking place in it.

Contemporary Indian society has many distinctive features, and these can be brought to light only by studying it comparatively and historically. Its distinctive features do not make Indian society unique or the social processes operative in India without historical parallel. The most striking feature of Indian society from the viewpoint of a student of inequality is the transition now taking place from a relatively closed hierarchical order to a relatively open democratic one. This is not the first historical instance of such a transition. Although each transition has its own distinctive features, a great deal may be learnt by examining similar transitions that have already taken place. The two striking features of contemporary Indian society are the marked and pervasive inequalities in social practice and the repeated assertion of

egalitarian values in political ideology. The book as a whole derives its
focus from the interplay of these two contradictory features.

Chapter 1 provides a broad and general survey of the field. It traces the
roots of inequality to some of the constitutive features of society,
notably evaluation and organization (Béteille 1977: 1–72). This is followed by a discussion of inequality in the different types of society,
simple and complex, including hunter-gatherer bands at one end and
advanced industrial societies at the other. Inequalities arising from
gender, race, caste, wealth, and occupation are discussed in the process.
The ideal of equality, and the tensions between that ideal and the reality
of social stratification are taken up in the concluding section.

Chapter 2 discusses the relationship between class and status comparatively, but with special reference to modern Britain. It draws attention to the ambiguities that arise from the simultaneous use of two
different conceptions of status, the first to refer to a dimension of social
stratification and the second to the legal basis of equality in modern
societies. How we view the relationship between class and status will
depend on which of the two conceptions of status we adopt. Inequalities
of esteem and prestige are present in all societies and operate to some
extent independently of those of wealth, power, and materiel advantage. In examining inequalities in a society we have to look to the
distribution not only of material capital but also of symbolic capital.
Equality of legal status, no matter how important in modern societies,
cannot cancel out the inequalities of esteem and prestige that arise from
differences in quality and performance.

The two following chapters are devoted to the changing face of caste.
They both deal with the meaning and legitimacy assigned to caste in
contemporary India. In chapter 3 on *varna* and *jati* I discuss the two
principal ways of representing caste, and the changes now taking place
in its representation. In the classical literature of Hinduism and until
quite recent times, caste was characteristically represented in the language of *varna*. That language is rapidly becoming obsolete, and when
people speak and write about caste today, they use the language of *jati*
rather than *varna*. I have argued that this betokens an erosion in the
legitimacy of caste as an intellectual and moral system.

The discussion of the meaning and legitimacy of caste is continued
into the next chapter. Here it is shown how, despite the new lease of
life given to caste by electoral politics, it is loosening its grip over many

areas of social life. The association between caste and occupation has weakened with the emergence of an increasing number of 'caste-free' occupations. Again, although inter-caste marriages are still infrequent, the sanctions against such marriages have steadily weakened. Finally, the multitudinous rules of purity and pollution by which the system was governed in the past are decisively in retreat. These changes are most in evidence among the middle classes that emerged along with the new educational and occupational systems. At the same time, members of these classes have themselves shown the way to reawakening the loyalties of caste for mobilizing political support at elections.

Chapter 5 discusses the relations between the private and the public. It seeks to identify the distinctive features of the public as a social and moral category by means of a contrast between a society of publics and a society of communities. A society of publics comes into being through the creation of new rights for individuals as citizens. But the detachment of the individual from the bonds of kinship, caste, and community does not lead to the creation of full or substantive equality for all. The development of citizenship marks the advance of legal equality but, as shown in Chapter 2, that has to accommodate economic and social inequalities of many kinds.

'Distributive Justice and Institutional Well-being' (Chapter 6) deals with the problem of redressing the bias of past social arrangements in the direction of greater equality. In more concrete terms, it examines the programme of positive discrimination in India and tries to assess its social costs as well as its social benefits. While it addresses questions of policy, the emphasis is on policy analysis rather than policy prescription. It draws attention to the fact that at the time of the Great Mandal Agitation beginning in August 1990, both the proponents and the opponents of reservations argued their cases from the premise of equality. This brings to light the antinomies of equality which are discussed more fully in Chapter 8.

The urge towards strong measures for social justice is impelled not only by the pervasive presence of inequality but also by the social reproduction of inequality. Not only are there many different levels in society, but the same kinds of faces are reproduced at each level from one generation to the next. I discuss in Chapter 7 the processes by which the reproduction of inequality comes about in modern societies in general and Indian society in particular. I assign a crucial role to the family in transmitting not only economic or material capital but also social and cultural capital across the generations.

In Chapter 8 I deal specifically with the antinomies of equality, returning to a subject I have discussed in more broad and general terms in a recent book (Béteille 2000). Here I examine not so much the contradictions between the amplitude of social ideals and the constraints of social structure as the contradictions within the ideal of equality itself. This leads to an examination of the conflict of norms and values and the conflict between law and custom. It is not simply that hierarchical values continue to be deeply embedded in social practice but also that there are acute tensions between equality of opportunity and distributive equality (Béteille 1985b).

The weakening of hierarchical social arrangements based on estates or castes does not lead to the disappearance of inequality as such. Competition and individual mobility create and sustain their own forms of inequality. Hence the distinction between 'hierarchical' inequality based on caste and gender and 'competitive' inequality based on education, occupation, and income. The two forms of inequality coexist in contemporary India, and, although they are sometimes mutually reinforcing, they also cut across each other.

I have argued throughout the book that there are many different forms of inequality. Not all of them are equally odious or reprehensible. We must learn to discriminate among the different forms of inequality, and not condemn them all and without exception in the pursuit of an utopian fantasy. Inequalities of education, occupation, and income cannot be eliminated but they can be regulated. It is more important to ensure that certain basic rights and capacities are made universally available than to seek to eliminate inequality in every form. Chapter 10, from which the book takes its title, makes the case for universality as against equality by arguing that the aim of achieving the former is often deflected by an excessive concern for the latter.

The book has two Appendices, both of them review articles dealing with subjects of central importance to it. Appendix I is a critical appreciation of Amartya Sen's work on inequality which raises questions dealt with by a variety of disciplines. Appendix II discusses problems addressed by a number of economists and others in a book devoted to meritocracy and economic inequality. A consideration of these two books has reinforced my belief in the importance of comparative and interdisciplinary approaches to the subject matter of the present work.

1

Equality and Inequality

General and Comparative

A striking feature of the modern world is the deep and pervasive disjunction between the ideal of equality and the reality of inequality. The ideal of equality is widely endorsed and, as Sir Isaiah Berlin has put it, 'The assumption is that equality needs no reasons, only inequality does so' (1978: 84). At the same time, there is extensive and sometimes extreme inequality in the distribution of material and other resources, and in the relations between individuals and between groups and categories of every conceivable kind.

In studying inequality systematically we have to keep in mind the fact that inequalities differ not only in degree but also in kind. Inequalities in the distribution of income or of wealth are difficult to compare directly with inequalities in the distribution of power, and those in turn with inequalities of status, prestige, or esteem. Moreover, the idea of equality is not at all a simple or a homogeneous one, so that when people say they value equality, they may not all mean the same thing. There are indeed striking differences of orientation and perception between those who emphasize equality of opportunity and those who stress distributive equality or equality of result. For these reasons it may be misleading to argue about the nature and forms of inequality without keeping in mind the various meanings of equality which in our age is also an ideal and a value.

While social theorists agree that the societies in which they live are marked by many forms of inequality, there is disagreement about the inevitability of inequality. Perhaps the majority of them believe that inequality is inherent in the very nature of collective life, and some would go even further and argue that inequality or stratification is not only inevitable but also has a definite social function (Davis and Moore 1945; see also Bendix and Lipset 1966: 47–72). Others maintain that inequality or stratification is not inevitable and that the egalitarian society is possible as a reality and not merely an ideal. Most of the latter would probably concede that what is attainable is what Tawney (1964) described as 'practical equality' rather than absolute or perfect equality.

Those who argue that, in spite of the wide prevalence of inequality, egalitarian societies are in fact possible, have sought to demonstrate either that such societies have existed in the past or that they can be constructed in the future, or both. Characteristically, the faith in the possibility of constructing such a society in the future has been sustained by the belief that equality and not inequality was the original condition of human life.

Among modern social and political philosophers, Rousseau was one of the first to argue that equality or near equality was the original or natural condition of human life, although Hobbes and Locke had put forward similar arguments before him (Béteille 1980). Rousseau did not deny the existence of natural or physical inequalities, but those he believed to be slight or insignificant. The inequalities that really mattered were political or moral inequalities which, being based on a kind of convention, could be abolished or at least reduced by a different kind of convention. Rousseau's views, which were considered radical in his time, left a lasting impression on succeeding generations in Europe and elsewhere (Haldar 1977; Ganguli 1975).

The writings of Marx and Engels gave rise to the doctrine that the first stage of social evolution was one of 'primitive communism'; and that the final stage would also be one of communism, both stages being marked, despite many differences, by the absence of classes. However, there was a difference in approach and method between Rousseau and the nineteenth-century proponents of primitive communism. Rousseau constructed his model from first principles, observing, 'Let us begin then by laying facts aside, as they do not affect the question' (Rousseau 1938: 175). Marx, and more particularly Engels, on the other hand, turned to the available evidence from primitive societies to demonstrate that classless societies existed in reality (Engels 1948).

The second half of the nineteenth century saw the emergence of the new science of ethnography based largely on accounts of primitive or pre-literate societies by explorers, missionaries, traders, and others. A whole new world was opened up for systematic investigation. The early ethnographers were enthusiasts of the comparative method which they

used for constructing large evolutionary schemes. Perhaps the most
famous of these schemes, and one which had a lasting influence in the
erstwhile Soviet Union, was the one formulated by Lewis Henry Morgan (1964). According to it, the first stage of evolution, designated as
savagery and represented by a number of surviving pre-literate societies,
was marked by the absence of inequality and class.

The theory of primitive communism aroused great interest in the
late nineteenth and early twentieth centuries. The discussion turned
invariably around the presence or absence of individual property in the
early stages of social evolution. The predominant view was that the
concept of property—and indeed of the individual—was absent in
primitive societies; and it was tacitly assumed that where there was no
individual property, there could be no classes, no strata, and no significant inequality. This view was challenged in a landmark study first
published in 1921 by the American anthropologist Robert Lowie
(1960). He showed by a meticulous examination of the ethnographic
record that primitive societies were far more varied and differentiated
than had been allowed for in the theories of his predecessors. Most
anthropologists are now skeptical about a universal stage of primitive
communism, although it was a part of the canon of Soviet ethnography
for well over half a century.

Skepticism about a universal stage of primitive communism does not
mean that anthropologists reject altogether the view that primitive
societies, or at least some primitive societies, may be genuinely egalitarian in their constitution. The term 'egalitarian societies' has been
recently used to describe a number of societies in which 'equalities of
power, equalities of wealth and equalities of prestige or rank are not
merely sought but are, with certain limited exceptions, genuinely real-
ised' (Woodburn 1982: 432). The use of the term 'egalitarian' in the case
of these societies is justified on the ground 'that the "equality" that is
present is not neutral, the mere absence of inequality or hierarchy, but
is *asserted*' (Ibid.: 431). Examples of such societies are provided by the
Mbuti Pygmies of Zaire, the !Kung Bushmen of Botswana and Na-
mibia, the Pandaram and Paliyan of South India, the Batek Negritos of
Malaysia, and the Hadza of Tanzania.

The egalitarian societies referred to above are all based on a foraging
or hunting-and-gathering economy. Indeed, according to Woodburn,
who is one of the principal contemporary proponents of the idea of the
egalitarian society, not all hunter-gatherer socieities are egalitarian,
but only those characterized by 'immediate-return' as against 'delayed-

return' systems (Ibid.: 431). Hunter-gatherers characterized by immediate-return systems live and move about in very small groups without
fixed membership and with a very rudimentary division of labour, close
to the outer limits of organized social life. It is very difficult to draw
any significant conclusion from their study for the future of equality
in organized societies.

Although evolutionary theories are no longer as popular as in the
past, those who study equality and inequality comparatively often
adopt an evolutionary perspective, either implicitly or explicitly. A
characteristic expression of the evolutionary perspective on the subject
is to be found in an essay by Ernest Gellner. Commenting on the work
of a well-known American author, he observed, 'The pattern of human
history, when plotted against the axis of equality, displays a steady
progression towards increasing *in*equality up to a certain mysterious
point in time, at which the trend goes into reverse, and we then witness
that equalization of conditions which pre-occupied Tocqueville' (Gellner 1979: 27). This view of the course of human history is in fact very
widely held, and it merits a brief discussion.

Implicit in the evolutionary scheme outlined above is a classification
of societies into three broad types: (i) primitive societies; (ii) agrarian
civilizations; and (iii) industrial societies. Primitive societies, including
bands, segmentary tribes as well as tribal chiefdoms, are small in scale
and relatively undifferentiated; though few of them are egalitarian societies in the strict sense, they are generally not divided into distinct
classes or strata. Agrarian civilizations of the kind that prevailed in
Europe, India, or China are or were hierarchical both in design and in
fact; their characteristic divisions were of the caste or estate type whose
boundaries were relatively clear and acknowledged by both custom and
law. Industrial societies, whether of the capitalist or the socialist type,
have a formal commitment to equality rather than hierarchy; their
characteristic divisions are classes or strata which must accommodate
themselves to the ideals of citizenship and equality of opportunity. It
is not that inequalities are unknown or even uncommon in industrial
societies but they depend, or are believed to depend, on achievement
rather than ascription.

The distinction between 'aristocratic' and 'democratic' societies, and
the historical passage from the former to the latter were described in
memorable prose by Alexis de Tocqueville in the early part of the
nineteenth century. He wrote: 'In running over the pages of our history, we shall scarcely find a single great event of the last seven hundred

years that has not promoted equality of condition' (Tocqueville 1956
I: 5). And again, 'The gradual development of the principle of equality
is, therefore, a providential fact. It has all the chief characteristics of
such a fact: it is universal, it is lasting, it constantly eludes all human
interference, and all events as well as all men contribute to its progress'
(Ibid.: 6). Tocqueville set out to demonstrate the progress of equality
in every sphere of life: in the material conditions of men and women,
in the pattern of their social relations, and in their ideas, beliefs, and
values.

It must be remembered that Tocqueville's argument about 'aristocratic' and 'democratic' societies was an historical argument, intended
to bring out the continuity as well as the contrast between the two.
The contrast has been extensively applied, both to different historical
phases in the life of the same society and to different societies independently of historical connection. The second mode of contrast does
not have any necessary link with the evolutionary perspective, and
might in fact explicitly reject such a perspective.

Western scholars have long been fascinated by the Indian caste system which has often been presented as the prototype of a rigidly hierarchical system. Some of them have seen in it an extreme form of
tendencies present in their own society, while others have viewed it as
a qualitatively different, if not an altogether unique, system. The
French anthropologist Louis Dumont developed a body of work in
which the contrast between *homo hierarchicus* and *homo equalis* was
presented in the sharpest possible terms, the former being exemplified
by traditional Indian society and the latter by the modern west (Dumont 1966, 1977a).

Dumont's contrast between *homo hierarchicus* and *homo equalis*
has been both admired and attacked. The contrast, as he makes it, is
confined largely to the plane of values, to what people believe or say
they believe rather than to what they do or practice. When Dumont
talks about *homo equalis*, what he means is that modern societies have
an egalitarian ideology—that they are egalitarian in intention—not that
they have attained or are likely to attain equality in the distribution of
material resources. This of course leaves open the whole question of
what we mean when we talk about equality or inequality in regard to
human societies.

How tangled the question is can be easily seen by going back briefly
to Tocqueville. When Tocqueville spoke of the providential advance
of equality, he clearly believed that equality was, in his own lifetime,

advancing simultaneously on all fronts. But that, plainly, was an illusion. We have no reason to believe that equality of condition, or equality in the distribution of material resources, always advances simultaneously with equality as a moral or political value.

An important aspect of inequality in all modern societies is inequality in the distribution of income. Now, it is a well-established conclusion that there was an *increase* rather than a decrease in income inequality in the early stages of economic growth in most, if not all, western countries (Kuznets 1955). In other words, inequality in one significant sense was increasing during precisely that period of western history when the modern egalitarian ideology was steadily gaining ground in the west. Not all societies have had or can be expected to have the same historical experience in every respect. But it is obvious that 'legal equality' and 'economic equality' do not have the same rhythms of change and might, arguably, move in opposite directions.

An additional difficulty arises from the fact that different concrete forms of inequality may coexist in the same society, for instance, an open class system and a rigid system of racial stratification. This was noted by Tocqueville for the United States (Tocqueville 1956 I: 331–434). Lack of internal consistency makes comparisons difficult, and the difficulty is compounded when the units being compared differ vastly in scale, for instance, a small foraging band and a large nation state. A society on a large scale with a complex pattern of stratification may contain within it component units which have an appearance of remarkable homogeneity and equality; and a small-scale egalitarian community, enjoying a degree of isolation and autonomy, may depend for its survival on its articulation with a large and complex system of stratification. Relatively egalitarian tribal communities have existed within the broad framework of the very hierarchical traditional Indian society.

The limitations of treating the nation state as an irreducible unit in the study of equality and inequality have become increasingly apparent. Societies are at all levels in continuous interaction with each other, and modern anthropologists no longer regard them as isolated or self-sufficient units with fixed and rigid boundaries. Recent studies have shown how the rise of European powers from the seventeenth century onwards was often at the cost of smaller or less developed or less powerful societies in Asia, Africa, and Latin America which they oppressed and exploited (Wolf 1982). One must not be too quick to characterize the former as egalitarian societies by looking only at the ideals they set for themselves and looking away from their actual treatment of others.

Approaches to the Study of Inequality

It is clear that when we compare different societies, we are dealing with inequalities that differ not only in degree but also in kind. There is no universally-accepted method which enables us to conclude that a given society corresponds more closely than another to some general standard of equality, and common sense is not always a very reliable guide. Economists often single out a specific aspect of the problem, e.g. inequality in the distribution of income on the ground that it lends itself most readily to quantitative treatment. But even here they find it difficult to declare unequivocally that a given distribution shows either more or less inequality than another (Sen 1973; see also Sen 1992 and Appendix I, this volume). And inequality of income has to be viewed along with other aspects of inequality which differ significantly among themselves.

The conclusion we reach from a comparison of different patterns of inequality will depend in part on our method and approach. Of the several approaches to the study of inequality, two are of particular importance. The point of departure for the first approach lies in the inequalities inherent in the distribution of traits among the individual members of a society; for the second, it lies in the inequalities inherent in their arrangement into an organized whole. The first approach stresses that individuals are unequal to begin with, and their unequal abilities, aptitudes, or propensities are bound to show no matter how or where they are initially placed (Herrnstein and Murray 1994); the second maintains that since individuals are unequally placed from the start, they develop and display unequal abilities (Béteille 1977, 1987a).

Individual variations are a matter of common observation, and they are to be found in every society. No two individuals are exactly alike, and identical twins are the exception that proves the rule. However, we must be careful to distinguish between difference and inequality, an obvious distinction that is easily overlooked by proponents of the theory of natural inequality (Béteille 1980). Two individuals may be different from each other without being in any meaningful sense unequal.

Do individuals differ to the same extent in all societies? It is difficult to give an unequivocal answer to the question. One might like to distinguish between variations in purely physical or biological traits and those in mental or 'moral' characteristics, or between 'natural differences of kind' and 'social differentiation of positions' (Dahrendorf

1968); but the distinction is by no means easy to sustain in a consistent fashion. Comparison of the degrees of individual variations becomes difficult where societies differ very greatly in scale. Moreover, variations among individuals of one's own kind always appear larger than among individuals of a different kind. Explorers, missionaries, and colonial administrators systematically underestimated individual variations, even as to physical characteristics, among the natives whom they observed and described.

Some sociologists take the view that the stress on individual distinctions, if not the very fact of it, is unique to modern societies, being underdeveloped or weakly developed in primitive and traditional societies. Émile Durkheim, whose work has left a lasting impression on the French school of sociology, put forward this view in his very first book, *The Division of Labour in Society*, where he argued that primitive societies (conceived of in a very broad sense) were held together by mechanical solidarity which was based on 'likeness' as opposed to 'complementary difference' which was the basis of organic solidarity characteristic of modern societies (Durkheim 1982). He believed that individuality was absent in the former to such an extent that even the differences between men and women, including their physical differences, were weak or rudimentary in them. This is an extreme position to which few would give assent today.

While individual differences are present in all societies, they may be culturally restrained in some and encouraged in others. They tend to be encouraged to such an extent in modern societies that individualism has come to be regarded as the dominant ideology of these societies (Dumont 1977a, 1983; Macpherson 1962). Tocqueville maintained that there was a close connection between individualism and equality (Tocqueville 1956 II: 98–100). But individualism has more than one implication just as equality has more than one meaning (Béteille 1986). To the extent that individualism stresses the autonomy and the dignity of the individual, it places itself against all forms of ascribed inequality. But to the extent that it stresses competition and achievement, it justifies and promotes inequality in other, sometimes extreme, forms (see Chapter 9; also Appendix II).

The preoccupation with individual achievement (and the individual qualities on which it is presumed to be based) has given a distinctive character to contemporary debates on equality and inequality. The logic of capitalism is that opportunities are *in principle* equally available to all individuals who, nevertheless, do not all benefit from them to the same extent because they differ in their endowments and their fortunes. Thus, for many it is this difference in individual endowments and individual fortunes that lies at the heart of the problem of inequality in modern societies (Hayek 1960: 85–102; Eysenck 1973; Herrnstein and Murray 1994). This creates a bias in favour of methodological individualism, seen most commonly in writings on inequality by economists and psychologists.

Methodological individualism faces many difficulties in the study of variation and change in patterns of inequality. It can perhaps account for the ranks attained by individuals on a given scale, but it cannot as easily account for the scale itself. An issue that all students of social inequality must face is what may be called the passage from difference to inequality. Why do only some differences count as inequalities and not others? Are they the same differences that count as inequalities in all places, at all times? What actually is involved when a set of differences is transformed into a system of inequalities? These questions cannot be addressed without considering some of the constitutive features of human society and culture.

The majority of sociologists and anthropologists take as their point of departure not the individual agent, but the framework of collective life within which he acts (Bendix and Lipset 1966; Béteille (ed.) 1969; Heller 1969). Every individual acts within a framework of society and culture which provides him with facilities and at the same time imposes constraints on him. The language he speaks, the technology he uses and the division of labour within which he works all exist to some extent independently of his will and inclination. The regularities by which language, technology, and division of labour are governed are different from the regularities of individual action.

Language provides us with a convenient example of the place of collective representations in human life. Human life, as we know it, would be impossible without language, and human language, in its turn, would not exist in the absence of collective life. But collective representations include much more than language. They consist of the entire range of beliefs and values shared by individuals as members of society. At this point it will be enough to say that collective representations include both cognitive and evaluative elements—which are, moreover, closely intertwined—so that the individual members of a society share not only common modes of thought but also common standards of evaluation. Indeed, it is difficult to see how collective life would be possible in the complete absence of shared beliefs and shared values.

Durkheim stressed the contrast between the amplitude and variety of the collective representations of a society and what it is possible for any individual mind to create or comprehend on its own. Subsequent investigations by anthropologists in the field have fully confirmed the truth contained in Durkheim's insight. People with a simple neolithic technology, such as the Bororo or the Nambikwara Indians of the Amazon basin, show a richness and complexity in their collective representations that seem to surpass what even Durkheim might have expected. The luxuriance of expressive life commonly encountered in the primitive world at the level of cosmology and taxonomy can scarcely be explained by the practical requirements of material existence (Lévi-Strauss 1966).

A seminal paper published by Durkheim and Mauss a hundred years ago opened up a new field of cultural anthropology devoted to the study of systems of classification (Durkheim and Mauss 1963). We now know that such systems, which are sometimes extraordinarily elaborate, are present in even the simplest of societies. They not only arrange the vast multitude of culturally-recognized items into broad classes but order them according to principles that may be explicit or implicit. This means that there are not only socially preferred items of food, dress, adornment, etc., but also recognized preferences in regard to colour and other attributes of nature. These preferences reveal the aesthetic and moral categories of a society. Once again, not only are such categories to be found in all known societies, but it is difficult to see how any human society could exist without them.

Now, it would be strange in a culture to have standards of evaluation that apply to food, dress, adornment, plants, and animals, but none that apply to human beings and their activities. In other words, where people are able to discriminate between good and bad food, they will also discriminate between good and bad cooks; where they judge some gardens to be superior to others, they will also judge some gardeners to be superior to others; where there are preferences as between artefacts, there are likely to be preferences also as between artisans. It goes without saying that I am talking now of culturally-prescribed, or at least culturally-recognized, preferences, and not the personal preferences of particular individuals.

Every culture, no matter how rudimentary, has its own bias not only for certain types of human performance but also for certain types of human quality. Quality and performance are of course closely related in the minds of people, but they may be given different priorities in different cultures. Men and women may be believed to have different qualities, and, where these qualities are themselves ranked, as they often are, men and women will also be ranked. Even where qualities are assigned priority, there is always room to take performances into account. For instance, women may be considered to excel in gardening and men in hunting, but then hunting may rate higher than gardening, in which case men will be ranked higher than women. The stress on quality tends to be associated with the segregation of distinct sections of society into distinct fields of activity so that their members do not compete with each other on a common ground. Where the stress is on performance, men and women—or, to vary the example, Whites and Blacks—may be allowed to compete for the same prizes and then ranked according to their performance, irrespective of gender (or race). But here again, success or failure will be attributed, at least in part, to the presence or absence of some quality such as intelligence. Moreover, the fact that Whites and Blacks (or men and women) may in certain spheres compete on equal terms and be judged on merit, does not mean that they will not in other spheres be treated differently or even unequally.

Thus, it is clear that what transforms differences into inequalities are scales of evaluation. A scale of evaluation is not a gift of nature; to borrow the words of Rousseau, 'it depends on a kind of convention, and is established, or at least authorized by the consent of men' (Rousseau 1938: 174). Even while invoking the name of Rousseau, it is important to guard against the excesses of constructivist arguments. The conventional scales by which human beings rank each other—their qualities and their performances—are rarely the outcome of conscious design. Most people use these scales as they use language, without a clear awareness of their structure.

Once we realize that scales of evaluation are not usually the products of conscious design and are not always clearly recognized to be what they are, we have to turn to the coexistence of a multiplicity of scales and the problem of their mutual consistency. Now, it is a common experience that where A ranks higher than B in scholastic ability, B may rank higher than A in athletic ability, leaving open the question of the overall rank of A in relation to B. Some occupations are more remunerative, others permit greater freedom of individual action; how are they to be ranked in relation to each other? How complicated the general problem is may be seen from a glance at the voluminous literature that has grown around so specific a topic as the social grading of occupations (Goldthorpe and Hope 1974; Goldthorpe 1987).

To assign a central place to evaluation in the explanation of inequality is not to deny that different values coexist in the same society. One can go further and argue that different values tend to predominate in different sectors of the same society. Manual workers and professionals may not rank occupations in the same way; Blacks and Whites may not assign the same significance to colour in social ranking; and men and women may show different kinds of bias in the individual qualities they value. While this is true, it should not lead to the conclusion that there can be as many scales of evaluation as there are individual members of society, for no society can survive without some coherence in the domain of values.

Those who have been called 'structural-functionalists' tend to stress the integration of values in the societies about which they write (Parsons 1954: 69–88, 386–439). One form of the functionalist argument is that, although there may be different scales of evaluation in the same society, these scales themselves can be arranged in a hierarchy, since every society has a 'paramount value' which determines the alignment of all its other values (Dumont 1980). This is a tendentious argument which should not be allowed to divert attention from the empirical investigation of the actual extent to which different values reinforce or subvert each other in concrete historical situations. Modern societies in particular are marked by deep and pervasive antinomies by which I mean contradictions, oppositions, and tensions among the existing norms and values (Béteille 2000a).

Where there are competing or conflicting values in society, each associated with a particular section of it, they do not always rest in a state of stable equilibrium. Of course, the discordance may be reduced through reflection, argument, and self-correction, and accommodation achieved on the plane of beliefs and values itself. But this is not the only or even the most typical way in which the problem of value conflict is resolved. Differences that cannot be resolved on the plane of values are typically resolved on the plane of power. Or, to put it succinctly, in the language of Marx, 'Between equal rights force decides' (Marx 1954: 225).

The resolution of conflicts, including the disagreement over values, through the exercise of power brings to our attention a second important source of inequality in collective life. The importance of coercion (as against common values) in maintaining order and stability in society has been noted by many, and there are some who would say that it is not only important but decisive (Dahrendorf 1968: 151–78). This is particularly true of those who deal with the place of the state in human affairs.

As Hobbes put it in *Leviathan*, 'And Covenants, without the Sword, are but Words, and of no strength to secure a man at all' (Hobbes 1973: 87).

The state provides the most striking example of inequalities in the distribution of power, but by no means the only one. Such inequalities are commonly found in many domains, including the domestic domain, that are a part of society but not, strictly speaking, of the state. No doubt it can be argued that where the state exists it provides sustenance to inequalities of power in every domain and that with the collapse of the state, these inequalities will also collapse. This has been a familiar argument among Marxists who have found support for it in a work published by Engels more than a hundred years ago (Engels 1948). At that time it was hoped that the argument would be confirmed by the imminent collapse of the bourgeois state. The bourgeois state has collapsed from time to time, though not quite as dramatically as the Soviet state, but the end of the inequality of power is nowhere in sight.

There is, besides, plenty of evidence of inequality of power in what are commonly described as 'stateless societies' (Tapper 1983). There are firstly the chiefdoms, varying greatly in size and degree of organization, with tribal or clan chiefs who might exercise considerable, though intermittent, authority in organizing people for collective activities. Much depends on the scale and importance of the collective activities that require to be organized. Pastoral tribes have leaders whose voices carry considerable authority in matters concerning the movement of men and animals, and in conducting and coping with raids (Barth 1959).

Then there are the segmentary systems proper—segmentary tribes as against tribal chiefdoms, to follow the terminology of Sahlins (1968)—which do not have chiefs in the accepted sense of the term. Here the system works not so much through a hierarchical distribution of power as through the balance of power between groups at different levels of segmentation (Evans-Pritchard 1940). There are two kinds of groups that are specially significant in such societies: descent groups and local groups. Where descent groups are corporations—whether among the patrilineal Tallensi (Fortes 1945, 1949) or the matrilineal Truk (Goodenough 1951)—the senior male members have a decisive say in the disposal of the productive and reproductive resources of the corporation, mainly land, livestock, and women. This is particularly true at the lower levels of segmentation where the descent group is functionally most effective as a corporation.

It is on the plane of the local group rather than the descent group that the crucial evidence for the kind of argument that I am trying to make will have to be found. The evidence seems to me to be clear, though perhaps not decisive. Evans-Pritchard, whose book on the Nuer was a turning point in the study of tribal political systems, deliberately excluded the internal organization of the village from his consideration of the political structure of the Nuer (Evans-Pritchard 1940). We can nevertheless say something about the exercise of power in maintaining the stability of such groups, even while conceding that this stability is itself a matter of degree.

The problem is of the following kind. Every stable group has a division of labour, no matter how rudimentary, which is regulated by rules regarding the rights and obligations of its individual members. It is in the nature of human life that these rules do not operate mechanically with clock-like regularity and precision. They are occasionally, if not frequently, violated, if only because individuals have divergent interests as well as divergent perceptions of the rules. These divergences, which are found in even the simplest local groups, may appear trivial from the lofty heights of an industrial society, but they are important in their own context. Disputes have to be settled, decisions that are binding on all have to be made, and that provides the basis for the exercise of power by some individuals over others. To be sure, matters may be settled from one situation to another by all the members of the group acting together so that no individual accumulates more power or authority than any other. But that would be the *limiting* case and not the *typical* case.

We may turn back to the egalitarian society based on an 'immediate-return' economy of hunting and foraging. It will be a little more clear now why I regard it as a limiting case. It stands at one extreme, the other extreme being the monolithic and authoritarian industrial state with its massive apparatus of coercion and manipulation which reached perfection, or near perfection, in the USSR under Stalin, and, more briefly, in Germany under Hitler. We can learn a great deal about equality and inequality from both types of society, although it is my judgement, which I cannot substantiate here, that they are both highly unstable.

Some Common Historical Forms of Inequality

In an important essay on the origin of inequality, Ralf Dahrendorf distinguished, first, between natural differences of kind and natural

differences of rank, and then again, between the latter and social stratification (Dahrendorf 1968: 151–78). We shall set aside for the moment
the question of 'natural differences of rank', or what is more commonly
called natural inequality (Béteille 1980). The relation between natural
differences and social inequality is a very important one, although it is
by no means as simple as might at first sight appear. Natural differences
do not present themselves to us directly, but are perceived in a highly
selective manner through the lens of socially-established systems of
classification (Lévi-Strauss 1966). What needs to be stressed is that not
merely the evaluation of differences but to some extent their very
recognition is a social process.

Differences that are assigned cardinal significance in one society may
be ignored or overlooked in another. The differences between men and
women are, however, taken into account in all human societies, and it
is difficult to see how it could be otherwise. This, of course, does not
mean that they are taken into account in the same way or to the same
extent in every society. Where men and women are given distinct social
roles they develop differences, and sometimes marked differences, in
temperament and ability; these differences in temperament and ability
are then taken—by women as well as men—as the reason for their being
given different roles. It is clear that much of this rests on convention
which varies from one society to another (Mead 1963). What is not clear
is whether, outside of procreation and parturition, there have been or
can be conventions for the social division of labour that ignore altogether the differences of gender.

Leaving aside the question of what is possible, we have to consider
how far in fact the differences of gender are treated as inequalities. This
is a vexed question where the facts are confusing and open to conflicting
interpretations. There is a vast literature on the position of women in
primitive societies which it is impossible to summarize here. In a lecture
delivered on the subject in 1955 and first published in 1965, Professor
Evans-Pritchard, then Britain's foremost anthropologist, observed that
the acrimonious debates on the subject belonged to the past and that it
could at last be discussed with scholarly detachment (Evans-Pritchard
1965: 37–58). That has turned out to be a monumental error of judgement, for no field of anthropology is more deeply embattled today than
the one that deals with gender and inequality (Ardener 1975; MacCormack and Strathern 1980).

The historical record of the development of the subject is roughly
as follows. Early anthropologists commonly subscribed to the theory

of the primitive matriarchate or the view that the first stage of social evolution was marked uniformly by the prevalence of matriarchy or mother-right. This view gradually became obsolete, particularly after Lowie's critique of it in *Primitive Society* (1960). At about the same time, Rivers also pointed out that power generally lay in the hands of men, irrespective of the mode of descent, and that there was no uniform relationship between the position of women on the one hand and modes of descent, inheritance, and succession on the other (Rivers 1924). The considerable body of empirical material available when Evans-Pritchard wrote his lecture seems to have borne out Rivers's basic point that women were in general subordinated to men in public life, and that parity between men and women was uncommon if not unknown.

The whole subject has been thrown open once again, mainly through the recent efflorescence of gender studies (Leacock 1978; see also the *Indian Journal of Gender Studies*, beginning 1994). New dimensions of it have been brought to light that were not perceived by even the most acute minds among the earlier anthropologists. These studies have implications, only now beginning to be explored, for the understanding not only of the disparity between the sexes but of inequality as a whole. I shall merely touch upon, and that too very cursorily, two such issues, one relating to power and the other to values.

It has generally been the case that those who have stressed the subordination of women to men have dwelt mainly upon the politico-jural rather than the domestic domain. Clearly, in even the most strongly 'patriarchal' societies, women have sometimes an important, not to say a crucial, role in domestic affairs. They may play the major part in everything concerned with food, health, and nurture, and exercise independent initiative in all these regards. As against the 'jural' inferiority of the wife to the husband or the sister to the brother, there might be the 'psychological' dominance of the son by the mother. Indeed, a contemporary Indian psychologist has argued about his own society, which is to all appearances strongly patrilineal, that 'the Indian lives in his inner world less with a feared father than with a powerful, aggressive and unreliable mother' (Nandy 1980: 107; see also Kakar 1978). All this, however, will require a reconsideration of the concepts of power and dominance as conventionally used in the social sciences to an extent that would take us far beyond the scope of the present essay (see, however, Béteille 2000a: 264–86).

Just as it may be unreasonable to assume the existence of a single homogeneous domain in which some individuals invariably exercise power over others, it may also be unrealistic to assume the existence of a homogeneous conceptual or moral universe whose categories of classification and evaluation are accepted in the same way by all. The important contribution of women's studies has been to draw attention to the existence of alternative beliefs and values whose implications for the *social* rank of individuals are yet to be fully explored.

Distinctions of race, though also marked by physical or biological traits, differ significantly from those of gender. They are less clear and less fixed and are not universally present. Only some societies have or recognize them while others do not. Within a given society racial differences exist and are perpetuated because they are assigned social values. If people simply ignored these distinctions in their social interactions and married without regard for them, the distinctions themselves would cease to exist or become markedly different (Béteille 1977: 101–28). The same can hardly be said about gender.

The term race has been so extensively misused either to express contempt or to incite hatred that extreme care must be exercised in its application (Montagu 1974; Baxter and Sansom 1972). There is a very large range of variation of physical features in the human species, much larger than in most animal species. However, variation by itself does not betoken the presence of distinct races: the variation has to be clustered in a particular way for races to become visibly present. Genetic diversity is a necessary but not a sufficient condition for race formation. There is, for example, enormous genetic diversity in the Indian population but it has proved impossible to classify that population into distinct races.

There are specific conditions under which genetic diversity manifests itself in the form of more or less distinct races. That happens when populations that are or appear to be biologically distinct are territorially separated to an extent which practically rules out interbreeding; or when, though sharing the same territory, they are prevented or discouraged from interbreeding by law or custom. The continued presence of distinct races in a society and their social segregation are, in a sense, two sides of the same coin.

Racial discrimination in its characteristic modern form is a feature of societies that owe their origin to historical circumstances of a particular kind. These are circumstances of sudden and violent encounter between populations differing sharply in physical appearance, language, and material culture, associated with the European conquest of

Africa and the New World (and to a much lesser extent of Asia). This is not to say that the violent penetration by people of one physical type into the territories of another never took place in the past. But the European penetration of Africa and the New World between the seventeenth and the nineteenth centuries was unique in its global character, in its swiftness and violence, and in the scale on which it led to population displacements (Wolf 1982).

Two distinct patterns of racial inequality, both involving Whites and Blacks, could be seen in the twentieth century, one in the United States and the other in South Africa (Béteille 1977: 101–28, Béteille (ed.) 1969: 297–334). In the United States racial inequality survives under a liberal democratic regime which has shown a fluctuating commitment to affirmative action. In South Africa many forms of racial inequality survive the overthrow of a minority racist regime committed to a policy of Apartheid (i.e. apartness). Apart from differences in constitutional history and orientation, there is an important demographic difference between the two countries. In the USA, the Whites are not only politically dominant, they are in a majority, having successfully overwhelmed other races by sheer technological and numerical superiority. In South Africa the Whites, who were until recently politically dominant, are numerically in a minority, being surrounded, moreover, by states hostile to the idea of White dominance. What is notable in the United States is the ambivalence of the Blacks, whereas what is striking in South Africa is the anxiety of the Whites.

Even where two distinct races are initially brought together by the use of force and are then kept segregated, at least to some extent by the use or the threat of force, their coexistence over successive generations leads them to share certain common values. To be sure, these 'common' values are largely the values of the dominant race, but the point is that they tend to be internalized, at least to some extent, also by the subordinate race. A striking example of this may be found in the extent to which upwardly-mobile Blacks in the United States have internalized White values and standards in regard to personal beauty, elegant dress, and refined speech (Frazier 1957). Where, on the other hand, the subordinate race fails or refuses to internalize the 'common' values of the dominant race, we have an unstable and a potentially explosive situation as in South Africa.

We have seen thus that the inequality of races is, in the typical case, established by the exercise of power and maintained by the hold of a common culture which assigns a higher value to the traits, characteristic of one race as against those characteristic of the other. There is nothing 'natural' about either of these processes. Indeed, if the present population of either the United States or South Africa were allowed to revert to its 'natural' state, all distinctions of race, or at least those distinctions now considered significant, would disappear with the passage of time. Even if for the moment we concede the argument of the ethologists about 'domination' (Ardrey 1966)—which few sociologists will be inclined to do—evaluation cannot in any meaningful sense be regarded as a natural phenomenon.

Caste and race are sometimes considered together as they are both regarded as extreme forms of rigid social stratification maintained by strict rules of endogamy. Both Lloyd Warner (1941), who pioneered the empirical study of social stratification in the USA, and Gunnar Myrdal (1944), who conducted a monumental study of the Blacks in the same country, found it convenient to use the metaphor of caste in analysing stratification by race. They both pointed out that neither the Blacks nor the Whites were a race in the scientific sense, that the whole system rested on social conventions, and that, therefore, to represent it in a biological idiom was misleading. They also felt that the barriers separating Blacks from Whites were qualitatively different from those between classes within each of these populations. Thus, the choice of the term 'caste' was to some extent dictated by negative considerations, since neither 'race' nor 'class' seemed appropriate.

While the nineteenth-century idea that the distinctions of caste are based on differences of race has proved to be scientifically untenable, something may be learnt from the analogy between race and caste. Some anthropologists have pointed to a number of similarities between the Indian caste system and the colour-caste system of the United States (Berreman 1960, 1966). One of these relates to attitudes towards women. Both Whites in the United States and upper castes in India have shown an obsessive concern with the 'purity' of their own women while engaging freely in the sexual exploitation of Black or Untouchable women. All of this can be related to ideas about bodily substance and the conditions appropriate to its exchange. The general importance of these ideas in American culture has been stressed by David Schneider (1968) and in the Hindu caste system by Marriott and Inden (1974). In other words, inequalities of caste are illuminated in the same way as those of race by a consideration of gender (Béteille 1990a).

There are fundamental differences between caste and race, and the tendency among contemporary anthropologists is to stress the differences more than the similarities (Dumont 1961; Reuck and Knight 1968). In any case, the Indian caste system is a sufficiently important historical example of inequality to deserve attention in its own right. Recent writers on caste have seen in it the most complete example of a hierarchical society, one which in its traditional form was hierarchical not only in fact but also by design and in which the hierarchical principle animated every sphere of life (Dumont 1966). Viewed in that light, the Hindu caste system had its analogue in the European estate system which too was governed by the 'hierarchic conception of society' (Huizinga 1924: chapter 3).

The caste system may be viewed at two levels, those of *varna* and *jati*, for both of which the same English word 'caste' has been commonly used (Srinivas 1962; see also Chapter 3). *Varna* represents the formal order of caste, the 'thought-out' rather than the 'lived-in' system, and the traditional discourse on caste has been typically in the idiom of *varna*. All mankind and, indeed, all created beings were in principle divided into four *varnas* which were both exclusive and exhaustive. The Manusmriti declares that Brahman, Kshatriya, Vaishya and Shudra are the four *varnas* and that there is no fifth (Manu 1964). The same four *varnas*, in the same order of precedence, were acknowledged by Hindus throughout India for more than two thousand years until disowned by the new constitutional and legal order.

The *varna* order is expounded in detail in the classical socio-legal literature known at the Dharmashastra, particularly in the Manusmriti or the Manavadharmashastra which goes back rougly two thousand years in time (Kane 1974). Anyone who reads this literature will be struck by the elaborate and comprehensive manner in which human beings—and their qualities and actions—and all things around them are classified and ordered. To take a well-known example, it is decreed that the sons of a Brahman shall inherit property in the following proportions: the son of the Brahman mother, four parts, the son of the Kshatriya mother, three parts; the son of the Vaishya mother, two parts; and the son of the Shudra mother, one part only. To be sure, the classification and ordering are highly schematic and present us with models rather than descriptions of reality.

The invariance and fixity characteristic of the *varna* model appear less conspicuous when we move down to the plane of *jatis*. *Jati* is a regional rather than a national system, the number of *jatis*, and also their names, varying from one part of the country to another; moreover, there is reason to believe that old *jatis* have disappeared and new ones come into being with the passage of time in each and every region. Although Hindu theory says that the whole of mankind is embraced by the *varna* order, *jatis* have in fact freely existed outside that order, among Muslims, among Christians and, to some extent, also among tribals (Bose 1975). The problem of the correspondence between *varna* and *jati* is a difficult one, although the assumption of such a correspondence was a part of Hindu beliefs about caste (Srinivas 1962; see also Lingat 1973).

Whereas the *varnas* are only four in number, the *jatis*, in each region, are very many; exactly how many it is difficult to say because they are frequently segmented in a way that has baffled census takers over the distinction between caste and subcaste (Béteille 1964). Suffice it to say that there may be in a single village as many as thirty-five subcastes (Béteille 1965). The *jatis* in a region are not merely differentiated from each other, they are also mutually ranked. This ranking manifests itself in a variety of social contexts through transactions of different kinds (Marriott 1959, 1968). Traditionally, a very large social distance had to be maintained between the Brahmans at one extreme and the Harijans or Untouchables at the other.

The ranking of *jatis* differs, and has always differed, from the ranking of *varnas* in a number of important ways. There is no clear linear order of *jatis* as there is of *varnas*. It is no doubt true that the Brahmans are at the top and the Harijans at the bottom, but each of these two categories is made up of a number of distinct *jatis* which themselves cannot by any means be easily placed in a linear order. As M.N. Srinivas pointed out many years ago, this ambiguity always left some room for mobility among castes and subcastes (Srinivas 1968). An upwardly-mobile *jati* not uncommonly phrased its claim to superior status in the idiom of *varna*.

While there is general agreement that the ranking of *jatis* is very elaborate and, compared with other systems of social ranking, also very rigid, there is considerable disagreement about the sources of caste rank. The actual ranks enjoyed by the different castes arise from a variety of factors, although the idiom in which caste ranking is phrased is typically a ritual idiom, more specifically the idiom of purity and pollution. This had led some observers to exaggerate the importance of ritual factors, giving the system an appearance of mechanical rigidity without any room for freedom of action.

Despite the impressive stability and continuity of the caste structure, Hindu ideas behind the ranking of persons are fluid and complex, and perhaps heteronomous. *Varna*, which may loosely be rendered as 'order' or 'kind', provides an overall framework, but it does not stand by itself. Besides the four *varnas* detailed in the Dharmashastras, there are the three *gunas* or 'qualities' discussed elsewhere, particularly in the Samkhya texts (Rege 1988, 1984; see also Larson and Bhattacharya 1987). The three *gunas* are: *sattva* (signifying light, purity, intellect), *rajas* (energy, valour), and *tamas* (darkness, inertness). The *gunas* enter as constituents into the make-up of different persons. In addition to *guna*, there is also *karma* which refers to action or works, what a persons does rather than what he is.

Guna and *karma* are commonly discussed in relation to persons rather than groups, although they may also be linked, more or less explicitly, to the four *varnas*. In the *Bhagvad Gita*, Lord Krishna declares, *caturvarnyam mayam sristam, guna-karma-vibhagasah:* the four *varnas* did I create, dividing (or distributing) the *gunas* and the *karmas* (Zaehner 1969: 4/13). Some modern interpreters of the Gita, including Tilak and Gandhi, have tried to argue that it represents an activist philosophy; however, it cannot be too strongly emphasized that throughout the long course of Indian history, individual action has been severely constrained by the social framework of caste.

Some contemporary western anthropologists have over-stressed the hierarchical completeness of Hindu society in order to bring out the distinctive features of their own (Dumont 1964). Modern societies do indeed have a number of distinctive features both in their organizational structures and in their value patterns. These features stand out when we contrast the modern west not only with traditional India but also with its own medieval past (Béteille 1987a: 33–77).

In the context of our present subject perhaps the most striking feature of modern societies is equality before the law. As an articulated principle governing the relations between persons, it has found its fullest expression only in modern times. It developed first in the west, in England, France and the United States, and then spread gradually to the rest of the world so that there are very few parts of it today where it is not acknowledged. The far-reaching implications of this should not be overlooked, for equality before the law requires equality not only between the rich and the poor or the high- and the low-born, but also between Whites and Blacks and between men and women. Medieval European society and, to an even greater extent, traditional Indian society, was a society of privileges and disabilities; as against that we have a society of citizens entitled to, if not actually enjoying, the equal protection of laws.

The acceptance, in principle, of equality before the law or of equality of opportunity does not mean of course that inequalities of status and power have ceased to exist. There is a vast body of sociological literature that shows beyond any reasonable doubt that such inequalities do exist in all modern societies (Bendix and Lipset 1966; Heller 1969; Béteille (ed.) 1969). Through the better part of the twentieth century there were acrimonious debates over the rigours of inequality between the proponents of socialism and the defenders of capitalism (Aron 1964). Socialist writers from the USSR and other East European countries argued that since inequalities derived primarily from the private ownership of property, they were to be found in their most extreme form in capitalist countries, notably the United States. Liberal writers from the west, on the other hand, maintained that the truly oppressive forms of inequality, being those that arise from the untempered concentration of power in the apparatus of state and party, were to be found in countries like the USSR.

We might begin on neutral ground with a consideration of the occupational structure of modern societies. It will be difficult to exaggerate the importance of that structure in industrial societies, whether of the capitalist or the socialist type. Occupations have become highly specialized, and the occupational system has become more elaborate, more complex, and more autonomous than in any society previously known to history. Industrialization is accompanied not only by a new attitude to work but also by a new organization of it.

The thousands of named occupations present in an industrial society are classified and ranked. The principles of occupational ranking have been discussed even more exhaustively by sociologists than those of caste ranking have been by anthropologists (Goldthorpe and Hope 1974). Studies in the United States have shown that, although new occupations displace old ones with great rapidity, the structure of occupational ranking shows a high degree of stability (Treiman 1977; Treiman and Robinson 1981). Moreover, comparative studies of occupational ranking in different industrial societies, of the capitalist as well as the socialist types, have shown that this structure is not only remarkably stable but also relatively invariant.

In general, non-manual occupations rank higher than manual ones, and this was true even in the Soviet Union where official theory assigned pride of place to manual work in the creation of value in the material product sense of value. Doctors, as independent professionals, rank higher than typists in the United States, but they also ranked higher in the Soviet Union where they were both employees of the state. Attempts to level out differences of income between occupations did not succeed beyond a point despite strong pressures from the state, and such attempts were later condemned by Stalin (Lane 1971).

The question why some occupations are ranked higher than others is in some ways as difficult to answer as the question why some castes are ranked higher than others. It is not enough to say that space scientists rank higher than plumbers because they receive higher earnings, just as it is not enough to say that Brahmans rank higher than Oil-pressers because they have greater purity. In the example on occupations one might just as well ask why the space scientist should have a higher earning than the plumber. Various kinds of explanations, none of them very satisfactory, have been offered in terms of 'scarcity', 'function', and so on (Bendix and Lipset 1966: 47–72). It is quite clear, as Parsons consistently stressed, that occupational ranking is governed by the value system of a society, and the more fully a given occupation embodies or expresses its core values, the more highly it is likely to be ranked (Parsons 1954: 69–88, 386–439; see also Chapter 2). There are only two qualifications to be added: firstly, occupations alone do not express the core values of a society, and, secondly, their ranking is also governed, at least in part, by considerations of power which are different from those of esteem.

Although occupational ranking may be as elaborate as caste ranking, the occupational status of the individual is different from his caste status. Caste status is ascribed whereas occupational status is, at least in principle, achieved. There is no guarantee that the individual will have the same occupation, or even the same occupational level, as his father, and the same individual may, in fact, move considerably from one occupational level to another in his own lifetime. Therefore, sociologists who study occupational structure and occupational ranking also study occupational mobility. Indeed, it would not be too great an exaggeration to say that the enormous literature on the social grading of occupations has grown largely in response to the problems of describing, analysing, and measuring occupational mobility (Goldthorpe 1987; Erikson and Goldthorpe 1992).

The literature on occupational mobility in industrial societies is not only very large but in parts highly technical, so that casual inferences drawn from it are likely to be misleading. Some of the studies have come to conclusions that at first sight appear surprising. In a pioneering study made in the 1950s, Lipset and Bendix stated at the outset that '*the overall pattern of social mobility appears to be much the same in the industrial societies of various Western countries'* (Lipset and Bendix 1967: 13). They found their own conclusion 'startling' in view of the universal assumption that the United States had much higher rates of mobility than European countries such as Britain and France. The earlier studies operated with such broad differences of level as between 'manual' and 'non-manual' workers; more refined analyses have naturally revealed variations in rates of mobility within the same overall pattern (Erikson and Goldthorpe 1992).

An important issue in the study of social mobility relates to its implications for the formation and stability of classes. Sociologists who deal with this question tend to approach it from two different points of view. There are those who maintain that the multiplicity of occupational levels together with high rates of individual mobility renders the formation of distinct and stable social classes difficult if not impossible in advanced industrial societies. Blau and Duncan argued in an influential book that high rates of mobility make most individual positions impermanent to such an extent that few individuals are likely to develop a commitment for life to any particular class (Blau and Duncan 1968). 'Class' then becomes a statistical construct rather than a socially significant category.

Marxists have traditionally had an ambivalent attitude towards individual mobility. On the one hand, they have questioned the fact that capitalist societies have high and even rising rates of mobility. On the other hand, they have maintained that rates of mobility have little, if anything, to do with the polarization of classes which is an historical tendency generated by contradictions inherent in capitalism (Poulantzas 1976). A reasonable position would seem to be that, while rising rates of individual mobility do alter the context of class conflict, they do not abolish class identity as such, and certainly not the identity of the working class (Goldthorpe 1987: 1–36, Goldthorpe 2000: 230–58).

Marxists, as is well known, contrast class with occupation (Dahrendorf 1959: 3–154) and assign far more importance to class than to occupation, at least in the analysis of capitalist societies. The importance that we assign to class in industrial societies in general, as against its capitalist variant specifically, will depend on what we mean by class (Ibid.; Aron 1964: 57–73). In the Marxian scheme, the inequality of classes is much less a question of status or esteem than of unequal power in the market. The inequality of power itself is seen as being rooted in a particular institution, that of private property. Thus, in this scheme, although inequalities of power are crucial and quite large in capitalist societies, they can, at least in principle, be greatly reduced, if not eliminated, by the abolition of private property.

Others say that property is only one of the bases of power which has other bases that survive the abolition of property and might in fact be strengthened by its abolition. They too tend to subordinate esteem or status to power in their analytical scheme, but in a way that is different from the Marxist way (Dahrendorf 1968: 151–78). In their view, power is a universal and inescapable source of inequality which permeates all areas of human life, particularly in societies organized on a large scale (Foucault 1975, 1980). To be sure, there are variations in the pattern of its distribution, and the inequalities can even be controlled or regulated to some extent, but never eliminated altogether.

Some have taken the further step of trying to redefine class by substituting power (or authority) for property. Thus, for Dahrendorf, 'the term "class" signifies conflict groups that are generated by the differential distribution of authority in imperatively coordinated associations' (Dahrendorf 1959: 204). The presumption behind this definition (like the one behind the definition it seeks to supercede) is that inequality of power (like inequality of property) generates conflict. Whether it does so or not, and under what conditions, to what extent, and in what forms are empirical questions that cannot be pursued any further here.

Equality as Concept and Ideal

We are now in a position to return to a consideration of equality as a concept and an ideal. There is no doubt that inequalities of status and power exist everywhere in the modern world, but they now exist in a greatly altered legal and moral environment. 'Hierarchy', wrote Marx and Engels, 'is the ideal form of feudalism' (Marx and Engles 1968: 190), and it was also the ideal form of other past civilizations. It is no longer the ideal form of society; people live with inequality, they may seek to explain or even justify it, but they no longer idealize it. This is true not only of England, France, and the United States, where the modern ideal of equality first took shape, but also of countries like India to which it later spread.

But the ideal of equality is no less perplexing a subject than the reality of inequality, and the confusion is worse confounded when we seek to consider it in a comparative perspective. Two questions may be asked at this point: firstly, whether the ideal of equality is indeed unique to modern times and, if so, in what sense; and, secondly, whether the ideal or, rather, the concept behind it, is a coherent one.

Some scholars believe that egalitarian values have not only originated in the west but are, moreover, somehow incompatible with non-western societies and cultures. Others maintain that they are neither uniquely western nor uniquely modern. We have already alluded to Woodburn's argument about 'egalitarian societies' (Woodburn 1982). References to egalitarian values are not uncommon in the general literature on tribes, including pastoral and agricultural tribes: Nuer egalitarianism has been made proverbial through Evans-Pritchard's vivid descriptions (Evans-Pritchard 1940). Then, on a larger scale, there is Islamic civilization which was in many respects more markedly egalitarian than medieval Christianity, not to speak of medieval Hinduism (Gellner 1981). However, Islamic egalitarianism lacked the universality characteristic of modern egalitarianism; it denied equality, even in the formal sense, to women as well as to adherents of other faiths. In the case of most tribal societies as well, this lack of universality goes hand in hand with such commitment to equality as there is.

Although modern societies have universalized the *idea of equality* and have elaborated it in moral, legal, and political discourse to an unparalleled degree, they have not come anywhere near to the *equality of condition* said to be common among many tribal communities, including those adhering to Islam. The modern idea of equality arose under specific historical conditions, in response to a society where hierarchy was deeply and firmly entrenched. It was under such conditions that 'equality of opportunity'—or, in Napoleon's famous phrase, 'careers open to talent'—became a powerful slogan. Equality of opportunity could hardly be a forceful idea in a tribal society where equality of condition, or near equality of condition, was common.

The idea of equality of opportunity, which was a new one in Napoleon's time, had already lost some of its shine a hundred years later. R.H. Tawney, one of the strongest advocates of equality in the interwar years, saw clearly that in a society marked by acquisitiveness and untempered competition, equality of opportunity by itself could do little to reduce the gap between the rich and the poor, and might in fact increase it (Tawney 1964). So he contrasted equality of opportunity with what he called 'practical equality' and sought to make the latter the central focus of social policy.

It is through considerations of social policy rather than abstract speculation that the ambiguities in the concept of equality have become manifest. We know today that legal equality, equality of opportunity, and even rising rates of mobility can coexist with increasing inequality in the distribution of income. As we have seen, equality of opportunity can be of significance only in a society based on the competition of individuals. But this means that there can be equality only *before* the competition, and not *after* it. From this it may be argued that the commitment to equality requires not only that the competition itself should be free, but also that the rewards of success should not be too lavish or the penalties of failure too severe.

Thus, equality may signify equality of opportunity, or it may signify equality in the distribution of benefits and burdens (Béteille 1985b; see also Chapter 7). It is true that modern ideology sets a high value on equality; it is also true that it is deeply divided on these two conceptions of equality. Several positions may be taken on this. One may argue that there is no real contradiction between the two, that the contradiction is only apparent. If we interpret equality of opportunity to mean 'fair' and not merely 'formal' equality of opportunity, we can more easily reconcile it with equality, or at least equalization, in the distribution of benefits and burdens (Rawls 1972: 83–9, 298–303).

Others would maintain that the idea of 'fair' equality of opportunity is subjective and arbitrary, and that the ideal of equality cannot be tested against any preconceived model of distribution. This being so, substantive equality is a kind of mirage whose pursuit is bound to be self-defeating. More important than that, it can subvert the ideal of formal equality, or equality before the law which, in this view, is where the essence of equality lies (Hayek 1960: 85–102; Joseph and Sumption 1979).

If we now look back on the transition from the 'aristocratic' to the 'democratic' type of society, or from the 'hierarchical' to the 'egalitarian' type, we realize how complex the issues are. When we look at the transition in Europe, and also elsewhere, we cannot but be struck by the crucial part played in it by the forces of the 'self-regulating market'. These forces broke down old barriers and created new cleavages. In Europe the old distinctions of estate, guild, and parish yielded before the expanding forces of the market to the extent that the latter took less account of social origin than of individual ability.

However, the market did not dissolve all the old distinctions, some of which survived, although in altered forms, and accommodated themselves to it. First of all, there are countries like India where market forces have not penetrated far enough and where what are called 'semi-feudal' arrangements based on caste and patronage are still in evidence. It can of course be argued that what survives from the past will inevitably decay as and when the market takes full command. But this argument loses much of its force when we see that distinctions of race and ethnicity, and sometimes marked disparities based on them, flourish even in such a mature capitalist society as the United States.

The market also sharpens old distinctions, and creates new ones, the most important being the distinction between capital and labour. The widening gap between capital and labour, the simultaneous enrichment of the few and immiserization of the many in mid-nineteenth century England were noted not only by Marx and Engels but by many others who witnessed the expansion of market forces at first hand. It is true that the worst excesses of this phase of capitalism have been corrected to some extent, at least in the advanced capitalist societies, but it is not true that they have all been corrected solely by the 'self-regulating market'. Few of those who are witnessing the expansion of market forces and experiencing the accompanying rise in economic disparity in India and other countries in Asia, Africa, and Latin America can seriously believe that they should wait for the market itself to correct these disparities in the long run.

The belief that the inequalities inherited from the past and those being generated at present can and should be corrected by some form of social intervention is widely held in countries like India, and also held by varying and fluctuating sections of society in countries like Britain, France, and Germany. Of course, such interventions may be of many different kinds, and opinion is, naturally, divided on who should intervene, to what extent, and in which areas of public life. A certain consensus on these issues, however fragile and momentary, was embodied in the institution of the welfare state created in a number of west European countries in the wake of World War II.

Given the full range of historical possibility and experience, the welfare state of post-war western Europe appears as a relatively mild instrument for the containment of inequality. Far more powerful apparatuses of state and government were devised in the USSR and other socialist countries, at least partly with the objective of lessening inequality. We should not ignore what they achieved. There were achievements in controlling unemployment, in giving the worker a better deal, and in regulating income differentials between manual and mental workers. Some advances were also made in reducing disparities between the different ethnic groups and nationalities which were very unequally placed at the time of the Bolshevik Revolution. The achievements of the socialist regimes should not be exaggerated, but they cannot be denied.

The gains to equality just mentioned above were achieved at some cost, which many, including those within the erstwhile socialist countries, now believe to have been excessively high. A consideration of this cost at once reveals one of the paradoxes of equality. The very attempt to regulate and reduce inequality through direct intervention in social and economic processes led, and some would say led inevitably, to a tremendous concentration of power in the apparatuses of state and party. In other words, the instruments for the suppression of inequality are not neutral, but generate their own inequalities. One could then ask whether, in moving from the inequalities of estate prevalent till the eighteenth century to the inequalities of class about which Marx wrote, and from those again to the inequalities of power of the twentieth century, any real or demonstrable gain was made for equality.

A monolithic structure of power imposes costs not only on equality but also on other social values, notably liberty. It may well be the case, as some believe, that in an ideal world there will be no conflict between liberty and equality, and that they will reinforce each other; but such an ideal world is not yet within reach, and perhaps for most, not even within sight. Libertarians do not question the principle of equality before the law or even of equality of opportunity to the extent that it is consistent with the former. But they do question the 'legitimacy of altering social institutions to achieve greater equality of material condition' (Nozick 1980: 232), whether in the name of distributive equality or of 'fair equality of opportunity'.

The stress on distributive equality may be viewed as a threat not only to liberty but also to efficiency. Few persons would place efficiency on the same plane as equality and liberty in the hierarchy of values. It is nevertheless true that efficiency has a central place in the economic ideology that dominates much of modern life. Some of the most crucial debates in the realm of social and economic policy relate to the comparative advantages of market and plan as two alternative forms of rationality (Dahrendorf 1968: 215–31). A major test of these advantages, even for those who believe that the two alternatives cannot be mutually exclusive, is the degree of efficiency attainable under each, either singly or in combination with some elements of the other.

Modern egalitarians have always argued that an order that tolerates extremes of inequality is not only socially unjust but also economically wasteful and inefficient. But the considerable experience now available of centrally-regulated economies has shown up the other side of the coin. In the socialist countries, the market was for decades viewed with deep suspicion for generating and sustaining economic inequality, and one of the main objectives of centralized planning was to restrict precisely that role. If the market is viewed with less suspicion today, it is not because that role has been completely lost to sight, but, rather, because the experience of 'real socialism' has made people more willing to accept some economic inequality as a price for the greater freedom and efficiency that go with some measure of competition.

Thus, although equality is undoubtedly an important value in modern societies, there is a considerable distance between a minimalist definition of it as equality before the law and a definition that also tries to take into account the distribution of income, wealth, and various social services, such as health and education. What must be kept in mind is that there are not only strong advocates of equality in these societies but also critics of it (Letwin 1983). These critics point not only to the high political and economic costs of realizing equality, but also to the conceptual ambiguity inherent in the very idea of equality. 'The central argument for Equality', a contemporary political philosopher has written, 'is a muddle' (Lucas 1965: 299). And even about the more specific ideal of 'equality of opportunity', a distinguished American educationalist has written, seemingly in despair, that it is 'a false ideal' (Coleman 1973: 135).

Perhaps equality is not so much a false ideal, as one which cannot be meaningfully conceived of in an historical vacuum. It can be meaningfully conceived of only in response to the specific challenge that a given society faces from its reflective members. Sometimes the challenge comes from an order established by age-old religious tradition, such as that of caste; sometimes it comes from a recklessly competitive economic system such as that of free-enterprise capitalism; or again, it may come from a monolithic political apparatus itself designed to solve the problem of inequality once and for all. Equality is today too powerful an idea to be set aside simply because it cannot be exactly defined. It is like the djinn which, once released from the bottle, cannot be put back into it again.

2

Class and Status

The relationship between class and status has for long been a subject of discussion and debate in the sociological literature, particularly among those engaged in the study of social stratification. It is important to our understanding of the nature and significance of inequality and the limits to which the ideal of equality can be reached in social practice. In what follows I will explore some of the ambiguities that arise from unstated differences among sociologists in the ways in which they represent the distinction between class and status.

I would like to underline the contribution made by analytical sociology, through empirical studies of class and status, to our understanding of the varieties of inequality and the reasons why policies and programmes for the advancement of equality are often frustrated. It is true that sociologists disagree about what they mean by status and by class. Nevertheless, they would generally agree upon the need to maintain as consistently as possible some kind of distinction between the two. This is because they seek a deeper insight than the lay person into the richness, the complexity, and the contradictions of social stratification even when they are not able to express their insights in a fully consistent terminology.

There are serious, not to say insuperable, difficulties in insulating the terminology essential for sociological analysis from the habits of everyday speech. The terms 'class' and 'status' are a part of everyday usage in which not only does each carry several meanings but the two are often used interchangeably. More than one sociologist has pointed out that when someone describes a person as being 'class conscious', what he often means is that the person is status conscious. But sociologists who know better also slip into such usage in their unguarded moments. For instance, a sociologist may speak of the 'class status' of a person when all that he has in mind is the person's class position.

There are also deeper ambiguities than the ones to which I have just referred, and it is to one of those that I will devote my attention here. The relationship between class and status has been viewed in analytical sociology in two distinct, not to say contrasting, ways. In the first view, class and status are opposed as two different and mutually irreducible forms or dimensions of inequality: here the stress is on distinctions of status expressing honour, dignity, worth and so on as against the disparities of wealth, income, and other forms of material advantage. In the second view, class and status are opposed as one might oppose inequality and equality: here the stress is on citizenship as a major factor in redefining the relationship between class and status in modern democratic societies. The two conceptions of status, the one focussing on unequal social esteem and the other on the equal rights of citizenship, cannot be related in the same way to class, no matter how we define that term; and they have very different implications for a general theory of social stratification. At any rate, it is not unreasonable to anticipate some difficulty when the same general concept is used to describe a major aspect of inequality and also an antidote to it.

To draw attention to the divergent implications of viewing status in terms of unequal esteem on the one hand and equal entitlements on the other is not to argue, at least at this stage, that one of the two views is correct and the other should be discarded. Both uses of the term are well established, not only in popular speech and writing but also in the scholarly literature. The legal usage is the older one and, with changes in the legal standing of the citizen, first in the western world and later elsewhere, the emphasis has tended to shift from the unequal status of estates (or castes) to the equal status of citizens. But a different usage that associates status with qualities, attainments, and actions that are unequally esteemed, irrespective of the legal standing of persons as citizens, is also well established in the sociological literature.

The oscillation between status as a form of inequality and as a warrant for equality expresses a deep ambivalence among western, and particularly British, sociologists about the meaning and validity of inequality in their own society. They fully recognize the presence of inequalities on the plane of facts, but are unclear and uncertain as to what they signify on the plane of values. They display a sure touch in dealing with inequalities of wealth, income, and other forms of material advantage, but falter in the face of disparities of honour, dignity, and worth which they tend to regard as residual, inconsequential, and some-what anachronistic. The point was forcefully made by Louis Dumont when he wrote: 'Differences of rank run contrary to our dominant ideology of social life, which is equalitarian. They are for us fundamentally meaningless' (Dumont 1967: 28). Are they?

In formulating my arguments here, I will turn repeatedly to the work of David Lockwood, particularly his later theoretical work, *Solidarity and Schism* (1992), but also his earlier empirical work, *The Black-coated Worker* (1958). His work on class and stratification is both rich and subtle, and it has the merit of keeping an eye on each of the two ways of looking at status with which I am concerned. There is a pervasive awareness, particularly in the early part of *Solidarity and Schism*, that status has to do with value and meaning, with proximity to (or distance from) the sacred centre, being thus associated with distinctions between superior and inferior in a hierarchical arrangement. There is also a detailed discussion of status in the later part of the same book in terms of the equal rights of citizenship created and maintained by the modern legal order (see also Lockwood 1996). What is not altogether clear is how the two conceptions of status, the one going back to Durkheim and the other derived from T.H. Marshall, should be related to each other in the study of social stratification as a whole.

Although my discussion of status, like Lockwood's, will be confined to the context of class and stratification, it is well to remember that a broader and more general use of the term is also common among sociologists. In this broader usage, 'status' means any socially-defined position, irrespective of considerations of rank. This usage is particularly common in American sociology where it has been developed by a line of scholars from Ralph Linton to Robert Merton. It is in this sense that one may speak of the 'ritual status', the 'marital status' and even the 'class status' of a person. This usage makes it difficult to distinguish between class and status as different dimensions of stratification.

In Linton's view, 'A status, as distinct from the individual who may occupy it, is simply a collection of rights and duties' (Linton 1936: 113). The same individual occupies many positions or statuses, simultaneously as well as in his passage through life. 'However, unless the term is qualified in some way, *the status* of any individual means the sum total of all the statuses which he occupies' (Ibid.). In a later work, Merton

(1957) developed the idea of the 'status set' as a composite of different statuses.

It will be seen that there is a certain affinity between the conception of status as 'simply a collection of rights and duties' and the definition of it in terms of the entitlements of citizenship. But there are two things to be kept in mind. Firstly, the point in defining status in terms of the rights of citizenship is that they are *equal* rights whereas nothing is presumed as to either equality or inequality in the rights and duties that define status in Linton's sense. Secondly, citizenship is not for Linton (or Merton) the defining component among those that together make up the status of the individual.

Let me now return to the conception of status as an aspect or dimension of inequality present in all human societies, or at least in all stratified societies. Most students of stratification would agree that social inequality is a multidimensional phenomenon that cannot be explained in terms of any single criterion. Here, as I have indicated, sociology has enriched our understanding by going beyond the categories of common sense through systematic comparative study. Common sense tends to reduce all forms of inequality to one single factor: class or the 'economic' factor in capitalist societies, power or the 'political' factor in some other type of society. Sociologists have never remained satisfied with the commonsense categories of capitalist societies and have sought to identify aspects, dimensions, or bases of inequality other than those of class that have an independent operative effect in their own and other societies.

Even where the empirical work has been rich and detailed, problems of terminology have made comparisons between different studies difficult. Earlier writings by American sociologists tended to use the concept of class in a very broad sense, and then to distinguish between 'economic class', 'political class' and 'social class'. The six classes in Lloyd Warner's pioneering study of Yankee City were not classes in the sense of categories defined primarily by economic criteria (Warner and Lunt 1941). In fact, Warner rejected the primacy of economic criteria in the understanding and explanation of class, and used patterns of consumption, styles of life, and people's own perceptions of where they and others stood in the social hierarchy in constructing his six-class model of Yankee City. As many have pointed out, Warner's study dealt more with status than class.

Most contemporary theorists of stratification use Max Weber as the starting point in analysing its different dimensions. Weber's writings on the subject are not always easy to interpret: when they are not cryptic, they are hedged in with all kinds of qualifications. But it was he who first pointed to the difference between distinctions based on production and market situation and those based on consumption and life style: 'With some oversimplification, one might thus say that classes are stratified according to their relations to the production and acquisition of goods; whereas status groups are stratified according to the principles of their *consumption* of goods as represented by special styles of life' (Weber 1978: 937).

Drawing largely on the work of Weber, W.G. Runciman has used the distinction between class and status in an important empirical study in Britain. For him, status and class are both dimensions of inequality, but they are different dimensions of it. ' "Status", by contrast, is concerned with social estimation and prestige, and although it is closely related to class, it is not synonymous with it'. Further,

Distinctions of status separate from class are visible among both non-manual and manual workers and their families. Within the same profession and therefore class, doctors or lawyers will belong to different status-groups according to social origin or secondary education or manner of speech (Runciman 1966: 38).

It can be easily shown that this usage which associates status with differential esteem or prestige—as against differential economic or material advantage—has been very widely adopted by sociologists writing about social stratification in the last four or five decades.

Runciman used the distinction between the inequalities of class and of status to good advantage in his study of relative deprivation in Britain. His study showed that disparities between manual and non-manual workers had declined in regard to both class and status. However this did not necessarily betoken a decline in relative deprivation. 'The magnitude and frequency of relative deprivation of status in the manual stratum has, on the whole, risen as inequality of status has declined' (Runciman 1966: 96). Furthermore, relative deprivation of status was perceived and experienced differently from relative deprivation of class by members of the same manual stratum. One may infer from Runciman's account that even when the real disparities of status between manual and non-manual workers become reduced, they do not necessarily become less significant than the disparities of class.

Differences of status between manual and non-manual workers had been discussed earlier by Lockwood in his study of class consciousness among clerical workers in Britain. There he had shown how the status situation of clerical workers differed from that of manual workers and combined with differences in market situation and work situation to sustain the social distance between the two sections of employees (Lockwood 1958).

In Runciman's formulation, as in many others, there are two oppositions that tend to get conflated. There is, firstly, the opposition between the 'economic' dimension governed by income, wealth, or some other economic criterion and the 'status' dimension (sometimes loosely described as the 'social' dimension) having to do with esteem, prestige, and the like. There is, secondly, the opposition between class and status-group. The two kinds of opposition are not the same, since classes, conscious of their opposed identities and interests, are never purely economic phenomena or governed solely by economic considerations; and status-groups, in their turn, can never be fully understood without taking economic differences between them into account. My view is that it should be possible to discuss distinctions of status irrespective of the presence or absence of the kinds of status-groups that were characteristic of the hierarchical societies of the past.

The conflation of the two oppositions just referred to is characteristic of Weber's writing which, as I indicated earlier, is the starting point of the analytical distinction between the 'class' and the 'status' dimensions of stratification in much of the current writing on the subject. Although Weber was acutely aware of the pitfalls of reducing all inequalities to purely economic ones and warned repeatedly against such a practice, his observations on the matter are embedded in his discussion of the distinction between 'classes' and 'status-groups' in which the 'economic' and the 'status' dimensions of inequality repeatedly intersect.

The English term 'status-group', unlike the German 'Stand', is a sociological coinage and not taken from the currency of ordinary speech or writing. English society was a 'society of estates' (or orders) till the end of the eighteenth century. By the end of the nineteenth it had become a 'society of classes'. This had not happened to the same extent in Germany. Hence it was natural for Weber to speak of 'Stand' and 'Standlische Lage' in a way in which it would not be natural any longer to speak of 'estate' or 'estate position' in England; and the contrast would be sharper if in place of England we put the United States which never had a hierarchy of estates.

The 'status-groups' of which Anglo-Saxon sociologists speak do not have the prominence or the visibility of the estates of the past. This is as one would expect from the repudiation by the legal order of the hierarchical distinctions of estate. It is true that the old distinctions between groups are maintained to some extent by custom and convention even when the law denies them, but the secular trend is for those distinctions to become muted. The question is whether new distinctions of esteem or prestige—as against the purely economic distinctions of class—do not arise even as the old ones of estate become attenuated. In other words, do modern societies generate their own distinctions of status that are peculiar to themselves? Or are all distinctions of esteem or prestige destined to wither away with the passage from a society of estates to one of classes?

There are obvious advantages in viewing social disparities in terms of the distribution of income and wealth. Income and wealth are important in their own right, and they can be used for acquiring symbols of status and instruments of power, though more freely in some societies than in others. Moreover, income and wealth lend themselves to measurement, and hence present an appearance of objectivity not easily matched by other indices and criteria. Comparisons between different societies or between different phases in the development of the same society can be made more readily in terms of the distribution of income than in terms of other aspects of inequality.

But the distribution of income, no matter how important, can easily be shown to be only one aspect of inequality whose significance, moreover, varies from one society to another. Persons in the same occupation do not necessarily have the same income, and persons having the same income may be in a variety of different occupations. More important than that, the social esteem enjoyed by an occupation is not governed solely by the actual or expected income from it. Judges, ambassadors, and scientists do not earn higher incomes than entertainers or traders, yet they are more highly esteemed by virtue of the occupations in which they are engaged.

It is now a sociological truism that the disparities between manual and non-manual occupations are matters of esteem and not merely of income. Non-manual occupations tend to be more highly esteemed than manual ones even when the pay is less. In the recent past this was as true of socialist as of capitalist societies even though the ideology of the socialist state placed a premium on labour and in particular manual labour. The disparities of both income and esteem between manual and non-manual occupations have declined steadily since World War II.

This is partly because the technological changes in the intervening period have altered the work situation to such an extent that the old distinctions between manual and non-manual workers no longer apply in the same way. The new manual occupations created by technological innovations are not disesteemed like the old ones, and they are better paid. But this does not mean that all occupations are now equally esteemed or even that there is any clear trend in that direction.

Some would say that the social rank of an occupation is governed not only by the income it provides but also by the authority vested in it. This is to a large extent true empirically, but little will be gained by making it true by definition. We may define authority in such a way that it incorporates not only command and obedience but also prestige, esteem, and deference. Authority in the strict sense of the term is inseparable from command and obedience, whereas deference is freely conceded and freely withdrawn. It is certainly not true that we esteem only those who have the authority to command or in the measure in which they have it, for in that case even junior ministers would enjoy greater esteem than the best scientists or writers. We may of course speak of the authority or even the power of science or literature, but that would be to speak metaphorically.

Even when it is agreed that inequality is not merely a matter of control over things and persons, it is not clear where exactly the other sources of it should be sought and what weight should be attached to them. One may note the lack of congruence between class and status but still maintain that it is not of any great significance since in modern industrial societies at least, the inequalities of esteem and prestige become aligned sooner or later with those of class. As against that, one might argue that the former are constitutive of human societies as moral and symbolic systems. That argument would lead us to examine the inequalities that arise in every society from distinctions of moral worth and find expression in symbolic representations. (Here 'moral worth' has to be clearly understood as what is perceived as such by the moral standards of the specific society under examination, without any judgement as to the universal validity of those standards).

Among modern sociologists, it was Parsons who stressed most consistently the centrality of evaluation in systems of stratification: 'Stratification *in its valuational aspect* then is the ranking of units in a social system in accordance with the standards of the common value system' (Parsons 1954: 388). And further, 'The valuational aspect must be analytically distinguished from the others entering into the total "power" system of a society' (Ibid.). Weber had made the same point in some-what different language:

Quite generally, 'mere economic' power, and especially 'naked' power, is by no means a recognized basis of social honor. Nor is power the only basis of social honor. Indeed, social honor, or prestige, may even be the basis of economic power, and very frequently has been (Weber 1978: 926).

What Weber repeatedly refers to as 'social honour' has to be considered separately from the unequal distribution of life chances in a formally free market.

Parsons sought to make explicit the link between social stratification and the moral order of society. 'In the first place, moral evaluation is a crucial aspect of action in social systems' (Parsons 1954: 70). And then, 'There is in any given social system an actual system of ranking in terms of moral evaluation' (Ibid.: 71). There is a difference, according to Parsons, between the actual system of ranking which is the 'system of stratification' and the normative structure which he calls the 'scale of stratification'.

In every society, inequalities of esteem or prestige are given shape and form by its system of classification. Lockwood has done well to draw attention to the central significance of classification in the sociology of Durkheim, although it is a pity that he has so little to say about the seminal essay on primitive classification by Durkheim and Mauss (1963). Now it should be clear that when Durkheim spoke of classification, he had in mind much more than what is generally meant by class in the sociological literature on stratification. To quote Lockwood, 'His concept of social classification refers not to class, in the Marxist or Weberian sense, but to a hierarchy of status' (Lockwood 1992: 76).

Lockwood seems to follow Durkheim closely in seeking to relate the distinctions of status to the very constitution of human societies as moral and symbolic systems. Further, he takes Durkheim to task for failing to make certain fundamental connections explicit. He says, 'In Durkheim's account of the social hierarchy there is a surprising omission: this is the connection of status with the scared' (Lockwood 1992: 84). He adds, 'But it is not only in the sacred, but in the morality of everyday life that the ineradicability of status consists' (Ibid.: 85). So what is being presented as ineradicable are the hierarchical distinctions of status arising from the idea of the sacred and the morality of everyday life.

What Durkheim pointed to only by implication has been made explicit and elaborated upon by other sociologists, notably Parsons and Shils to whose writings Lockwood also refers. I have already pointed to the significance assigned by Parsons to evaluation in the functioning of social systems. Evaluation is a matter not only of differentiation but also of ranking, since the units of any differentiated system tend to be differentially ranked. Two such units may of course be equally ranked, but that is the limiting and not the typical case:

The theoretical possibility exists that not only any two individuals but all those in the system should be ranked as exact equals. This possibility, however, has never been very closely approached in any large-scale social system (Parsons 1954: 71).

This should hold true *irrespective* of the prevalent legal order.

A similar conception of status has been presented by Edward Shils through the ideas of centre and periphery. Lockwood gives credit to Shils for bringing to light the relationship between 'what is held sacred by society' and 'the differential coefficient of social worth'. He goes on to say,

The sacredness of charisma which emanates from what Shils calls the 'centre' of a society towards its 'periphery' may be more or less concentrated, but there is no known society in which such a central religious zone is indiscernible; and it is unlikely that any society will lack one (Lockwood 1992: 84).

This again is a forceful statement on the universality of status as ineradicable hierarchical distinction. The opposition of centre and periphery speaks of social distance and social exclusion, and the differentiation associated with it is by its nature hierarchical distinction. The centre is the zone of maximum dignity and worth, and they diminish as we move outward towards the periphery. When we are talking about the 'differential coefficient of social worth', we are clearly not talking about class or material advantage; it is difficult to know what we are talking about if not status.

Shils (1981) has tried to show that the idea of the sacred centre need not be tied to any established religion in the restricted sense of the term, but may be associated with a broad 'secular' tradition. In modern societies, occupation and education are important, not to say crucial, elements in the coefficient of social worth. 'The most esteemed occupations in societies are those which are in their internal structure and in their functions closest to the centres' (Shils 1975: 279). Again, educational attainment is important because it betokens 'an assimilation into a pattern of values and beliefs which are part of the centre of existence' (Ibid.: 282).

Ideas of the sacred and of everyday morality draw their sustenance from tradition, and no society can exist without tradition, not even those in which established religions are or appear to be in decline. There is a close relation between tradition and distinctions of status. Shils (1972) has in particular examined the place of tradition in the sciences and the arts, and shown how these activities, characteristic of 'secular' modern societies, generate more or less stable conceptions of differential social worth. The deference accorded to scientists, writers, and composers is in principle different from the obedience due to the state and its functionaries. What I have in mind as the free and willing expression of deference may be illustrated by Jude's fascination for Christminster, or Oxford, in Thomas Hardy's novel. Oxford was the sacred centre of his imagined world, even while he accepted his own exclusion from it on the periphery of that world.

Distinctions of status are created and maintained through social exclusion, which may act in a variety of different ways. It may be open or disguised, conscious or unconscious, formal or informal, operating in some cases through the strict enforcement of rules and in others through the discreet manipulation of symbols. Social exclusion is not always designed to secure material advantage but may, on the contrary, be willingly practised at some material cost.

Lockwood is undoubtedly right in drawing attention to the connection between the hierarchy of status and the idea of the sacred. That idea confronts many obstacles in a secular society, or a society that has experienced the disenchantment of the world. Hence the preoccupation with power, material advantage, and class as the only real and enduring bases of inequality in a world where most persons, including sociologists, believe that ideas of the sacred centre, of institutional charisma, and of the differential coefficient of social worth are somewhat anachronistic. They will readily concede the importance, even the primacy, of such ideas in other places and other times, but are uneasy about doing so in the world in which they themselves live and act.

Where inequality comes to be viewed essentially in terms of the distribution of material advantage, the concept of status may be put to a different use by replacing the hierarchical idea of it with one that stresses equality of status as defined by law. The definition of status as legal standing is, as I have indicated, also in accordance with established usage. But while in the past there were legal orders—or estates—based on hierarchy, the accent in the modern world is no longer on hierarchy but on equality: equality before the law, equal protection of the laws, and equality of status for all citizens. This kind of legal order is indifferent, if not hostile, to the idea of the differential coefficient of social worth. If we are to see that coefficient at work, we have to look behind or beyond the legal order.

Lockwood speaks of status not only in terms of the differential co-efficient of social worth, but also in terms of the entitlements of citizenship. Here he is using a concept of status derived from T.H. Marshall rather than Durkheim, although he was preceded by Parsons (1965) in this. Following Marshall, he tells us that 'the basic constituent of status in capitalist societies is citizenship' (Lockwood 1992: 229). But the modern concept of citizenship repudiates the idea of a legally-sanctioned social hierarchy. Its basic premise is contained in the Benthamite maxim that every man is to count for one and no one is to count for more than one. In such societies either the evaluative and expressive aspects of social disparities have become atrophied; or they continue to exist and operate, but outside the areas of social life governed specifically by the entitlements of citizenship.

It has to be pointed out that Marshall himself was well aware of the ambiguities contained in the idea of status. He was not against the use of the term in the broad sense to indicate 'social position'; at the same time, he felt it would be best to keep in sight the distinction between 'social status' and 'legal status'.

'Social status', according to Marshall (1977: 191), 'refers to one aspect of the phenomenon of stratification in society'. As against that, 'legal status' refers to 'a position to which is attached a bundle of rights, duties, privileges and obligations, legal capacities and incapacities, which are publicly recognized and which can be defined and enforced by public authority and in many cases by courts of law'. Further, 'many legal statuses have little to do with stratification, for instance such statuses as those of minor, doctor, innkeeper or married woman' (Ibid.: 193). There is only a limited overlap between legal status and social status as an aspect of stratification. The divergence between the two may be best understood by examining societies historically and comparatively.

In Marshall's landmark study of citizenship and social class, the development of citizenship status with its drive towards equality is presented as a counterpoint to the inequalities of class generated by the market. Here class stands for inequality whereas status betokens equality. Where in this argument should one look for the moral and symbolic aspects of inequality, or those aspects of it that Lockwood brought to the fore in his discussion of the ideas of Durkheim, Parsons, and Shils? Following Marshall, Lockwood contrasts 'the divisive solidarities of class and the status common to citizens of the wider society' (Lockwood 1992: 253). Here, to follow Marshall's own distinction referred to earlier, 'status' stands for 'legal' rather than 'social' status; and class and status are opposed as divisiveness and commonality are opposed, or as inequality and equality are opposed. Hence the mismatch between status and class may be represented, with only a little simplification, as the mismatch between the ideal of equality and the reality of inequality. The ideal of equality, or even 'the status common to all citizens' takes little account of 'the differential coefficient of social worth'.

The argument about citizenship and social class here loses sight of status as a fundamental aspect of social stratification whose significance is elsewhere underlined by both Marshall and Lockwood. In that argument, inequality is conflated with class; its roots lie in market forces and not in the moral and symbolic systems of society. Status, on the other hand, is conflated with legal status whose basic premise is equality. Inequalities of 'social' status are either swallowed up by those of class or neutralized by the advance of citizenship.

There can be no denying the many changes in the real positions of men and women in society brought about by the ideal of equal citizenship. Citizenship is an unmediated relationship between the individual and the state which disregards the traditional social hierarchies such as those based on estate, caste, and kinship. Changes in the legal order do bring in changes in social perception; and the moral, and not merely the legal, climate of a democratic society is different from that of an aristocratic one, as Tocqueville (1956) had pointed out more than a hundred and fifty years ago. It was the same trend of change to which Alfred Marshall later drew attention:

The question is not whether all men will ultimately be equal—that they certainly will not—but whether progress may not go on steadily if slowly till the official distinction between working man and gentleman has passed away; till by occupation at least, every man is a gentleman. I hold that it may, and that it will (Pigou 1956: 102).

To do away with the *official* distinction between working man and gentleman is one thing; to ensure that all occupations enjoy equal esteem is another.

In his discussion of citizenship and social class, T.H. Marshall sought to develop the ideas of Alfred Marshall. Agreeing substantially with his predecessor's view about the advance of equality, he observed:

> The basic human equality of membership ... has been enriched with new sub-stance and invested with a formidable array of rights. It has developed far beyond what he foresaw, or would have wished. It has been clearly identified with the status of citizenship (Marshall 1977: 77).

T.H. Marshall's argument here was that the basic equality inherent in the status of citizenship was not incompatible with the inequality of class, although such equality could not be created or sustained without some interference with the processes of the market. He believed—and hoped—that the welfare state would play an active part in restricting the inequality of class by expanding the content of citizenship. The forces of the capitalist jungle would be domesticated by the policies of the welfare state.

Marshall sought to explain the significance of citizenship by showing how new rights were added so that its content became progressively enriched. The three sets of rights that came to be successively built into the status of citizenship were civil rights, political rights, and social rights. These rights have provided an increasingly secure basis to the status of citizenship not only in Britain but in many other countries as well. However, the rights of citizenship do not automatically extinguish the pre-existing hierarchy of esteem as may clearly be seen in a country such as India where the most extensive legal rights coexist with a multitude of invidious social distinctions.

It is important not to lose sight of the fact that we have to contend with three, and not just two, terms. These are, (a) equality of legal status; (b) inequality of class position; and (c) inequality of social esteem. Marshall's own distinction between 'legal status' and 'social status' is very much to the point here. Not only did he make the distinction, he drew attention to the hazards of confusing the one with the other. Speaking about the estate system in Europe, he had observed, 'Legal status rights did not permeate the whole of social life, and a description of stratification in terms of these rights alone is jejune and artificial' (Marshall 1977: 195). And it is well to remember that in a society of estates, which is a hierarchical society, one would expect far greater congruence between legal status and social status than in a modern capitalist democracy.

Marshall had been preceded by Weber in the argument about the limits to which the legal order can constrain a system of social stratification. According to Weber:

Power, as well as honor, may be guaranteed by the legal order, but, at least normally, it is not their primary source. The legal order is rather an additional factor that enhances the chance to hold power or honor; but it can not always secure them (Weber 1978: 926–7).

If the legal order cannot always secure the distinctions of social honour in a hierarchical society, it can regulate only to a limited extent the distinctions of social esteem in a democratic one.

Does the expansion of equal rights in the broadest sense—civil, political, and social—secure full equality of status for all citizens? Everyone appears to be agreed that equality of legal status can accommodate the inequalities of class to a greater or lesser extent. But what other kinds of inequality can it accommodate? It is easy to be beguiled by the temptation of equality that the idea of citizenship places before us. Parsons used that idea as his guiding thread in assessing the social situation of the Blacks in the United States. He expressed a rather positive view of the prospects of 'full citizenship' for them (Parsons 1965), but had very little to say in his analysis of the obstacles to its realization embedded in the evaluative and expressive systems of American society.

Lockwood himself is skeptical about Parsons's idea of 'full citizenship'. But he dwells at the same time on the expansion of 'status rights within the existing social order', and points to 'the expansion of the franchise, the establishment of collective bargaining, and the enlargement of social welfare entitlements' (Lockwood 1992: 255). 'Citizenship is (*sic*) an institution which embodies values that are more exploitable than most because of its diffuse egalitarian promise, the limits of which are highly uncertain' (Ibid.: 260). Referring to the Scandinavian model of citizenship, he notes that it contains 'a more robust notion of equality of opportunity' (Ibid.: 261–2). Here we are far away from the ineradicable bases of the distinctions of status in the morality of everyday life and in the idea of the sacred.

The experience of the second half of the twentieth century shows that the egalitarian promise of the institution of citizenship remains highly diffuse and highly uncertain. What citizenship can achieve by way of the advance of equality depends not only on the nature of the state but also on the divisions that run through society. The Scandinavian countries are different from the United States in both respects. Citizenship is no doubt an important force for equality, but it has to contend not only with the divisions of class but also with those of race, caste, and ethnicity, and much more so in some societies than in others.

Lockwood sees that the status rights attached to citizenship can only promise but not fully establish equality, hence he is skeptical of the idea of 'full citizenship' proposed by Parsons. But he does not tell us what, other than the inequalities of class generated by the market, is to stand in the way of its establishment. The normative order, which had secured the ineradicability of the distinctions of status, seems to have been turned around by the advance of citizenship into being a guarantor of equality (Lockwood 1996). In such a situation, inequality can only be about the control over things and persons, i.e., economic and political power.

Though skeptical of the idea of full citizenship, Lockwood has sought to distinguish between 'substantive citizenship' and 'formal citizenship': 'Substantive citizenship is therefore qualitatively different from formal citizenship, since it is built on values that run counter to the market and point beyond this mode of income distribution' (Lockwood 1992: 262). It is not clear in what sense 'substantive citizenship' differs from 'full citizenship' or whether the one is more easily attainable than the other. Formal citizenship has clearly played a part not only in restraining the excesses of class but also in undermining many of the traditional distinctions of status. But old social distinctions often survive, however transmuted, and new ones emerge. We are likely to lose sight of these if we focus only on what the state can do to secure equality of status in the face of the inequalities of class generated by the market. Market and state are important in the life of society, but they do not make up the whole of it.

No doubt the relationship between the inequalities of income generated by the market and the equal rights of citizenship created and protected by the state tells us something very important about social stratification in modern societies. But an acknowledgement of the importance of that relationship should not lead us to deny or ignore the connection of status with the sacred. It is true that the legal order has itself a sacred character and is at the same time an important source of core values. But while the legal order of modern societies can tell us a great deal about the pursuit of equality, it cannot tell us very much about the continuance and renewal of inequality.

Here I find it useful to turn to the distinction, which we owe to Parsons, between norms and values, and more generally to the antinomies of society. 'Norms' are for Parsons 'regulatory rules'; they are primarily social and their structural locus is the legal system. 'Values', on the other hand, are 'generalized ends', and they connect the social with the cultural system (see Béteille 2000a: 208–37). Although they are distinct analytically, the term 'normative order' is often used by Parsons to cover both, not without some confusion. The emphasis in his essay on full citizenship for the American Black was on norms or regulatory rules; the emphasis in his two earlier, more general, essays on social stratification was on values or generalized ends.

Norms and values are rarely, if ever, in a state of stable equilibrium. This is particularly true during the passage from a hierarchical to a democratic system which is marked by deep and pervasive antinomies, by which I mean the contradictions, oppositions, and tensions within the 'normative order' in the broad sense. The equilibrium of norms and values characteristic of stable hierarchical systems is rarely re-established in democratic ones. The historical experience has been that it is much easier to change the legal norms of a society than its underlying social values. This is strikingly demonstrated in the case of India in the last fifty years where formal citizenship has had to steer a very uneasy course in a social environment permeated by traditional hierarchical values. The Indian case is exemplary because it brings out strikingly the disjunction between norms and values, a disjunction that is present in more muted and less visible forms in every modern society.

T.H. Marshall did well to bring to light the opposition of citizenship and social class. But the normative order itself, of which citizenship is but one expression, is permeated by deeper tensions and contradictions.

There are distinct limits to the utility of rights-based concepts in the analysis of systems of stratification in modern societies. The simple reason for this is that social stratification goes against the grain of the legal order in 'democratic' as against 'aristocratic' societies, to use Tocqueville's terms. But that is not to say that it has no basis in the evaluative and expressive aspects of these societies. No matter how diligently we seek to refashion the concept of citizenship, it remains at its core a rights-based concept. T.H. Marshall, who drew pointed attention to the distinction between 'legal' and 'social' status, was well aware of this. The concept of citizenship is of enormous utility in the comparative and historical study of societies. We have only to compare India and France in the nineteenth century, or to follow the passage of Britain from the eighteenth to the twentieth century to appreciate this. But although it can illuminate broad differences in a very striking way, its utility in accounting for the unequal social positions of different persons and different categories of persons is limited.

Students of stratification in modern societies have devoted a great deal of attention to the social grading of occupations (Goldthorpe and Hope 1974). Occupational differentiation and ranking are among the most significant features of these societies. The legal order can tell us very little as to why physicians or architects are consistently rated higher than gardeners or porters. The consistency of occupational rank-ing shows that there is an underlying system of values which discrimi-nates between physicians and architects on the one hand and gardeners and porters on the other. The law does not discriminate among them, and, as citizens, they enjoy equality of legal status; but they do not by any means enjoy equality of social status. Perhaps Alfred Marshall's hope that they will all come to be regarded as gentlemen will soon be realized. But by then the category of 'gentleman' will have been emp-tied of content, and new social distinctions come into operation.

How should we account for the unequal esteem attached to different occupations, not only in the sphere of work but also outside it? Here there is a strong temptation to abandon all arguments about the expres-sion of core values, the proximity to sacred centres, and the differential coefficient of social worth, and to revert to the hard common sense of capitalism which sees all inequality as resting ultimately on the distri-bution of income, wealth, and material advantage. That would still leave unexplained why Blacks and Whites, or women and men, are unequally esteemed even when education, occupation, and income are held constant. We cannot even begin to understand these matters with-out taking account of the symbolism of colour and of the human body in western societies of the past and the present. To say that the Ameri-can Black does not as yet enjoy full citizenship but is moving towards it does not seem to be a very fruitful way of addressing the problem of unequal social esteem in a complex society where contradictory values coexist.

It is true that equality of esteem cannot be enjoyed in the absence of equality of rights. But the converse is not true: it is not possible to guarantee equality of esteem simply by legislating equal rights for all citizens, no matter how extensively those rights might be defined. Status may be a matter of rights, but it is also a matter of esteem, and the two do not necessarily move in step with each other.

The problem of status is complicated in modern societies by the disjunction between the legal order and other aspects of the social order. There have been societies in the past, based on caste, that were hierarchical both in fact and by design: to borrow a phrase from Huizinga (1924), Europe in the late Middle Ages was suffused by 'the hierarchic conception of society'. There social distinctions between superior and inferior—or the differential coefficient of social worth—did not act against the grain of the legal order, but were supported, reinforced, and expressed by it.

The modern concept of citizenship was alien to the hierarhcial societies of the past, whether in Asia or in Europe. The best known historical example of such a society was the one that existed in India for two thousand years (Dumont 1966; Bose 1975). It was a society marked by privileges and disabilities between groups rather than equality among individuals as citizens. Society was divided and subdivided into groups that were unequally ranked. The boundaries between these groups and their unequal ranks were maintained by marriage rules and distinctive styles of life that were upheld by religion, morality, and law. Social distinctions, and the differential coefficient of worth associated with them were discussed, explained, and justified in an elaborate body of literature known as the Dharmashastra which was the basis of Hindu law until recent times.

The division of society into castes gave a framework for the distinctions of status. To be sure, those distinctions enjoyed legal sanctions, but the law provided only a framework within which a great many distinctions having to do with food, dress, deportment, and many other matters took root and proliferated. The same appears to have been true by and large of the law of estates in medieval Europe, and Huizinga has dwelt particularly on the aesthetic and expressive aspects of the distinctions of status within that order. Again, while the law might provide a useful, indeed an indispensable, starting point for the study of social hierarchy among the Hindus, distinctions of status in Hindu society acquired a life of their own, and were elaborated and reproduced in a thousand different ways to many of which the law was at best indifferent. Similar distinctions, though less elaborate and less rigid, also prevailed among the Muslims in India who were not governed by the Dharmashastra but by a different kind of law.

Distinctions of status not only have a life of their own outside the law, they sometimes grow by mimicry even against the spirit of the law. This may be seen by comparing styles of life and patterns of social exclusion among Hindus and Muslims on the Indian subcontinent. Muslims borrowed many distinctions of status, including some of those associated with caste, from the Hindus among whom they lived despite the differences between Hindu law and Muslim law, and even where the Muslims were the rulers. Again, at the height of imperial rule, educated middle-class Indians added to their own distinctions of status many of those characteristic of Victorian England. Symbols of status, to borrow Whitehead's expressive words, 'have a tendency to run wild, like the vegetation in a tropical forest' (Whitehead 1959: 61).

The law has changed in India. The change began in the middle of the nineteenth century and reached its high watermark in 1950 with the adoption of the Constitution of India. The hierarchical distinctions of caste no longer have any legal standing. The only context in which the Constitution allows caste to be taken into account is that of positive discrimination whose objective is not to support the old distinction of status—or hierarchical distinctions of any kind—but to render them inoperative. Today in India, as in many parts of the world, citizenship has become an important component of the legal order. In the Indian Constitution, the parts on Fundamental Rights and on Directive Principles of State Policy both place strong emphasis on the protection and promotion of equality among citizens (Béteille 1987b).

It will be incorrect to say that the entitlements of citizenship have made no difference at all to the texture of social life in India. In the last five decades, law and politics have done something to alter the relations among castes. But no one can seriously claim that the legal rights of citizenship have expunged all the distinctions due to caste. The contemporary Indian case shows very clearly how a certain commitment to the equal rights of citizenship may go hand in hand with a keen sense of the differential coefficient of social worth.

Some of the distinctions of status due to caste have disappeared; some have become muted; and some remain clear and well marked. The law can abolish discrimination due to caste in only certain fields; it cannot even attempt to do so in every field. Meanwhile, new social distinctions based on education, occupation, and lifestyle have emerged and become intermeshed with the old distinctions of caste. The new distinctions of status operate in many ways like the old ones, although they do not enjoy the kind of legal sanction that the latter did under the law of the Dharmashastra. One may certainly describe them as 'conventional', but that should not be taken to mean that they are, from the social point of view, trivial.

I have already referred to the confusion caused by the conflation of 'status' and 'status-group'. Status-groups with legally defined or recognized identities are a particular form of the crystallization of distinctions of status, just as classes with a clear sense of their opposed interests are a particular form of the crystallization of economic differentiation. Even where they are associated with legally enforceable privileges and disabilities, status-groups do not exhaust all the distinctions of status recognized in a society. This was as true of the European system of estates as of the Hindu system of castes.

One might of course argue that the distinctions of status that remain pervasive in contemporary Indian society are residues of a past in which the legal order upheld a hierarchy of status-groups. To the extent that tradition is an important guarantor of distinctions of status, one should not discount those residues of the past in any society. They continue to play an important part in maintaining and reproducing the inferior social, as against legal, standing of Blacks in the United States and of ethnic minorities from the non-western world throughout Europe. There is also the unequal social standing of men and women in most if not all industrially advanced countries: is this a question of class or of status in societies where rights of equal citizenship, irrespective of gender, have been established?

More important than the question of how long and in what forms the residues from the past are likely to survive in advanced industrial societies is the question whether these societies have the capacity to generate new distinctions of status. Leaving aside distinctions based on race, caste, ethnicity, and gender, modern societies have shown enormous capacity to generate new social distinctions based on occupation, education, and lifestyle. Students of social stratification in Europe and America have done well to point out how complex and elaborate the social grading of occupations is in advanced industrial societies; but they have not always pointed out how new, in a broader historical perspective, all of this is. The differentiation and ranking of occupations were relatively simple matters in western societies until a couple of hundred years ago; today they are a fertile source for the proliferation of all kinds of social distinctions. These are not residues from the past; they are innovations.

The modernization of society by which the advance of the equal rights of citizenship is driven renders obsolete many of the traditional symbols of status and puts an end to age-old modes of social exclusion. But modernization creates its own symbols of status and its own modes of exclusion. It will be a mistake to believe that modern societies know how to innovate only in the technical and not in the symbolic domain; or that they create only symbols of inclusion and not of exclusion.

Modern societies are prolific in the creation of new cultural symbols, maintaining a continuous differentiation of lifestyles. Compared to stable hierarchical societies where it enjoyed legal or quasi-legal sanctions, social exclusion in democratic societies acts in diffuse, implicit, even surreptitious, ways, often under the cover of privacy. Some of the most interesting work on social stratification in recent years has been about the elaboration of cultural and social distinctions and their reproduction through the use of symbolic capital (Bourdieu 1984, 1988; Bourdieu and Passeron 1977). Parsons had rightly pointed to the central significance of moral values in the structure of social ranking. But, as the work of Bourdieu has shown, social gradation in contemporary societies is not only about moral judgements; it is also about judgements of taste. Moral judgements and judgements of taste lend themselves to continuous elaboration and innovation, and they can be constrained only to a limited extent by the equal rights of citizenship. These judgements sustain and are sustained by the differential coefficient of social worth, unequal esteem, and unequal social status.

The equal rights of citizenship are of the greatest importance in the modern world. It may not be too much of an exaggeration to say that they are the defining features of modern societies. At the same time, they have to contend not only with the inequalities of class or the market but also with those that arise from the evaluative and expressive systems of society, no matter by what name we decide to call the inequalities of the second kind.

3

Varna and *Jati*

I would like to use the present occasion to discuss some important changes taking place in the caste system in our time. The focus of attention will be on caste as a system of representations, and I would like to justify my approach by referring you to Durkheim whose view was that social facts are things, but they are also, and at the same time, representations.

The social morphology of caste continues to be one of its important features. The division of Indian society into innumerable castes and communities has been noted by the many Backward Classes Commissions set up in independent India, and Mr Mandal's Commission listed as many as three thousand seven hundred and forty-three. More recently, the monumental People of India project undertaken by the Anthropological Survey of India has drawn public attention to the continuing significance of the divisions of caste and subcaste in contemporary India. But I will dwell less on these divisions and subdivisions themselves than on the ways in which they are perceived, particularly among the intelligentsia whose role in contemporary Indian society should not be discounted.

My argument is a simple one. In the classical literature of India, caste was represented as *varna* and for two thousand years, when Hindus wrote about it, they did so characteristically in the idiom of *varna*. This is no longer the case and caste is now represented much more typically as *jati*, or its equivalent in the regional language. This displacement of *varna* by *jati* indicates much more than a simple linguistic shift. It indicates a change of perception, a change in the meaning and legitimacy of caste even among those who continue to abide by the constraints imposed by its morphology on marriage and other matters. This change has not as yet received the systematic attention from sociologists that is its due. It is a truism that caste is not merely a form of identity, arising from birth in a particular group; it is also a matter of consciousness. It was believed by many at the time of independence that with economic and political development, with a secular Constitution and with the spread of education and a scientific outlook, the consciousness of caste would decline or disappear, at least from public view. It is quite evident that caste consciousness has not disappeared, and many would even question that it has declined. But what we have today is a somewhat different kind of consciousness, with *jati* rather than *varna* in the foreground.

I do not wish to suggest that the consciousness of *jati*, or the idea of it is a new one, only that it had a subordinate place in representations of the caste system. Much of the reality of everyday life must have turned around the divisions and subdivisions of *jati*. It may have been the case even in the distant—as in the more recent—past that peasants, artisans, and labourers gave little thought to the larger scheme of things expressed by the concept of *varna*. My attention today is on India's long intellectual tradition. Within that tradition, the literati, those who reflected on what we call caste today, and wrote about it, represented it in the idiom of *varna* rather than *jati*. When their contemporary counterparts write and speak about it, they make use of a different idiom.

I would like to turn now to the path-breaking essay by M.N. Srinivas (1962: 63–69) called 'Varna and Caste' published more than forty years ago. It may be noted that the title pre-empts, at least by implication, the term caste for the designation of *jati*. Srinivas was reacting against the Indological representation of caste as *varna* which he felt gave a distorted view of the Indian reality: 'The *varna*-model has produced a wrong and distorted image of caste. It is necessary for the sociologist to free himself from the hold of the *varna*-model if he wishes to understand the caste system' (Ibid.: 66). My point is that Indians are in fact freeing themselves from the hold of that model. The conditions under which this disengagement is taking place were not discussed by Srinivas, but they merit serious attention.

Srinivas's impatience with the *varna*-model was a response to the dominance in Indian writing about society of what he called the 'book-view' which he was eager to replace with the 'field-view'. He pointed out, with great success, that the way people actually live is very different

from how they are supposed to live, and that sociologists should concentrate on the former and not the latter. This was true of the Indian
village community, the Indian joint family and, of course, also of caste.
But then, people everywhere have some conception of how they ought
to live. Today in particular, they are acutely aware that they do not
always live as they ought to, and it would be a mistake for the sociologist to ignore how people think they ought to live, and dwell only on
how they actually live. It is in this sense that I consider representations
to be an important part of the social reality.

No matter how we argue, we cannot turn our back on the book-view
of Indian society which may be regarded as a particular form of collective representations. Of course, collective representations have to be
studied even where there is no book-view, as Durkheim did in his work
on the Australian Aborigines who had no book, hence no book-view.
But India is not just an aggregate of tribal and peasant communities. It
is and has been a major civilization in which the book-view, or, rather,
different and even competing book-views have existed for two thousand years and more. The social reality on the ground rarely changes
without some change in collective representations; and when those
change, the book-view also undergoes change.

Just as the social reality on the ground and its morphological framework change, so also do collective representations and the authoritative
texts in which they are encoded. The authoritative texts of the past no
longer enjoy their old authority today. Their influence has declined,
although it has by no means disappeared. Here it is useful to remember
that the late Professor P.V. Kane found a place for the Constitution of
India in his monumental work on the history of Dharmashastra. Nor
am I talking only of the Dharmashastra, with or without inclusion of
the Constitution. Today, the book-view of Indian society may be found
in a variety of texts: legislative debates, judicial decisions, political
manifestos, essays, pamphlets, and books of a great variety of types.
Caste figures in many of these documents, but it figures more commonly as *jati* than as *varna*, in contrast with the ancient and medieval
texts.

Sifting this vast and amorphous mass of material for convincing
evidence of a clear direction of change in the social perception of caste
is no easy task. It is not something that can be accomplished single-hand-
edly by any individual scholar. I cannot say that I have even made a
proper beginning of a systematic enquiry. The only point I would like
to make very briefly here is that the really crucial evidence of the shift

in representations of caste will be found not in English but in the Indian languages. I can claim some competence in only one of those languages, namely Bengali, and I have been struck for some time that Bengalis, particularly of the younger generation, hardly use the term *varna* (or *barna*) in either speech or writing. Casual enquiries from those whose mother tongue is Hindi seem to indicate that something similar is happening there as well; beyond that, I am not able to even suggest anything further.

The idiom of *varna* has no doubt been used extensively in the present century in the process of upward social mobility described as Sanskritization (Srinivas 1966). It is possible that the new opportunities provided by censuses and ethnographic surveys since the end of the nineteenth century may even have revived to some extent the language of *varna* among groups aspiring to upward social mobility. But the impression is that this trend reached its peak in the earlier part of the twentieth century and is now on the decline. When so many castes with manifestly inappropriate antecedents claim that they are Kshatriyas, the category itself is bound to become devalued. Where sixty years ago a caste would claim to be Kshatriya, today the same caste might prefer to be designated as backward. This is not a change of small significance.

Srinivas seemed to suggest that there was an error in describing caste as *varna* and that it should be described as *jati*. My view is that this is not just a recognition of error, but also a response to change. A decade before the publication of Srinivas's paper on *varna* and caste, the social historian Niharranjan Ray (1945) published a book in Bengali entitled *Bangali Hindur Barnabhed*, meaning caste among the Bengali Hindus. Similarly, the anthropologist, N.K. Bose, who wrote much in Bengali (1949a; 1949b; 1975), often for literary magazines, freely used the term *barna* in describing caste. There is a repertoire of terms relating to *varna* or *barna: barnabyabastha*, the affairs of caste; *barnabinyas*, the arrangement of castes; *asabarnabibaha*, inter-caste marriage; *barnasankar*, offspring of mixed unions; and so on. My impression is that these terms are now far less commonly used among Bengalis than in the 1930s and 1940s.

What appears remarkable in retrospect is the continuing use of this language in a social context that was making its categories obsolete. Bose, in particular, was tireless in pointing to the forces that were disrupting the design of traditional Hindu society. Both he and Ray were well aware that the actual divisions of Bengali Hindu society did not fit at all well into the traditional scheme of *varnas*: there were only

Brahmans among the three upper *varnas*, the rest being in some sense or other Shudras. Such has been the actual state of affairs for decades or even centuries, yet the old language continued in use right until our own time.

Much of Bose's description in fact related to such functional castes and subcastes as Telis, Kumhars, Lohars, and so on, which he would certainly recognize as *jatis*; yet he commonly used the language of *varna* to refer to such general features of their social arrangement as division of labour, rules of marriage, and so on. One of the reasons in his case might have been his interest in the distinction between tribe and caste, and in what he called the Hindu method of tribal absorption (Bose 1941). He repeatedly argued that Hindu society had a distinct design, and that non-Hindus, from both within and outside, had fitted themselves into it. He continued to use the language of *varna* because of his interest in that design even while he pointed out that it was being undermined by internal and external pressure to an extent that had no precedent in the country's history.

Srinivas (1962: 69) said at the end of his brief essay: '*Varna* has provided a common social language which holds good or is thought to hold good, for India as a whole'. What I am arguing here is that it is this language that is now, before our eyes, becoming obsolete and anachronistic. When Bengalis speak or write about caste, they no longer use *barna* as commonly as before, but *jat* in the spoken language, and also *jati* in the written form. Their experience and perception of caste has changed, and this change is expressed in the shift of vocabulary.

When I discuss the caste system with young, educated, upper-caste Bengalis now, I am struck by their lack of familiarity with the old vocabulary pertaining to inter-caste marriage, hypergamy, offspring of mixed unions and so on. Part of this is due to the reduced attention paid in schools to the teaching of Sanskrit which was the basis of Bengali grammar and etymology; another part is due to the obsolescence, or at least the attenuation, of an old social code which upper-caste Bengali children imbibed at home without conscious effort; and part of it is due to a shift of attention brought about by the enlarged role of caste in politics.

Both *varna* and *jati* are polysemic terms, and therefore it is natural that there should be a large overlap of meaning between the two. Many writers on the subject took colour to be the primary meaning of *varna*, and sought its origin in the distinction between the light-skinned Aryas and the dark-skinned indigenous population (Ghurye 1950; Srinivas

1962: 63–9). But Mrs Karve (1968: 50–2) rightly pointed out that the term had other connotations in the early sacred literature and grammatical works. It is best to adopt her suggestion to use the word *varna* in the sense of hierarchical order, and to refer to the four *varnas* as the four orders of society. This would be in conformity with the European usage which spoke of the orders of society, or the three orders or estates (Duby 1980). That usage continued in the English language until late; Adam Smith, for instance, spoke of orders rather than classes. It was only in the nineteenth century that the concept of order was displaced by that of classes in response to major changes in society.

N.K. Bose drew attention to the varieties of categories to which the concept of *varna* was applied. He wrote: 'The division into *varna* is not confined to human society; it is widely known that even lands or temples are classified into Brahman, Kshatriya and so on' (1975: 91). Earlier he dwelt in particular on the classification of temples into *varnas* (Bose n.d.). He concluded, 'In effect we may regard the *varna* system as a particular method for dividing into classes various kinds of phenomena, beginning with human society' (1975: 91). It was, in other words, the pre-eminent scheme of social classification established by Hindu cosmology.

Conceptually, the order of *varnas* is not only exclusive, it is also exhaustive. The Dharmashastra says Brahman, Kshatriya, Vaishya, Shudra, these are the four *varnas* and there is no fifth; this means that in principle all of mankind can be fitted into one or other of the four *varnas*. According to Bose, this was regularly done in the past when *varna* was an active principle of social classification. 'Whenever in ancient India men came in contact with different communities, they tried to find a place for them in one or another *varna* according to their qualities and actions' (1975: 91). *Varna* has ceased to be an active principle of social classification; it has been displaced by other principles.

It is obvious that *varna* did not cease to play an active part in the arrangement and rearrangement of groups in society all at once. What is now happening seems to be the culmination of a very long and tortuous process. When the British established their empire in India, the new rulers could no longer be accommodated within the scheme of *varnas*: here one might find significant differences between British India and the princely states. The process had started earlier, with the Islamic conquest, although Muslim rulers adapted themselves to the Indian social climate much better than their European successors. Nevertheless, both Muslims and Europeans had other models of rulership, and where their authority became established, the category of Kshatri-yas inevitably became emptied of some of its meaning.

Where large sections of the population became converted to Islam, as in the Punjab and Bengal, it became difficult to fit those sections into the scheme of the four *varnas*. To the extent that social divisions such as those between Rajputs, Jats, and Ahirs survived the conversion to Islam, some continuity with the old forms of representation was main-tained. People recognized the gaps and inconsistencies, but still used the language of *varna* in writing about caste.

The idea of *jati* is also an old one and has been used, along with that of *varna*, for a very long time to refer to caste. But the connotations of the two have perhaps always been a little different. The term *jati* refers more to the units that constituted the system—the castes and commu-nities—than to the system viewed as a whole. It did not provide the kind of basis for a universal social classification that *varna* did. Unlike the *varnas*, the *jatis* were not thought of as being exhaustive in a formal sense. We have noted that the Dharmashastra named the four *varnas*, and said that there was no fifth. One cannot draw up a complete list of all the multifarious *jatis* and declare categorically that none exists be-sides those listed. New *jatis* could always be added on, but not new *varnas*.

Perhaps the term *jati* has been used more commonly than the term *varna* for a very long time. It is also a polysemic term, and I am suggesting that today it can be stretched to accommodate all kinds of units that cannot be accommodated by *varna*. For instance, it would be strange to describe the Muslims as a *varna* or a segment of a *varna*, whereas it is common to hear them being described as a *jati*; their subdivisions, whether of the sect or the caste type, may also be de-scribed as *jatis*. There being no fixed number of *jatis*, the word allows itself to be used for denoting a group as well as a subdivision of it.

Whereas *varna* refers primarily to order and classification, the pri-mary reference of *jati* is to birth and the social identity ascribed by birth. It is thought of as a natural kind whose members share a common substance, although the sense of that may be weak or strong, depending on how broadly the group is conceived. *Jatis*, unlike classes, are thought of as organic divisions, self-generated and self-reproducing.

The term *jati* is, if anything, even more elastic than its counterpart, *varna*. It may refer to a very small group, such as a subcaste or a sub-subcaste; it may refer also to the whole of humanity. Bengalis speak commonly of the Sadgope or the Kayastha *jati*, but also of *manabjati* or *manushyajati*. In current Bengali usage, the term may be applied to Europeans, Germans, American Blacks, Muslims, Madrasis (meaning south Indians), or Punjabis. The idea always is that the members of a *jati* share some qualities in common which give them a distinctive identity that is somehow present even when it is not visible. Men and women may be referred to separately as *jatis—strijati* and *purushjati—* but not, so far as I am aware, capitalists and workers.

Anyone who has tried to conduct an ethnographic census among Bengalis in the Bengali language will know how frustrating it can be to secure comparable information on caste. The entries under that column frequently contain such items as Jain, Oriya, Sayyad, Sikh, Adivasi, Santal, and so on, in addition to the names of castes as understood in the sociological literature. Census-takers with tidy minds have always found this to be a nightmare.

Every anthropologist has at one time or another been outwitted by his informants, and I too have my own tale of woes. When during my fieldwork in Burdwan, I asked my informants to which *jat* they belonged, some of them naturally put the same question back to me. The answer that I did not belong to any *jat* was rarely taken seriously. Puzzled by my name, they would ask whether I was not in fact a Bengali. When I pointed out that that had to do with my mother tongue, not my caste, they would say, 'Ah, then you are a Christian.' If I denied that, a sarcastic bystander might ask, 'Then I suppose you are a Frenchman?' The point is that my informants—and indeed many of my Bengali friends—believed that if I could not say that I was a Brahman or a Kayastha, I should admit to being a Bengali; if not that, at least to being a Christian. Practically anything might serve; what does not serve is not having any *jat* at all.

It is true that even today, the vast majority of Indians think of a person without a *jati* as an anomaly; indeed, they suspect that such a person probably has something to hide. At the same time, it must be recognized that *jati* here includes other kinds of units besides those that are listed and ranked as castes in works of ethnography. In this wider sense, *jatis* are not always or necessarily ranked. Many upper-caste Bengali Hindus speak of Bengalis (meaning Bengali Hindus) and Muslims (including Muslim Bengalis) or Christians (including Christian Bengalis) as different *jats*, but that does not mean that they think that Hindus, Muslims, and Christians are unequally ranked. Similarly, when they speak of Oriyajati and Telegujati, they think of them as different rather than unequal.

At first sight, such units as Brahmans, Sadgopes, Muslims, Bagdis, Oriyas, and Santals appear to be extremely heterogeneous. They cannot be thought of as the differentiated parts of any kind of system based on the division of religious functions. Hence they cannot be thought of as *varnas* or fitted into the order of *varnas*. But such units are precisely the ones that are increasingly competing with each other in the political process. In Bengal certainly, and perhaps in other parts of the country as well, when people think about caste today, they think less about religion than about politics. Hence they find it more natural to represent caste as *jati* than as *varna*.

In the 1960s, some anthropologists argued that when castes compete with each other in the political arena, they act in contravention of caste principles (Leach 1960). One might perhaps say this about caste in the sense of *varna* but hardly about caste in the sense of *jati*. The competition for power between castes and between coalitions of castes and communities is perhaps the most conspicuous feature of contemporary Indian politics. Here it would be misleading to represent the contending parties as *varnas*, but quite appropriate to describe them as *jatis*. The order of *varnas* necessarily entails a hierarchy of ranks, whereas the competition for power takes place between equals, or near equals. What one caste lacks in ritual status, it may make up by strength of numbers; where its members are wanting in educational attainments, they may advance through superior capacity for organization.

Castes have become increasingly involved in politics, but they have not ceased to be castes (Béteille 1969b). Electoral politics increases the consciousness of caste, and at the same time creates networks of relations across caste (Srinivas and Béteille 1964). The old cleavages between castes are continuously redefined by the formation of new coalitions among them. The sense of a common identity defined by birth and of a shared substance among members of the same caste provides a strong basis for the mobilization of electoral support (Kothari 1970). At the same time, the momentum of democratic politics creates coalitions between all kinds of groups, only some of which can be plausibly related to the traditional order of *varnas*.

All these different types of groups—castes, tribes, sects, denominations, religious and linguistic minorities—may, depending on context and situation, be designated as *jatis*. There is little sign of any decline in their active participation in the competition for scarce resources.

Nor are they active only in politics. We shall presently see how attachment to the group also provides a sense of economic security to its individual members.

I have pointed out that all these various groups—those listed by Mr Mandal's Commission and those being catalogued by the Anthropological Survey of India—may be called *jatis*, at least in the Bengali language. But can they all be legitimately designated in the English language as castes? There appears to be a problem of translation here. The term caste answers only partly, but not fully, to what Bengalis mean by *jat* or *jati*, which may refer also, according to context and situation, to tribe, sect, and religious or linguistic minority. It is in this light that we have to view the increasing use of such terms as ethnicity, ethnic identity, and ethnic group by sociologists and others to describe a significant feature of contemporary Indian society and politics. I am not suggesting that these are the most suitable terms, but they seem to answer better than the term caste to the mixed bag of social groupings to which I have been drawing attention.

Recently, Professor Srinivas has observed, 'In the future too caste will remain important in Indian life. But it will be conceived more in terms of ethnicity' (Padgaonkar 1993). That sums up very nicely what I am now trying to say. Those who had feared that the organic unity of society represented by the order of *varnas* would be disrupted by the new economic and political forces have had their fears confirmed, for it has become increasingly difficult to use *varna* as a standard of reference for describing the relations between castes. But those who had hoped that the new economic and political forces would lead to the demise of caste also have had their hopes belied, for the collective identities represented by the idea of *jati* have shown remarkable tenacity.

Writing in the 1920s and 1930s, Mahatma Gandhi (1962) represented the moral order of Hindu society in terms of *varna*, and still hoped that it could be revived and renovated for the benefit of all. It is that memory, filtered no doubt through rose-tinted glasses, that lingered in the minds of many Hindu intellectuals who wrote about caste until almost the time of independence. Today, it is difficult to invoke even the memory of a moral order in writing and speaking about caste.

When people now write about caste, they do not write about morality but about politics, the two being viewed as widely different, if not opposed in their nature. But is not loyalty to the community of one's birth, whether viewed in terms of language, religion, caste, sect, or tribe, itself a moral fact in the sense given to the term by Durkheim?

Here, the matter is somewhat complex because while people might concede that loyalty to language, religion, sect, or even tribe may be legitimate, they seem less prepared to make the same concession for loyalty to caste. The reason for this is that no matter how strong the pull of collective loyalties may be, our Constitution and our laws give primacy to the rights of the individual. Those rights might be required to accommodate the claims of religion and culture to some extent, but it is difficult to see why they should yield to the demands of caste which seems merely to divide without providing anything beyond some un-defined sense of security to its individual members.

We should not underestimate the moral force of the sense of security that attachment to caste and community gives to the individual in a changing and uncertain world. It is to this that N.K. Bose drew atten-tion in one of his later writings, a brilliant essay on the motley assort-ment of castes and communities that make up the city of Calcutta. He described the various castes among the Bengali Hindus—Kayasthas, Kansaris, Namshudras—living cheek-by-jowl with Oriyas, Sikhs, Urdu-speaking Muslims, Bengali-speaking Muslims, Gujarati Baniyas, and many others, all regarding themselves and regarded by others as so many different *jats*. He drew attention to the economic compulsions that kept them together, reinforcing in each a sense of its distinct identity:

Because there are not enough jobs to go around everyone clings as closely as possible to the occupation with which his ethnic group is identified and relies for economic support on those who speak his language, his co-religionists, on members of his own caste and on fellow immigrants from the village or district from which he has come (1965: 102).

The continuing strength of these collective identities is a reflection of the failure of the institutions of civil society to take root and gather strength in independent India. Civil society requires a variety of open and secular institutions—schools, universities, hospitals, municipal corporations, professional bodies, and voluntary associations of many different kinds—to mediate between the individual and the wider so-ciety of which he is a part. At the time of independence, it was hoped that these open and secular institutions would give shape and substance to democracy in India and at the same time drive back the consciousness of caste and community. They have failed to provide what was expected of them, and it is no surprise that the older forms of collective identities have not only held their ground but become increasingly assertive.

4

Caste in Contemporary India[1]

Meaning and Legitimacy of Caste

The subject I have selected is a very large one, and I am anxious therefore to indicate at once the limits within which I shall try to confine the discussion. Caste has been a subject of continuous interest to ethnographers, historians, and sociologists for the last hundred years, and attempts have been made to identify its fundamental structure, either in terms of a set of enduring groups and the enduring relations between them (Mayer 1960; Berreman 1963), or in terms of some principle of opposition, for instance between purity and pollution (Dumont 1966; Marriott 1990). I have myself written on the subject from time to time (Béteille 1969a, 1991), opposing some views and supporting others, but I will not enter into an extended discussion here of the social morphology of caste or the cultural oppositions on which it is based.

My primary concern will be with questions of meaning and legitimacy. What does it mean in India today for a person to belong to a particular caste or subcaste? What demands can it make on him or her and in what contexts, and to what extent is he or she prepared to meet those demands? We know very well that individuals do not always meet the demands made on them, that they are subjected to contradictory

[1] A first, very preliminary version of this chapter was presented as a lecture at the University of California, Berkeley, in April 1992 where Professor G.D. Berreman, who was in the chair, made a number of observations from which I have greatly benefited. I am grateful also for the many helpful comments I received when it was presented in London in July 1993, and would like in particular to thank Professor Jonathan Parry and Dr C.J. Fuller for their comprehensive written comments which have helped me in making extensive revisions.

pulls and pressures, and that they sometimes subordinate social obligation to personal interest. We know also that there are sanctions of
various kinds against the violation of prescribed or generally accepted
codes of conduct. What are the sanctions available to the caste or
subcaste today to ensure the conformity of the individual with the
codes prescribed or acknowledged by it?

It is quite obvious that being a member of a caste or subcaste does
not have the same meaning today for all individuals everywhere, if it
ever did in the past; nor do caste sanctions operate with the same force
in all sections of Indian society. I shall not attempt to provide a key to
the understanding of caste as a whole or as a 'total social system' in
either the past or the present, being mindful of the fact that such
attempts have usually come to grief. I shall confine myself largely to
urban Indians in what may be described as modern occupations, leaving
aside, except for occasional comments, the large majority of Indians
who inhabit the rural areas and derive their livelihood from agriculture
and related occupations. This does not mean that my argument does
not have some implications for the latter, but those implications are
not as yet fully clear.

I do not wish to circumscribe too narrowly the class or section of
society on which I seek to focus attention. It may be referred to loosely
as the 'urban middle class' or even the 'urban middle classes'. More
recently, the terms 'intelligentsia', 'professionals' and 'service class'
have been employed to refer to roughly the same category of persons
(Rudra 1989; Bardhan 1984; Béteille 1989; see also Chapter 7). These
terms are useful, not because they are accurate, but because they draw
attention to the growing importance of this class or stratum in contemporary India. Here numbers are important but not necessarily decisive.
If we adopt a narrow definition and take into account only civil servants, managers, and higher professionals, we will still be dealing with
a population that runs into hundreds of thousands. If we extend the
conception to include schoolteachers, clerks, and other white-collar
workers, as some are inclined to do, we will have a much larger category, numbering 50–75 million persons or more. Of course, these
distinctions have to be made much more carefully if we are to achieve
precision, but I am not now in a position to do so.

There is a reason why it is necessary to have some sense of the
numbers involved even when it is not possible to give precise numbers.
It is sometimes said that the underlying structure of caste remains what
it was, and that if there are changes in caste practice, they are superficial

and confined to a handful of urban, or educated, or westernized individuals who are in any case not truly representative of Indian society and culture. I wish to emphasize that the class or stratum that I am talking about, whether conceived broadly or narrowly, does not comprise a mere handful of individuals, and that socially, if not demographically, it is a very important part of contemporary India.

Again, I am anxious to avoid the impression of making too large a claim for my argument. What needs to be stressed as much as the social significance of the class or section in question is its great social diversity in terms of language, region, and religion—and, what is as important, in terms of wealth, occupation, and education. Limiting ourselves only to the professionals, there is all the difference in the world between a senior member of the Calcutta or Bombay bar and a small-town advocate; or between the research scientist in the Indian Institute of Science and the science teacher in a mofussil college. The stratum as a whole is so large and so diverse that any statement made about it could be either wholly true or wholly false for at least some of its individual members. Caste cannot possibly have the same meaning or the same legitimacy for all the individual members of such a large and diverse population, but that in a sense is the point I wish to make against those who would represent it as a kind of uniform medium that constrains all individuals in the same way.

Growing Ambivalence of Upper Strata

In viewing the section or stratum of society referred to above, whether narrowly or broadly conceived, we observe a characteristic ambivalence in the orientation to caste as it exists today. It is very marked among academics—sociologists, political scientists, historians, economists, and so on—but may be noted also among judges, lawyers, journalists and others, and is probably very widespread and extends beyond the section of society with which I am particularly concerned. The ambivalence is easy to recognise and not difficult to describe, but it has not received the scholarly attention it deserves. It can lead the same individual to deny any significance to caste at one time and to give it exaggerated importance at another.

European and American visitors to India often remark that when they ask educated Indians about caste, they are told that it does not exist any more. It would be a mistake to think that this is always an act of conscious deception. There is certainly an element of self-deception here, and we must ask why this form of self-deception is so commonly encountered. Of course, educated Indians know that caste exists, but they are unclear and troubled about what it means for them as members of a society that is a part of the modern world. No one can say that it is easy to give a clear and consistent account of the meaning and significance of caste in India today.

In a presidential address of 1957, entitled 'Caste in modern India', M.N. Srinivas (1962: 15–41) drew attention to the continuing if not increasing importance of caste in public life. The *Times of India* of 21 January 1957, commenting editorially, said that the role of caste had been greatly exaggerated in the address. It was pointed out that caste barriers were falling, both in ordinary interchanges among persons and in ceremonial life. However, the same newspaper reported shortly afterwards that caste loyalties were being extensively used for mobilizing political support in the second general election that followed in a few weeks.

Facts on the ground aside, Srinivas's view of caste was not in tune with the general intellectual climate in India in the wake of independence. I may say on the basis of personal experience in both Calcutta and Delhi, that the intelligentsia in general then had its mind on other things than caste. The preoccupation of the social anthropologist with the subject was on the whole viewed with disfavour by all those who believed that India was on the move, and that the eye should be to the future and not upon the past.

At the time of independence, most reflective Indians felt that they had come to a watershed on the other side of which were many new possibilities which it was up to them to seize and turn to the country's advantage. They had a new Constitution, a new Five-year Plan, and they felt that, given the will-power, they could do many things to bring about justice, equality, growth, and well-being for the people of India. Certain things needed to be put out of the way in order to achieve these objectives: poverty, hunger, malnutrition, illiteracy, ignorance, and superstition. The caste system too was counted among the obstacles in the way of progress. Certainly, it would be fair to say that those who fashioned the Constitution and the Plans did not wish to give a new lease of life to caste.

Caste proved to be much more obdurate than it was judged to be. Perhaps the will-power was not adequate to the task of its removal or containment. But we can also say now, with the advantage of hindsight, that there was a basic misperception of its strength among Indian intellectuals. It is important for us today to examine, honestly and with the maximum possible detachment, the reasons behind this misperception.

We have to go back to the period immediately preceding independence in order to form an idea of the different perceptions of caste and the changes in those perceptions. Caste had become a subject of debate and discussion before independence, and more than one view was formed regarding its pervasiveness and strength. At the risk of some oversimplification, I will pick out two among them that were in many ways the opposites of each other. There was the view of the colonial government and its many able administrators that caste was not only the pre-eminent institution of India, but that it permeated every area of life, and the idea that caste could be dispensed with was wishful thinking. As against this was what I may call the nationalist view, to which Indian intellectuals by and large then subscribed, that the importance of caste had been greatly exaggerated by the colonial administration, that it was clearly on its way out, and that its decline would be greatly hastened once India became independent. Here I must point out that a change in the orientation to caste had come about in the course of the nationalist movement itself. Indian intellectuals did not condemn caste as widely a hundred years before independence as they were ready to do when independence came.

The Indian perception of caste at the time of independence had been shaped, at least to some extent, by the dialectic between the colonial and the nationalist views regarding its place in the present and future society of India. For the Indian intellectual, it had become a matter of pride to confute the colonial view that, however eloquently they might talk about democracy and development, Indians were and would remain under the grip of caste with its exclusiveness, its hierarchy, and its ineluctable fragmentation of civil society.

But the misperception of caste among Indian intellectuals was not based solely on national pride; it had another more tangible, if not more credible, basis. Indians could use the evidence the colonial administrators themselves provided to argue, with some plausibility, that caste was definitely and irreversibly in decline. The predominant western view was that caste was basically a matter of religion and ritual, and educated Indians could see that that side of caste was withering before their eyes.

Religious Definition of Caste

The centrality of caste in Indian society and the religious definition of it became a part of the conventional wisdom of comparative sociology, so that social stratification—or, if one prefers, social hierarchy—was perceived as being essentially a religious phenomenon, emanating somehow from the very nature of Hinduism. This became the predominant view of Indian society among those who were specialists on India and also among those who were not. Nirad C. Chaudhuri (1979: 7) has written bitingly about the 'Western legend of Hindu spirituality', and argued that many educated Indians found it convenient to acquiesce in the legend and even to promote it. It gáve them a kind of comfort in the face of India's manifest economic and political inferiority to the west to feel that they were spiritually superior. Chaudhuri's own erudite work on Hinduism pays very little attention to caste.

Émile Senart, who published an influential book on caste at the end of the nineteenth century, wrote, 'Hindu society is regulated by religious custom, and the law-books are essentially collections of religious precepts' (1930: 91). Henry Maine (1950: 14–17), writing in the second half of the nineteenth century, had found it difficult to detach Hindu law from Hindu religion, and the belief became widely established that Hindu society was unchangeable because it was rooted in immutable religious observance.

Max Weber, perhaps the most outstanding comparative sociologist of all time, clearly defined the social identity of the Hindu in terms of caste, and of caste in terms of ritual. 'Caste, that is, the ritual rights and duties it gives and imposes, and the position of the Brahmans, is the fundamental institution of Hinduism. Before everything else, without caste there is no Hindu' (Weber 1958: 29). Even those who would broadly accept this view might point to significant exceptions: Hinduism always had a place for the renouncer, and the *sannyasi* might still be considered a Hindu, although without caste or clan.

Like Weber, Bouglé too was an outsider to Indian studies for he had not done fieldwork in India or learnt any of its classical or modern languages. Yet his work on caste has had great influence among scholars. Pointing to the remarkable historical continuity of the system, he wrote, 'The caste system allows all regimes to pass over its head; it alone remains' (Bouglé 1971: 65). He drew attention repeatedly to the inseparability of caste and Hinduism. 'All observers are agreed on this: caste is basically a religious institution' (Ibid.: 65). And again, 'Hinduism is defined more by the observance of caste rules than by fidelity to some precise dogma' (Ibid.: 66). Louis Dumont (1966) has carried Bouglé's perspective further forward and greatly enriched it by his mastery of Indian ethnography as well as his knowledge of Indian languages, both classical and modern.

The assumption about Hinduism in much of the early sociological writing is that in it religion and social structure are inseparable so that Hinduism stands not only for a particular religion but also for a particular social structure, that structure being caste. Western writers on religion, including western sociologists, rarely make such an assumption about Christianity, for they see quite clearly that Christianity as a system of beliefs and practices has a certain autonomy in the sense that it can be transferred, more or less easily, from one social or historical context to another. On the other hand, we are shown a somewhat peculiar feature of Hinduism that makes it appear quite different from Christianity, Islam, or Buddhism. This poses an intriguing problem for the sociologist of religion. To be sure, there is everywhere some relationship between religion and social morphology, but why should the two be inseparable in only one particular case? This assumption of inseparability leads directly to the question whether Hinduism is at all a religion in the true sense of the term.

The 'Western legend of Hindu spirituality' was more a creation of nineteenth-century Orientalists and Indologists than of twentieth-century ethnographers and sociologists. By the time ethnographic studies came into their own in the early decades of the twentieth century, the legend of Hindu spirituality had largely evaporated. It was displaced by a view in which ritual observances of every conceivable kind were given pride of place. The view of Hinduism that dominates the ethnography of the late nineteenth and early twentieth centuries may be best summed up in the words of Herbert Risley (1969: 233) as 'magic tempered with metaphysics'. Today's anthropologists have learnt to become more circumspect than the civil servants and missionaries who were their predecessors, but if we look closely into their accounts of Hinduism, we will encounter Risley's ghost at many places.

The evidence on which anthropological accounts of caste and Hinduism were based was impressive. The British had built an administrative system in India which was remarkable in its own way. One of its permanent achievements was the decennial census, now more than a hundred years old, and the massive apparatus associated with the ethnographic mapping of the country. From the end of the nineteenth century onwards, a voluminous body of literature began to be built up which described extensively and in detail the castes and tribes in the different parts of the country (Risley 1892; Thurston 1909; Enthoven 1920–2). The official accounts of the civil servants were supplemented by accounts by missionaries. This whole body of literature is an invaluable record of the customs, usages, and practices of the people of India.

The ICS ethnographers, if the phrase be permitted, included men of considerable scholarship such as Ibbetson (1916), Risley (1969), Gait (1913), Blunt (1931), O'Malley (1932), Hutton (1946), and many others. They were in India not merely to collect taxes and maintain law and order, but also to observe, describe, and interpret, with patience and care, and not always without sympathy, the new social world they had come to inhabit. In addition to the detailed descriptions of particular castes and tribes, they provided a number of general accounts of caste as the framework of Indian society.

These detailed and voluminous accounts repeatedly bring caste to our attention, and do so in their own distinctive way. There is a continued emphasis on the religious basis of caste, so that the system appears to be pervaded by a general aura of ritual and ceremony. Even when such subjects as endogamy, exogamy, division of labour, occupational specialization, craft practices and so on are being discussed, we are never far away from the world of religion, magic, and superstition.

Description and analysis are saturated with accounts of purity and pollution, and the manifold taboos or interdictions associated with them. These struck the attention of administrators, missionaries, and others in the nineteenth century, and every successive generation of ICS ethnographers tried to dig a little deeper in order to get to their roots. Most of them gave a central place to the rules relating to food and drink in their accounts of caste. These rules were so elaborate and so complex that one could fill volumes merely by listing them. Another favourite topic was the maintenance of distance and the avoidance of physical contact between members of different castes and subcastes.

Since many of the ICS ethnographers had antiquarian interests, their accounts of caste, apart from the general stress on ritual, purity, pollution, taboos, interdictions and so on, carried a certain archaic flavour. Now, educated Indians in the 1930s and 1940s naturally felt that if this was the essence of caste—*kacca* food and *pakka* food, 36 paces between Tiyan and Nambutiri, 12 paces between Tiyan and Nair, and so on— then, going by their own experience and observation, caste was clearly in retreat. These manifold customs which had been practised in the past, though perhaps not exactly as described in the ethnography, were rapidly losing their meaning and significance among educated Indians, and those who continued to practice them, at school or at work, were sometimes ridiculed by those who did not. Dwelling mainly on the ritual side of caste, it did not appear too implausible to maintain that it was irretrievably in decline.

Thus, the misperception of caste common among the Indian intelligentsia at the time of independence was due partly to the misplaced emphasis on ritual in accounts of it by civil servants and others in the preceding decades. Was there a misperception among the latter as well, and how can we account for it? Whatever place religion may have had in it in the past, the future of caste lay not with religion but with politics. I think that on the whole—for different reasons, and with notable exceptions—both sides failed to read the signs of the future. The ICS ethnographers like Hutton failed to read them because, before independence, they were themselves too closely involved in preparing the very ground on which caste was taking its place in politics. And if, immediately after independence, the Indian intelligentsia failed by and large to dwell on the future role of caste in politics, wishful thinking had something to do with it. They knew that it was there, but hoped that it could be made to wither away—through rapid economic development, through the spread of education, and through science and technology.

Erosion of Legitimacy

The concentration in the anthropological (as against the Indological) literature on Hinduism, as I have shown, has been on ritual, purity, pollution, taboos, interdictions, and so on—what pertains largely to magic rather than religion in the proper sense of the term. There is also another side of religion, concerned with morality, that has received rather less attention. It is characteristic of educated Indians today that they find it difficult to acknowledge, not only before outsiders but also among themselves, that caste might have had something to do with morality. N.K. Bose (1975, 1967) was one of the few anthropologists who, despite his deep antipathy to caste, tried to understand and interpret its moral and ethical basis in the traditional social order. But he also pointed out that that basis was being irrevocably undermined.

Indians have not always been shy of writing about the moral basis of caste. It was expounded in the nineteenth century by such men as Bankimchandra (1961); and as late as in the 1930s, Gandhi (1962) wrote in support of the morality of caste, at least in the form of *varna*. Gandhi favoured *varnadharma* to the extent that it stressed the community rather than the individual, co-operation as against conflict, and duties rather than rights. His conception of *varnadharma* was somewhat remote from reality as it did not take into account considerations of superior and inferior rank.

The student of comparative sociology, on the other hand, views caste society as above all a hierarchical society, in fact the prototype of all such societies. There social distinctions of certain kinds not only exist, but are widely acknowledged as right, proper, and desirable. Law, religion, and morality all serve to strengthen and reinforce the subordination of the individual to the group and the ranking of groups as superior and inferior (Lingat 1973). In such a society, the individual has certain obligations to the group of which he is a member by birth, and the group as a whole to other groups according to their respective ranks.

It is true that religious reformers from Buddha to Chaitanya and after have questioned the significance of these distinctions, and have asked what meaning they have for man's dignity and worth, and for his inner life (Bose 1975: 116–36). There were continuous fluctuations in the force and significance of caste, and it was not the inflexible, invariant, and unchanging system it has often been made out to be. Nevertheless and despite these fluctuations, it retained for many centuries a very distinctive character. There is no other way to account for the correspondence between representations of caste in the ethnographic record of the late nineteenth and early twentieth centuries, and in the record of classical Indology (Bose 1975; Dumont 1966).

The point to stress here is that when we first encounter caste in the writings of nineteenth-century observers and scholars, we encounter it as a more or less complete system. We encounter not only the existential order of caste, as something that might be observed on the ground from the outside, but also its normative order, as something regarded by its individual members as both meaningful and morally binding. This is not to say that there was perfect consensus regarding the values of caste, but that caste distinctions were considered significant and legitimate by most members of society, and particularly by those belonging to the upper castes whose descendants in contemporary India are precisely the ones who are most ambivalent and troubled about its meaning and legitimacy today.

Since the Indian intelligentsia is today most troubled about the hierarchical distinctions of caste, it needs to be emphasized that in the past and up to the middle of the nineteenth century, those distinctions were, at least among the Hindus, acknowledged, upheld, and reinforced by law, religion, and morality. Things began to change thereafter, as a result of the British presence as well as the Indian response to it. It would be seriously to misrepresent the dialectics of that change if we were to attribute it solely to the colonial intervention and ignore the nationalist response to it (Ganguli 1975). As I have noted elsewhere, Indians probably learnt more about equality from the colonial practice of inequality than from the British theory of equality (Béteille 1979).

Caste undoubtedly exists in contemporary India, and I shall speak in a while of its continuing influence in marriage and its marked, if not increasing, presence in politics. It does not, however, exist as a complete system any more, but—if the phrase be permitted—as a truncated system. The first and most decisive casualty has been the legal basis of caste (Sivaramayya 1984). No two texts can be more divergent in their orientation to caste than the Manusmriti, which we may take as the charter of traditional Hindu law, and the Constitution of India, which may be regarded as the charter of contemporary Indian law. As we have seen, comparative sociologists from Weber to Dumont have dwelt on the intimate connection between caste and Hinduism, regarding it as the social expression of the Hindu religion. But many of the modern proponents of Hinduism, such as Vivekananda, have attacked caste instead of defending it. There are very few contemporary proponents of Hinduism who would be prepared to argue that caste has to be saved in order to strengthen the Hindu religion.

The question of caste morality is more difficult to dispose of briefly, for the evidence is often unclear and sometimes contradictory. One of its principal components was the sense of obligation that the individual carried towards the caste into which he was born, to abide by its customs, to adhere to its style of life, and to pursue the occupation allotted to it. Perhaps that sense of obligation, though not easily articulated, is still quite strong among cultivators, artisans, and others in the rural areas. But it has weakened considerably in the urban areas and among those sections of contemporary Indian society to which I said I would largely confine this discussion. The compulsions of occupation operate rather differently in the different sectors of the Indian economy. Among engineers, doctors, scientists, civil servants, and managers, the obligation to one's occupation exists independently of the obligation to one's caste and to some extent displaces it. The schoolteacher, the clerk, or the electrician no longer feels very strongly that he has a duty to encourage his offspring to persevere in his own occupation or the occupation of his forefathers as the village blacksmith, carpenter, or potter might have felt in the past.

Nothing could be more mistaken than to believe that caste was something that for two thousand years Indians merely lived by, without giving thought to its meaning or its rightness, that it existed merely as practice and not as theory. We must not lose sight of the intellectual tradition of India in which theoretical reflection and dialectical skill were used for describing, explaining, and justifying the distinctions of caste by generations of intellectuals. Dumont (1966: 56) was right in drawing attention to the systematic thinking on which caste observances were based; but he was plainly wrong in suggesting that 'Hindus of today and of past times' think about caste in the same systematic way. Until the nineteenth century, Hindu intellectuals could argue with force and conviction about the significance and value of caste. Their counterparts of today, who are still mainly of upper caste, have lost the capacity not only to explain and justify caste, but even to describe it coherently.

Endogamy and Reproduction of Identity

It is often said that no matter how loudly Hindus might proclaim their indifference or even hostility to caste, when it comes to marriage, all of them—educated and uneducated, urban and rural, professional and peasant—turn to caste. Many have in fact maintained that the regulation of marriage and the social exclusiveness associated with it—something akin to a sense of race—are what make caste what it is. Risley stressed this aspect of caste far more than religion: 'Race dominates religion; sect is weaker than caste' (1969: 80). Obviously, we cannot associate caste with race as a biological fact, as Risley was inclined to do, but only with a sense of race more or less widely felt in society.

It will be of little avail to argue about the decline in the legal, religious, and moral basis of caste if it turns out that on such an important issue as marriage, nothing has changed at all. One hears both kinds of arguments among the intelligentsia today: some say that inter-caste marriages are now quite common while others maintain that they are rare and exceptional. Sometimes one hears a person argue vehemently that inter-caste marriages are impossible in Indian society, only to learn that he himself has married outside his caste. More common perhaps is the man who declares himself passionately against caste in every form, but nonetheless opposes strenuously the marriage of his children outside his caste.

Some changes are in fact taking place in marriage rules and practices among educated Indians in the higher occupational strata, but we are hindered in our assessment of them by the paucity of systematic data. People frequently take recourse to casual empiricism, selecting one or another set of examples to argue for and against the same proposition. No clear conclusion can be reached in the absence of statistical data that tell us something about rates and frequencies. But rates and frequencies are not enough; for where it concerns marriage, we have to attend not only to practices but also to rules and to enquire whether these rules continue to carry the same sanctions and the same meanings as before.

In a recent interview with the editor of the *Times of India*, M.N. Srinivas noted the changing role of caste in marriage. 'Equally significant as regards pan-Hinduism, Professor Srinivas says, is the diminishing importance of caste in marriage. Inter-caste, inter-regional and even inter-religious marriages are on the rise' (Padgaonkar 1993). What is remarkable about the observation is not that Srinivas is India's leading sociologist, but that he has repeatedly cautioned the Indian intelligentsia against underrating the strength and resilience of caste.

Similar observations were made thirty years earlier by C.T. Kannan in the only satisfactory full-length study of inter-caste marriage:

Just twenty-five years ago the instances of intercaste marriages were very few; and those individuals who dared to marry outside the caste had to undergo truly great hardships. Today the situation is altogether different. Not only has the prevalence of intercaste marriage become considerable, but even the difficulties the intercaste marriage couples have to face have become comparatively quite mild (Kannan 1963: vii).

Kannan limited himself to 200 couples formed by inter-caste unions (and 50 others formed by inter-community unions), and therefore his study cannot tell us very much about rates and frequencies that are statistically significant. At the same time, it does draw attention to significant social processes that had been set in motion at least a decade or two before his study was published.

In discussing these questions we must remember that not all inter-caste marriages are of the same kind. A marriage across two sub-subcastes of Smarta Brahmans would be an inter-caste marriage in some sense, but it would be very different from a marriage between any Brahman and an Adi-Dravida. In an earlier paper (Béteille 1966), I had suggested that there are ambiguities in the very idea of inter-caste marriage. There I had drawn attention to the slow and gradual way in which even for arranged marriages, the horizons of endogamy were being extended from sub-subcaste to subcaste, and then to caste among the Tamil Brahmans. I am not suggesting that there never was any ambiguity in the past, but the ambiguity over what constitutes the unit of endogamy has almost certainly become more pervasive now, particularly among the upper castes.

It is possible that a more permissive attitude towards caste in the selection of spouses is being accompanied by a greater attention to other restrictions such as those relating to education, occupation, and income. Many different criteria are taken into account in the selection of a spouse, and in the case of someone who is highly desirable on a number of important counts, one may overlook the traditional restrictions of caste if the person belongs to a different subcaste of the same caste or even to a different but cognate caste. It is only rarely that caste considerations are ignored altogether.

One can get a good sense of the diversity of the categories at play by looking at the matrimonial advertisements in the Sunday papers. These advertisements are classified, but not according to any single or consistent plan. The categories of caste are very prominent, but those of religion, such as Sunni, Sikh, and Muslim, and of language, such as Sindhi, Bengali, and Tamil, are also found. Cheek by jowl with these are categories belonging to other sets, such as 'doctors', 'engineers', 'MBA/CA', 'postgraduate' and 'cosmopolitan'. One should not be misled, however, because caste is frequently indicated, directly or indirectly, even under 'cosmopolitan'. But then again someone may indicate his own caste, in case the other party finds it relevant, even if he writes, 'Caste, dowry no bar', to show that he does not regard it as relevant for himself.

To be sure, even in the past, people took many factors into account in addition to caste, but those factors were taken into account after keeping caste constant. One always looked for an appropriate family in seeking a match, but one took it for granted that such a family would be of one's own caste. An advertisement in the *Sunday Times* of 19 December 1993 reads, '32/167, C.K.P. well-settled businessman from educated family seeks alliance from good-looking, cultured girls with good family background. Caste no bar'. (The man was 32 years old, 167 cm in height and of the Chandraseniya Kayastha Prabhu subcaste.) I have been much struck by the insistence on 'good family', 'cultured family' or 'status family' even in advertisements that do not give any specification as to caste.

I would like to return very briefly to the traditional rules of marriage through which the identities of caste, subcaste, and sub-subcaste were maintained and reproduced. As is well known, there was not one single rule, there were several rules. Of these, two are of particular significance, the rule of endogamy and the rule of hypergamy. The rule of hypergamy not only distinguishes between castes (or subcastes) but also ranks them, and on that ground it has sometimes been regarded as even more distinctive of caste than the rule of endogamy (Dumont 1966: 152–61). It should be pointed out that the rule of hypergamy (or *anuloma*) was not universally or even extensively observed in all places in all times (Karve 1968: 16), although it was clearly acknowledged by the shastras whereas its opposite or *pratiloma* was universally condemned.

Where inter-caste marriages do take place among the intelligentsia, ignoring for the moment the question of frequency, such marriages are in general as likely to be of the *anuloma* (or sanctioned) as of the *pratiloma* (or unsanctioned) type. More than that, in some areas where hypergamy was widely prevalent, the rule appears to have lapsed altogether. I can say from personal knowledge that many Bengali Brahmans, of both the Rarhi and the Barendra castes, well-known until the middle of the nineteenth century for the observance of hypergamy (associated with the notorious system known as Kulinism), have now little or no knowledge of the traditional rule and its implications. The attack on Kulinism in nineteenth-century Bengal and its gradual disappearance throw an interesting light on the relationship between caste, hierarchy, and marriage rules.

It seems clear to me that Kannan's assessment of the weakening of collective sanctions against inter-caste unions in urban India was on the whole the right one. His data show that the collective pressure of the caste or the subcaste against inter-caste unions among the urban middle classes is neither very strong nor very effective. In risking a wrong alliance, the primary focus of anxiety is the family or perhaps the 'kindred of co-operation' (Mayer 1960), itself more restricted in the city than in the village, whereas caste figures only dimly in the background. There are of course exceptions, and these must be noted. Newspapers sometimes report instances of brutal violence in small towns or villages against certain unions, typically where the woman is of a high caste and the man a Harijan or a Muslim. These acts are reminiscent of the lynchings that took place in the American South until forty or fifty years ago when a black male sought union with a white female. Otherwise, inter-caste marriages in metropolitan cities are not accompanied by any significant public violence, although there is no lack of urban violence in contemporary India.

Political Uses of Caste

I mentioned earlier that in the 1950s, most Indian intellectuals believed that caste was on the way out, while only a few said that it was there to stay. Even those who said that it was gaining a new lease of life could point to evidence from only a single domain, that of politics, to support their argument. No one could seriously maintain that, to use the language of Hutton, the strictures and sanctions of caste were becoming stronger, or that the many ritual injunctions and interdictions relating to food and physical contact were gaining in strength; or that the association between caste and occupation was growing closer; or even that the rules of endogamy were being more strictly defined and observed. In all these domains, caste was growing weaker, very slowly, almost imperceptibly in some cases, more clearly and noticeably in others.

It is only when we turn to politics that we get a very different picture. When Srinivas argued in his 1957 address that caste was getting a new lease of life, all of the evidence that he provided, or almost all of it, came from the domain of politics. But only a few years earlier, Radcliffe-Brown (1952 : x), reflecting the views till then common among anthropologists, had observed as follows in his Foreword to Srinivas's book on the Coorgs: 'A caste is in its essence a religious group, membership of which entails certain ritual observances. The rules of caste behaviour are rules of religion'. Clearly, some changes were under way which had not come to the attention of Radcliffe-Brown, although he had registered his interest in political anthropology as early as in 1940.

Caste did not enter politics all at once with independence, but it made its presence strongly felt in the first general election, and increasingly with each successive election. Although the subject of caste and politics was initially of interest to only a handful of social anthropologists, it soon attracted the attention of political scientists and others (Kothari 1970; Frankel and Rao 1989–90), and there is now a large literature on it. Even after the subject had been taken up by scholars in various disciplines in the 1960s and 1970s, some differences remained between the ordinary run of social scientists who saw and stressed the importance of caste in politics, and what are called 'left intellectuals' who were inclined to treat it lightly. Today, many more scholars, both Marxists and non-Marxists, acknowledge the importance of caste in politics, although they draw different policy conclusions from it (Centre for Social Studies 1985; Béteille 1992).

It will not be possible for me in the brief space remaining to review or even summarize the principal findings of the very large literature that we now have on caste and politics. I will only draw attention to certain processes that are known to be quite widespread, and indicate very briefly how those processes are viewed, explained, and justified by some of the principal actors who participate in and give shape to them.

In an essay written more than 30 years ago (Béteille 1969a:152–69), I had, after making a distinction between problems of distribution and problems of process, tried to identify the basic processes through which caste becomes involved in politics. The loyalties of caste are used for the mobilization of political support in a number of ways: by a generalized appeal to caste sentiment, by activating networks of kinship and marriage, and by the organized activities of caste associations. Studies conducted in the last 30 years have shown the extensive use of caste for the mobilization of political support during elections and in between elections, although there are significant regional variations.

As Srinivas showed, caste came to be used in the electoral process from the first general election, and indeed it had entered the political arena even before. But the question is not simply of the extent of the use of caste in electoral politics, but also of its meaning and legitimacy for the different sections of Indian society. Clearly, those who yielded to the appeal of caste loyalty and voted for candidates of their own caste, could not have all thought that it was a bad thing to vote according to caste. By and large, the intelligentsia showed an ambivalent attitude. They were troubled by 'casteism' in politics even though they might support someone from their own caste. They were inclined to treat this kind of caste preference more as an aspect of Realpolitik than of political morality.

In the 1950s and 1960s, the leaders of all political parties condemned in public the use of caste in politics. Politicians freely acknowledged that caste was being extensively used in the politics of post-independence India, but they said that it was being used by other parties, not their own. When it was shown that their party too was using caste, their reply was that they did not start the process but were being forced to accommodate caste in order to survive, for in politics, or at least in Indian politics, one could not afford to be too idealistic if one wished to remain in business. In other words, they sought to defend the use of caste (unlike, for instance, the use of class) on tactical rather than ethical grounds.

A change in the orientation of political leaders, and with them of other members of the intelligentsia, appears to have started in the 1970s when the politics of backwardness took a new turn with the installation of the first non-Congress government in New Delhi in 1977. It began to be argued that caste needed to be given a place in public life not so much on grounds of Realpolitik as on grounds of social justice. The lower castes had been stigmatized and exploited in the past, and they should be given special protection through extensive quotas in every domain of public life. The argument was not new; it had been an important component of colonial policy in the decades preceding independence (Irschick 1969; Béteille 1992). What was new was its increasing appeal to social justice and its increasing vehemence.

Again, I cannot enter into a discussion of the principal features of the politics of backwardness on which I and others have written extensively, but would like to point out that it has acquired a markedly ideological tone since 1990. The ideological tone was given a new articulation when the left parties decided to join hands with Mr V.P. Singh's Janata Dal in pressing for the extension of caste quotas in the cause of social justice. This made it in effect impossible for any party openly to oppose caste quotas, so that caste has, at least for the time being, strengthened its grip over politics. But it still is an unsteady grip for neither the supporters nor the opponents of caste quotas say that caste itself should be revitalized. In fact, the strongest supporters of caste quotas are, paradoxically, also the strongest opponents of caste as a hierarchical system.

Ethnicity and the Metaphor of Caste

Those who are given to moralizing sometimes observe that democracy has been debased in India by the pernicious influence of caste. The issue for the moment is not how caste has altered politics, but how politics is altering caste. Edmund Leach (1960: 6–7) had already asked more than fifty years ago whether castes cease to be castes when they compete with each other for political power. My view then (Béteille 1969b) was that there were obvious and significant continuities between the castes of the present and those of the past; something so complex and deeply entrenched as caste does not cease to be itself as soon as one or even a few of its basic characteristics change. I would now like to examine some of the shifts that are taking place in the ways in which caste identities are defined.

As is well known, conventionally caste has had at least two distinct (though related) meanings, *varna* and *jati*. While it is true that most Indians recognize both meanings of caste, they now think of it more as *jati* than as *varna*; that would be consistent with the shift in emphasis from religion to politics in matters relating to caste. In an influential paper, Srinivas (1962: 63–9) had drawn attention to the distinction, and argued that caste has been frequently *mis*represented as *varna*. Srinivas's own argument was perhaps one-sided, but it was timely, for it came at a moment when educated Indians were probably beginning to think of caste less as *varna* than as *jati*. They probably thought of it as *varna* much more commonly until after independence when the role of caste became increasingly prominent in politics. A few years before the publication of Srinivas's paper, the historian Niharranjan Ray (1945) wrote a book on caste in Bengali which he entitled *Bangali hindur barnabhed*,[2] meaning distinctions of *varna* among Bengali Hindus. He was following a well-established usage for the representation of caste, a usage which was, however, changing.

There are other ambiguities besides those that might arise from the confusion of *varna* and *jati*, for there are collective identities that are not identities of caste in the strict anthropological sense, but are nevertheless represented as such. Though most frequently paired with *varna* in the ethnographic (and Indological) literature, the term *jati* (or the more colloquial *jat*) has other associations as well. It is commonly used to cover a series of identities of increasing degrees of inclusiveness from sub-subcaste through caste to religion and language.

Those who use data from large-scale censuses and surveys have often

---

[2] In transliterating Bengali words, I have gone by the sounds of spoken Bengali, and not followed any consistent scheme. Thus, I have written 'Barendra' and not 'Varendra', and hence '*barna*' and not '*varna*' which is the more common north Indian form and also closer to Sanskrit.

to deal with lists of castes (or *jatis*) that are very heterogeneous indeed. While conducting a survey in 1958 for the Indian Statistical Institute in Giridih town and its surrounding villages in Bihar, I encountered in the entries under 'caste', in addition to the names of castes in the restricted sense, such terms as 'Marwari', 'Oriya', 'Jain', and 'Muslim'. Later, in 1963 and 1964 in the villages in Burdwan district in West Bengal, I was told that the inhabitants included Brahmans, Baidyas, Sadgopes, Aghuris, Bagdis, Santals, and Muslims.

We have moved some distance away from caste as *varna* when we are dealing on the same plane with such disparate groups and categories as Baidyas, Sadgopes, Telis, Bagdis, Santals, Oriyas, and Muslims. The disparate assemblage of clans, sects, castes, tribes, religious communities, and linguistic groups that can all, according to context and situation, pass as *jatis* fits at best awkwardly into the clear and symmetrical design of the four *varnas*. It would be unwise to declare that these modes of representation are all new, without any roots in past social experience and practice. At the same time, new perceptions of collective identities are forced upon people by the political process which uses the distinctions of language, religion and caste in the same way for the mobilization of political support.

The operation of caste along with language and religion in the political arena has led some to speak in a rather inclusive sense of 'ethnic groups', 'ethnic identities' and 'ethnic loyalties'. This is to signal a shift in the meaning of caste brought about by its increasing role in a new field of activity. Srinivas has recently been quoted as saying, 'In the future, too, caste will remain a predominant feature of Indian life. But it will be conceived more in terms of ethnicity' (Padgaonkar 1993).

The movement from caste as *varna* to caste as ethnic group has been seen by some as the 'substantialisation of caste' (Dumont 1966: 280; Deliège 1993: 107–10). This may be somewhat misleading in so far as the notion of substance conveys a sense of homogeneity, whereas in fact each caste is becoming progressively differentiated in terms of occupation, education, and income. Clearly, some shifts are taking place in the meanings that people assign to caste. When journalists and political commentators refer to castes as ethnic groups, they have in mind not so much hierarchical distinctions of status as differences in bargaining power and in life chances in general.

Few will deny that caste has become increasingly salient in the political arena, or that in that arena hierarchical distinctions of status count for less than differences in life chances. Does that mean that distinctions of status are losing their meaning and significance for Indians? It would be rash indeed to answer that question categorically in the affirmative. For one thing, we cannot say for certain what meaning and significance the innumerable ritual restrictions of the past had for distinctions of status among persons; the ethnographers have tried mainly to explain either the origins of those restrictions or their formal structure, but rarely asked what they meant for those who applied them or to whom they were applied. For another, distinctions of status continue to enjoy a luxuriant life among all social strata in contemporary India.

Some of the best accounts of distinctions of status and their meaning (or lack of meaning) in contemporary Indian life are to be found in literary as against ethnographic writing. V.S. Naipaul (1964) has left a memorable account of his encounter with rank and status in settings that are characteristic of modern India. Naipaul's *An Area of Darkness* caused much resentment among educated Indians, no doubt in part because many of them found something of themselves in his account.

Contemporary Indian life provides numerous occasions for the play of status in the factory, in the office, in hospitals, in laboratories, and in banks; in work and outside work; and in both public and private places. I am speaking now not simply of the distinctions of rank that are an inherent feature of every modern association, institution, and organization, but of patterns of deference and invidious distinction that grow within and around them in great and sometimes unexpected profusion. It is this luxuriance of status distinctions that some are inclined to regard as the characteristically Indian part of modern Indian life. They point out that all the professions of equality in the Constitution and the laws are but words in the face of the Indian's undying preoccupation with hierarchy, rank, and status.

It is natural to ask about this preoccupation with rank and status in contemporary Indian life whether it is anything more than a new manifestation of the old hierarchy of caste. The concept of caste has always been elastic, and the concept of status even more so. It is of course possible to speak of caste both literally and metaphorically, and in the latter case to describe every form of invidious distinction and social exclusion as a form of caste. But then one must be careful to note when one is speaking of caste in the restricted sense of distinctions of status based on specific ideas of purity and pollution, of birth and inherited bodily substance, and when one is speaking of it in the broad and general sense of rigid and elaborate social distinctions.

Even when an Indian is acutely conscious of his own caste and also of his status, he may not make distinctions of status among others solely or even mainly according to their caste. The social world of the professional, the civil servant, and the executive in the large metropolitan city is different from the social world of the village or even the small town. It would be rash to declare that the city is less animated by a concern for status than the village, and, indeed, from the villager's point of view, the case may appear to be the opposite. That apart, the definition of status, its symbolic form, and its social expression are not the same for the two. There are innumerable tales of persons from the village or small town being bewildered by the intricate conventions of status among their upper-class relatives in the metropolitan city.

In addition to caste, the things that count for status in the sections of society about which I am writing are education, occupation, and income, and the subcultures of the profession, the office, and the association. The latter are by no means unrelated to caste in the traditional sense, but they can hardly be regarded merely as aspects or expressions of it. The social world created by education, occupation, and income, the office, the firm, the law court, and the laboratory cuts across the social world of caste. The social circle of the Brahman judge, diplomat, engineer, civil servant, or manager is not the same as that of the Brahman clerk, schoolteacher, or cook. Particularly among the higher occupational strata, many relationships are formed that cut across caste, as may be easily seen from the patterns of residence in large metropolitan cities where housing goes directly with occupation and income, and only indirectly with caste.

There are, to be sure, many continuities and linkages between the new status distinctions prominent among the intelligentsia and the old ones based largely on considerations of purity and pollution. Different criteria of status, different symbols of distinction, and different strategies of exclusion now coexist in various sectors of Indian society. It is clear that they do not all fit neatly into a single, unified hierarchical design; whether and to what extent they did so in the past are questions that cannot be addressed here.

If we are to reach a proper understanding of variation and change in contemporary Indian society, we have to be on our guard against the unreflective switch from the literal use of the term caste to its metaphorical use as, for instance, in the phrase that the Boston Brahmans are an acutely caste-conscious set. It is of course well known that western writers from Alexis de Tocqueville (1956) to Michael Young (1961) have used the metaphor of caste while commenting on their own societies. No great confusion or misunderstanding is likely to result from the metaphorical use of caste to describe status, the sense of distinction, or the strategies of exclusion in western societies; few readers are likely to think that the court of Louis XVI or the playing-fields of Eton were teeming with Brahmans of different kind, carefully calculating what kinds of boiled vegetables they might share and with whom without serious risk to the purity of their bodily substance. Yet such misunderstanding repeatedly arises when the metaphorical use of caste is extended to contexts in contemporary India where caste in the traditional sense has ceased to have its old significance.

Conclusion: Imputed Meaning and Actor's Meaning

I began by pointing to the highly ambivalent attitude to caste among certain influential sections of Indian society, and some will no doubt object that I have ended by trying to show that caste no longer has any legitimacy at all. How can certain identities remain so manifestly durable if they have no meaning and no legitimacy for their bearers?

I would like to state clearly and firmly in conclusion that I do not believe that caste has disappeared or is likely to disappear from even the sections of society about which I have written; but I do believe that shifts are taking place in the meaning and legitimacy of social relationships and social activities among many members of it. We are likely to miss the significance of those shifts if we continue to think of caste—or, indeed, Indian society—in the old way, relying mainly on the ethnographic record of village studies or the Indological record of the classical texts. The problem in the past has been that anthropologists often came to India in search of the eternal, and that is why so many of them were drawn, instinctively as it were, to the remote village and the classical text. I have tried to redress the balance somewhat, but there is always the danger of going to the opposite extreme and, by focusing attention on a relatively small though very influential section of society, losing sight of the larger body of people.

The exercise I have undertaken above has to be seen primarily as an effort to redress the balance among anthropologists. To draw attention to the growing ambivalence towards caste is not to say that caste has become or is becoming meaningless, but to indicate that there are now both positive and negative components of evaluation that sit uneasily together. The negative components of evaluation have not in my view received sufficient attention from social anthropologists who study caste, and that is why I have dwelt on them at some length. It is of course true that meanings do not always lie on the surface but may be latent or hidden, and meanings that appear inconsistent on the surface may in fact be resolved at a deeper level. Psychoanalysis and some forms of structural analysis deal with these latent or hidden or imputed meanings, whereas my concern has been more with the empirical or observed meanings (Kolakowski 1982), or the meanings that actors themselves assign to their actions (Weber 1978). All that I can say is that if caste today has a single or homogeneous meaning, I have failed to discover it either in my own observation and experience or in the writings of other anthropologists.

It would be strange if something that occupied such a central place in society were to lose all positive significance for its members simply because they have changed their laws, or acquired a different system of education, or taken to new occupations. Evidence of some positive attachment to caste may be found in almost every sector of Indian society, among doctors, lawyers, and scientists, not to speak of administrators, managers, and businessmen. I said at the very beginning that the statement from educated Indians that caste does not exist any more should not be taken at face value. The attachment to caste may lie very deep indeed, so that a person may not even be fully aware of it; but then it might find expression suddenly and unexpectedly when, for instance, a daughter declares that she wants to marry a man from a very low caste, or when a man of a different caste boasts about the achievements of that caste. Much patience and care are required for collecting such evidence in a systematic way, and going back to the village or the classical texts cannot be a substitute for it.

It is easy enough to show that caste has both a positive and a negative significance for many members of contemporary Indian society. What is difficult is to weigh and measure these different components and draw an accurate balance sheet. Where the evidence is contradictory and points in different, even opposite, directions, the sociologist is very likely to draw on it in accordance with his own bias, and that bias may lead him either to exaggerate or to underrate the contemporary significance of caste. For the last twenty-five years, I have been told by anthropologists in London, Cambridge, and Chicago that I ignore evidence of the significance of caste in contemporary India, and by scientists, economists, and others in Calcutta and Delhi that I exaggerate it, and, indeed, that as a sociologist I am paid to do so.

In 1990, Indian intellectuals became deeply divided over the significance of caste in contemporary Indian society. The division was over
an issue of policy, that of caste quotas in education and employment
(Béteille 1990b; Guhan et al. 1990). It has been said that those who
opposed quotas minimized the significance of caste, sometimes deliberately. But it must not be assumed that those who supported quotas
thought that caste was a good thing which ought to be strengthened;
on the contrary, they said that caste was an evil but believed that the
best way of doing away with it in the long run was by having quotas
in the short run. No doubt personal interest played some part in this,
but it would hardly be reasonable to suppose that Indian intellectuals
are unique in the world in supporting or opposing policies solely on
the basis of personal interest. At any rate, those who supported the
quotas belonged to diverse castes, and Indian intellectuals, who are
predominantly of upper caste, both supported and opposed the quotas.

If among the intelligentsia, individuals differ in their perception of
caste or in the significance they give to it, it may well be that these
differences have some relationship to the differences in their positions
in the hierarchy of caste. Where some individual mobility is possible,
the burden of caste may weigh more heavily on the lower- than on the
upper-caste person. In certain contexts, caste might matter more for
Harijan than for Brahman intellectuals as race seems to do more for
black than for white intellectuals in the United States (Carter 1991;
West 1993). But this again would be a kind of reversal of the traditional
order where caste matters were ultimately the responsibility of the
upper and not the lower castes. That at least is my reading of the
literature relating to village India and to classical India. If we are to
understand what is happening to caste in contemporary India, we will
have to look for new types of data, devise new concepts, and, above all,
approach the subject with a more open mind that does not seek either
to ignore the distinctive features of Indian society or to maximize the
difference (Molund 1991) between India and the west.

5

The Public as a Social Category

Private faces in public places
Are wiser and nicer
Than public faces in private places
W.H. Auden

The term 'public' has many and diverse meanings. In the western historical tradition, the term—and its offshoot the 'republic'—has been in use since classical antiquity, and no doubt there are corresponding terms in other historical traditions such as the Islamic, the Indian, and the Chinese. It has undergone modification, elaboration, and differentiation in the course of its evolution from ancient to modern times and its diffusion from one social environment to another. The various meanings of the term flow easily into one another and it is difficult to keep them strictly apart. Therefore it is important to specify the context of its discussion here in order to minimize the confusion of meanings. The sense in which we use the term when we compare and contrast monarchy, aristocracy, and republic is not the same as the one in which we use it when we contrast the public with the private.

The context of the present discussion is provided by the emphasis on democracy, citizenship and, I would like to add, civil society. The idea of the public has a specific significance in the context of democratic society and politics and it is that significance which I will make the focus of the present chapter. If it is obvious that democratic society must value the public, it is equally obvious that it must respect the private. Thus in modern societies the public and the private become linked together and it is difficult to conceive of the one in isolation from the other. The two are distinct yet they are inseparable, somewhat like an object and its shadow.

It follows from the above that we may speak of the public in at least two different ways. We may use the term in the substantive or empirical sense to mean all the members of the community or the society as a whole; in this inclusive sense the public becomes coterminous with society itself. But the same term may be used also in an analytical or normative sense to refer to a particular sphere or domain of activity to which a particular significance or value is socially assigned. In the second sense the term is no longer identical with society as a whole for society as a whole includes and values the private as well as the public.

Given the context of the present discussion, I will dwell on the second, analytical and normative sense of the term. It seems to me that in that sense the term 'public' stands for a historical and not a universal category of social experience. It is present and valued in some societies and not in all. As a distinctive domain of social action, it has a significant presence in modern democratic societies but not in every kind of society.

Why does it make sense to speak of a distinctive public domain in modern France but not in a tribal community? After all, we can speak in either case of the people or the community as a whole, and perhaps more easily in the case of a tribal community than of a modern nation state. But it is only in the second and not the first case that we can speak of a public domain that is distinct from the private. The public becomes a distinct social category only when the legitimacy of the private comes to be socially acknowledged. Where it is difficult to distinguish the one from the other, the public has an uncertain existence as a social category; we may then speak of the community rather than the public.

What I wish to stress is that the public and the private are both social categories and that it will be a mistake to treat only the public and not the private as one. The respect for privacy is a social fact but it is not equally developed in all societies; where it is poorly developed, as in peasant communities, what is commonly encountered is secrecy rather than privacy. In those societies in which both the public and the private are acknowledged as fundamental social values, the same individual is expected to act in both domains, for instance as a citizen in the public domain and as a householder in the private.

The separation of private and public is a part of the differentiation of societies which is a long-term evolutionary tendency. This has to be understood in its proper perspective. To say that differentiation is a long-term evolutionary tendency is not to mean that every society becomes differentiated to the same extent or in the same way. On the

contrary, evolution in the strict sense is a process of *divergent* development. This means two things: firstly, that each society is likely to be
more differentiated internally in later than in earlier phases; and secondly, that we find more types of society as we move from the past to
the present.

If we look at the world in which we live and at our own times, we
are likely to be struck by convergence more than divergence in the
development of human society and culture. It is a truism among anthropologists that diffusion contributes as much to the development of
society and culture as does evolution. Technical know-how, ideas, beliefs, values, and institutions grow as much by the unfolding of their
own inner potential as by diffusion, adaptation, and accretion. This has
been the case in India since time immemorial and Mrs Karve (1968) has
pointed to the special significance of accretion in the Indian cultural
tradition. The point to be noted here is that any given society may
become internally differentiated not only by virtue of its own internal
dynamic but also through the process of accretion. Material and non-
material elements of culture travel from one corner of the world to
another with unprecedented rapidity today; but it will be rash to conclude from this that human societies are becoming more homogeneous
or more alike.

If we take a long-range view of the development of mankind, it will be
difficult to deny that past societies were less differentiated than present
ones. Economics, politics, kinship, and religion enjoy less institutional
autonomy in tribal and peasant communities than in industrial societies. It is not surprising that private and public are in the former less
clearly differentiated than in the latter. It is well known that in tribal
communities life is lived largely in the open, and the individual who
seeks to withdraw from the community to live his own life is regarded
as a deviant if not a sorcerer or a witch.

The separation of the economic domain from the domain of family
and kinship is far more marked in modern than in pre-modern societies.
This does not mean that the two domains were inter-linked in the same
way or to the same extent in all societies of the past. Pre-modern societies
differed greatly among themselves in their systems of kinship and affinity. Indeed, there were great variations within India itself. There were
patrilineal and matrilineal communities; communities which allowed
polygyny and those which allowed polyandry; communities which

preferred cross-cousin marriage and those which preferred parallel-cousin marriage, and yet others which allowed neither. But in all these communities the claims and obligations of kinship seeped into economic, political, and religious activities in a variety of different ways.

The separation of work and home first began in the west, particularly in the Protestant countries, at the dawn of the modern age. Perhaps the seeds of the separation were already present in England, Scotland, Holland, and other Protestant nations, and what was latent became manifest with the growth of capitalist enterprise and industrial organization. As the new economic order extended its influence to other parts of the world, it began to alter in one way or another the relationship between work and home there as well.

The differentiation of the economic domain from the general social matrix has been a subject of much discussion and debate. Louis Dumont (1977b: 33) opened his discussion of the subject with the following words: 'The modern era has witnessed the emergence of a new mode of consideration of human phenomena and the carving out of a separate domain, which are currently evoked for us by the words, *economic*, and *economy*'. It does not follow from this that the economic domain becomes disconnected from the rest of society, but only that it begins to be thought of as a distinct domain to which a distinct social value comes to be assigned.

The differentiation of the economic from the political domain has not taken the same course in all industrially advanced societies, not to speak of the industrially backward ones. This becomes clear when we compare the trajectories of the United States and the Soviet Union for the better part of the twentieth century (Aron 1962). The decline of socialism in eastern Europe might appear to strengthen the argument in favour of the autonomy of the economic domain, but the last word on the subject has not been said as yet. In India too the balance between the 'public' and the 'private' sectors is altering, but no matter where the balance is struck, the need for making a clear distinction between the two has by now come to be generally acknowledged.

When we talk of the differentiation of the economic from the political domain, we are dealing with questions not only of fact but also of value, not just with what people undergo but, in addition, with what they desire and seek to bring about. The regulation of economic life by political authority—and its deregulation—has become more conscious, more planned, and, in that sense, more 'rational' in modern times. But the political regulation of economic life cannot reverse entirely the tendencies that are the unintended consequences of the everyday actions of millions of ordinary persons.

The differentiation of the religious domain from other domains of society is a long-term historical tendency to which the term 'secularization' has generally been applied. This tendency was analysed in a classic study in the mid-1960s by M.N. Srinivas (1966), and he attributed its operation to a variety of acts, both intended and unintended but mainly the latter. The historical tendency towards secularization may be accelerated, slowed down, or reversed by the conscious actions of intellectuals and ideologues. Just as some ideologues favour greater political regulation of economic life, so too others favour closer regulation of political life by religion.

In speaking of the long-term tendency towards the differentiation of economics and politics, of religion and politics—or of the private and the public—we must not underestimate the strength of the ideologies that set themselves consciously against such differentiation. The course of human history is a disorderly movement in which there are currents as well as counter-currents. At the time of independence there was some consensus about the political regulation of economic life whereas now deregulation appears to enjoy greater favour. By contrast, intellectuals then seemed by and large to favour the separation of religion and politics whereas now more of them appear to be in favour of bringing them closer together. Long-term evolutionary tendencies can tell us little about what may happen in the next decade or two.

I would now like to return to the observation that the public emerges as a significant social category only when a distinct social value is assigned to privacy and the private. Societies which lack a well-formed idea of privacy are unlikely to assign much significance to the public in the sense adopted here. There is abundant ethnographic evidence to show that the idea of the private is at best weakly developed in many societies. It is more difficult to show this in the case of the public because there is no society in which the public in the substantive sense of 'all the members of the community taken together' is absent. Yet in the sense that I would like to give to the term, the public is not identical with the community; in some respects it is its opposite.

If in the modern world there is a particular institutional setting reserved to the private, it is the family or the home. The home and the outside world serve as metaphors for the private and the public. At the same time, family and home are not and have not been insulated from the outside world to the same extent in all societies or at all times. The historical process of this insulation marks an important chapter in the development of the idea of privacy.

In many modern western societies the elementary family comprising parents and unmarried children accounts for the better part of kinship. Within the elementary family the obligations of kinship—between spouses, between parents and children, and between siblings—are strong and intense; outside it those obligations tend to be weak and undefined and they easily fade away. No doubt there are variations according to class, race, and religion. But the boundaries of the middle-class western family are extremely well marked, and they may not be infringed even by other relatives such as cousins, uncles, and nephews who might elsewhere be regarded as near.

The western family system had acquired a set of distinctive, not to say unique, social characteristics by the beginning of the eighteenth century, i.e., before the age of capital and before the age of industry (Laslett 1972, 1977). It is possible that they contributed something important to the emergence of the 'private' and the 'individual' as significant social values. Outside the west and before the twentieth century, these characteristics were in evidence to some extent, and in their own distinctive forms, only in Japan.

In other societies the elementary family lacks the clear definition that it had acquired in the west by the time of the industrial and the democratic revolutions. In both India and China it was embedded in a wider system of kinship and marriage, and the home was not insulated to nearly the same extent as in the west. This is still true by and large in rural communities throughout the world.

The Japanese anthropologist, Chie Nakane has recorded her surprise on finding how porous the boundaries of the home were in a Bengali village where she had gone to do fieldwork. She had hardly settled into the village when a young unmarried woman took her in hand and showed her not only into her own home but also into the homes of many of her relatives:

As soon as we entered a house, the young and the old, men and women, gathered round me and warm conversation flowed as I was offered coconut juice and other drinks. Then she began to show me round every corner of the house, including storerooms and the kitchen, without asking permission of the mistress of the household, as if it was her own home (Nakane 1975: 19).

As an ethnographer Nakane was of course delighted, but as a Japanese she was dismayed by the disregard for boundaries.

The action of Nakane's young friend would be interpreted very differently in different cultures. In the west it would be viewed as a gross violation of privacy. But in the Bengali village, the issue was not of privacy but hospitality, and there hospitality overrides privacy, at least among relatives and with regard to any special friend a relative might bring. Were the mistress of the house to deny access to her kitchen and her storeroom to her young relative, it would indicate either that she had some secret to hide—and there are plenty of secrets in a village home—or that there was bad blood between the two families.

In the Indian village, although the ties of kinship extend far and wide, they cannot extend indefinitely. They have to stop short at the boundaries of caste. But then the ties of caste extend beyond the village, and they might extend quite far. Through repeated intermarriage all members of a subcaste become related to each other or at least have to be treated as if they were. To invoke the right of privacy against a member of one's own caste or subcaste might be to incur the opprobrium of the community. Do intra-caste interactions fall within the private or the public domain? Where obligations to communities of birth are far-reaching, the distinction between the private and the public is likely to be tenuous.

In China the major morphological divisions of society are those of clan rather than caste (Hsu 1963). Whereas a caste is an endogamous division, a clan is exogamous. Hence at least in principle the obligations of kinship could extend much further in China than in India. The obligations of clanship are to this day extensively used both on the mainland and overseas, and for linking mainland and overseas Chinese. Again, the question we asked about caste has to be asked about clan: are actions governed by the norms of clanship to be regarded as private or as public?

It is difficult to determine exactly when in the transition to the modern age the idea of the home as the bastion of privacy and the private became established. The historical evidence suggests that the home was not viewed in the same way in western Europe everywhere and at all times. In his study of childhood, Philippe Ariès has presented some interesting material about the use of space in the European home before the eighteenth century. He observes:

It is easy to imagine the promiscuity which reigned in these rooms where nobody could be alone, which one had to cross to reach any of the communicating rooms, where several couples and several groups of boys or girls slept together (not to speak of the servants, of whom at least some must have slept beside their masters, setting up beds which were still collapsible in the room or just outside the door), in which people foregathered to have their meals, to receive their friends or clients, and sometimes to give alms to beggars (Ariès 1962: 395).

It is true that Ariès was speaking here of the houses of notables; but it is unlikely that privacy would have been more highly valued among the peasantry in the period he was describing.

Where the distinction between the private and the public has become a part of common sense, if the domestic stands as the metaphor for the private, the political stands as the metaphor for the public. The public faces in the epigraph above almost certainly refer to politicians for whom Auden rarely concealed his allergy.

Not only does the political system become progressively differentiated from other social systems, but that system itself becomes internally differentiated. There are variations from one society to another in how politics actually operates, and also in how its agents think it operates and should operate. The same term has different meanings even in neighbouring countries. The French have only one term for what in English is described by two separate terms, 'politics' and 'policy' (Aron 1965: 21–2). When Max Weber spoke of *Politik als Beruf*, or *Politics as a Vocation*, he had both politics and policy in mind. He believed that politics in both senses of the term belonged to the public domain, and he certainly did not assign a wholly negative meaning to it.

Politics and kinship are not differentiated to the same extent in all societies. In some societies they are scarcely differentiated at all in either practice or principle. Lewis Henry Morgan wrote in the nineteenth century that the earliest societies were organized on the basis of kinship and not territory, and that territory only gradually replaced kinship as the basis of political organization (Morgan 1964). There was a kernel of truth in this observation although it came to be discredited later because Morgan did not have a clear enough understanding of the relation between kinship and locality. All societies are territorially organized, but in some the local group is in effect an extended kin group.

Morgan's observations were refined and extended in the twentieth century by Meyer Fortes (1970) whose analysis of the relationship between kinship, territory, and politics stands as a landmark. In the simpler societies studied by Fortes, kinship has a domestic or familial dimension, but it also has a politico-jural dimension. He tried to develop a technique whereby the two dimensions of kinship which the actor traverses easily and effortlessly may be separated analytically.

Fortes used the Australian Aborigines as his example of what he called the 'kinship polity'. To be sure, the Australian Aborigines provide the extreme example of the inerpenetration of kinship and politics—of the private and the public—but a study of the example throws light on the emergence of the private and the public as distinct domains. In the kinship polity, the boundaries of the politico-jural domain are coextensive with those of the domain of kinship: 'The jural domain and the familial domain are coterminous, unified by the common body of norms and the overriding ethic of generosity' (Fortes 1970: 110). There are in such societies no separate norms regulating the 'private' and the 'public'.

In the case of segmentary tribes with well-marked lineages, one may make a distinction in principle between the lineage system based on genealogy and the political system based on territory (Evans-Prithard 1940). Evans-Pritchard's classic study of the Nuer of east Africa showed how political order was maintained in such a system in the absence of any centralized authority vested in chief, council, or court. But even here, although the territorial system is distinct from the genealogical, 'political' relations between territorial sections are expressed typically in terms of relations between the lineage segements of the dominant clan. This led Dumont to question whether it was at all valid to speak of a 'political system' in the case of the Nuer: 'The so-called political system has neither head nor tongue: it expresses itself almost exclusively in the language of clans, of lineages, of ancestral myths' (Dumont 1971: 71, my translation).

Besides segmentary tribes there are of course tribal chiefdoms as well as tribal states. Whereas there are no constituted authorities in a kinship polity or even in a segmentary political system, there are chiefs, counsellors, headmen and so on in the tribal chiefdom and even more so in the tribal state. But although chiefs and headmen perform political functions, they are by no means the only functions they perform. Even at the highest point of the socio-political pyramid, 'household' and 'office' are never clearly separated. The chief cannot deny the claims of his kinsmen on his cattle and his granary on the ground that they are his 'private' wealth: nor can he say that they constitute 'public' wealth in the disposal of which he cannot favour his kin (Gluckman 1955).

When we move from tribe to peasantry, the picture is not very different. Peasant communities have been described as 'part-societies' with 'part-cultures' (Redfield 1956). This is because, though relatively isolated and self-sufficient, they have links of one kind or another with centres of civilization. Both in medieval Europe and until recent times in China and the Islamic world, everyday life in the community was governed by its own internal rhythm. Peasant communities were relatively homogeneous and undifferentiated in most parts of the world, though never quite like 'so many potatoes in a sack of potatoes'. The Indian village, as we know, was stratified on the basis of caste, but that is different from the kind of institutional differentiation I have been speaking of so far. At any rate, the subordination of the individual to the group—village, caste, and joint family—was no less marked in India than in other agrarian communities.

I have used the distinction between the home and the outside world to illustrate the distinction between the private and the public. But is there any society in which the home—or the privileged site of the private, wherever it may lie—is insulated completely from the outside world? This is clearly impossible, because the same individual has necessarily to act in both domains. Here I may refer to the distinction between the sacred and the profane as formulated by Durkheim (1915). The sacred and the profane are distinct and must ordinarily be kept apart; yet there has to be communication between them in socially prescribed ways. (It must be noted that whereas the opposition between sacred and profane is universal, that between private and public is not).

It is generally acknowledged in modern western societies that the relations between husband and wife or between parents and children are their private affair. This does not mean that they are outside the reach of the law: the divorce court and the juvenile court are very much within the public domain. What it does mean perhaps is that the neighbourhood or the community should not intercede in the internal affairs of the family. Private affairs may be publicly regulated but only through specified channels and in prescribed ways.

In agrarian societies generally, disputes within the home are legitimate concerns of the neighbourhood and the community. One may say that the diffuse sanctions exercised by the community act against disputes within the home reaching the point of crisis where only a legal settlement is possible. In the typical Indian village, elders feel free to advise and even to discipline younger members of the community on matters that would in other societies be regarded as private. In all these matters of course distinctions of caste and gender have to be kept in mind, but those distinctions do not correspond to the one between the private and the public. Here it is important to distinguish the community not only from the private but also from the public. In rural society how the elders of the community think and feel is certainly important: but is that the same thing as public opinion?

Apart from the diffuse sanctions of the community, there are more specific mechanisms for the settlement of disputes. In rural India these mechanisms took two main forms: the village panchayat and the caste panchayat. The village panchayat was probably less common and less active than is generally presumed. Caste panchayats, on the other hand, were often active and vigorous, although not all castes had equally effective panchayats. What have been regarded as village panchayats were in effect often panchayats of the dominant caste of the village. Such bodies, no matter how effective, were very different from what would be regarded as public organs in a modern democracy.

Returning to the home and other domains of modern society that may properly be regarded as private, we have seen that they cannot be kept outside the reach of the law: this is because the private no less than the public is a part of society, being both defined and regulated by it. While it is true that all aspects of modern societies, both 'public' and 'private', are regulated by law, it is also true that the differentiation of society is accompanied by the differentiation of law. It was Durkheim's profound insight that societies based on what he called the division of labour (but what it may be better to describe as the differentiation of institutions) are characterized by legal systems that are enormously more complex than the legal systems of societies based on mechanical solidarity, in other words on clan, caste, and community.

The emergence in the eighteenth and nineteenth centuries of what in English is known as 'civil society' and in German as 'Bürgerlichegesellschaft' was accompanied by far-reaching innovations in the legal system. Civil society is impossible in the absence of a differentiated legal system with its great variety of laws: administrative law, commercial law, contract law, patent law, procedural law, and so on. But while there is an increase in the volume and variety of laws, the initiative for legal action passes more and more from the state or the community to the individual or private party; in Durkheim's language, there is a displacement of repressive law by restitutive law.

The law of contract, and even more the idea of contract, provided the basis for the free and unfettered pursuit of private interests by otherwise unrelated individuals to their mutual advantage. Individuals became free to enter into contracts that they considered to be to their advantage without consideration of birth, station, or rank. Bernard de Mandeville's phrase about 'private vices, public benefits' was meant ironically, for the orderly pursuit of private interests was ceasing to be viewed as a vice or a mark of dishonour as it had been in the earlier social code (Hirschman 1977). This sense of the transition from one kind of order to a different one was captured in Sir Henry Maine's dictum that the movement of progressive societies has hitherto been 'a movement *from Status to Contract*' (Maine 1950: 141).

Is a society based solely on contractual relations between private parties without the state or other public institutions casting any shadow on them possible? The prospect of such a society lurked behind Adam Smith's idea of the invisible hand and Herbert Spencer's idea of contractual solidarity. In a brilliant polemic against Spencer and the English utilitarians, Durkheim (1982) demolished the idea of a social order, no matter how much freedom it gave to private parties, without any regulation by public institutions. Private and public, Durkheim would argue, are not enemies of each other, they are mutually reinforcing; differentiation does not weaken the fabric of society, it strengthens it.

A particular contract may be a private matter between two individuals, but the law of contracts, which alone makes it binding, belongs in the public domain. A contract is private in the sense that I am free to enter or not enter into it and to choose the person with whom to enter into it, without leave of my clan, caste, or community. It is public in the sense that no contract is valid unless it meets the requirements of the law of contracts which exists independently of the parties to the contract. With the increase in the number and variety of contracts, there has been a corresponding elaboration of the law of contracts.

The value placed on privacy or the private grows along with the value placed on the individual or person. Tocqueville had underlined the central part played by the growing social recognition of the individual in the passage from an aristocratic to a democratic society: 'Individualism is a novel expression to which a novel idea has given birth' (Tocqueville 1956: II, 98). It signalled the replacement of a social order based on the privileges and disabilities of estates (or castes) by one based on the rights and duties of individuals as citizens. It is my argument that the emancipation of the individual from clan, caste, and community is crucial to the modern conception of not only the private but also the public.

I have argued that the private and the public are complementary categories and that they are held together by the value placed on the individual as citizen. Citizenship is both an individualizing and a universalizing concept, and the progress of democracy is intimately linked to the enlargement of citizenship.

Citizenship is an individualizing concept in the sense that its entitlements are the entitlements of the individual irrespective of 'religion, race, caste, sex or place of birth'. These entitlements are diminished by the arbitrary exercise of the coercive power of the state. But they may also be stunted by the bondage of the individual to clan, caste, and community. In India, the individual has been for centuries subordinated to the group: village, caste, and joint family. While the subordination of the individual to the group was not unique to India, it was carried further there than perhaps in any other society known to history. Before independence it was the colonial state that appeared as the main obstacle to the growth of citizenship. Today the demands of caste and community appear as the main impediments to that growth.

The enlargement of citizenship may be understood in two senses. Firstly, hitherto excluded sections of society are granted citizenship which in that sense becomes more inclusive. In a purely formal sense, the extension of the franchise provides a good example of this. If we look at the history of western democracies in the last two hundred years, we will find that initially the franchise was restricted by property, by gender, and by race. Citizens consisted at first of a small and exclusive section of society and it was that section that constituted the political public from the democratic point of view. In nineteenth-century America, women and Blacks did not form a part of the political public. As the franchise became extended in the twentieth century, citizenship became enlarged and the public more inclusive.

I have used a purely formal criterion of citizenship to illustrate my point about the public becoming more and more inclusive. What took two hundred years and more in the west was accomplished overnight in India where subjects were transformed into citizens with the adoption of a republican constitution. But while all Indians are in a purely formal sense citizens under the Constitution of India, the public in any politically meaningful sense of the term is still highly restricted. The disabilities of subjecthood have been removed, but the abilities essential for effective citizenship have not been created. There has been a quantitative enlargement of citizenship without much qualitative advance.

Marshall (1977) realized that in Britain the enlargement of citizenship did not follow a smooth or uniform course, and a later commentator has pointed out that 'full' or 'substantive' citizenship is still some distance away (Lockwood 1992). Nevertheless, the enlargement of citizenship, both quantitatively and qualitatively, has made the public in Britain far more inclusive now than it was in the eighteenth century, and inclusive in a more meaningful sense than it is in India.

It hardly needs to be emphasized that the substance of citizenship is outside the reach of millions of Indians. Apart from the divisions of caste and community referred to earlier, society is deeply stratified by income, occupation, and education. Poverty, hunger, disease, and illiteracy are widespread. If there is a public domain in which decisions relating to the major institutions of society are made, it is inaccessible to very many Indians.

This brings us back to the substantive concept of the public: the public not as a domain of activity distinct from the private, but as the 'people', as all the members of the society or nation taken together. Is there any society in which the public in the sense of the people as a whole acts effectively and meaningfully in a single, homogeneous, and undifferentiated public domain? This certainly does not happen in either India or the Unites States, and it is difficult to see how it can possibly happen in any large and complex modern society. The idea of equal participation in the political process of all members of the public may be the dream of the political philosopher but it has very little foundation in sociological reality.

Is the idea of the public, in either the analytical or the substantive sense, incompatible with social differentiation and social stratification? Were it so, it would be unviable from the start. I have argued that all modern societies are internally differentiated and they are in general more differentiated than societies of the past. They are also stratified in terms of income, esteem, and power. But social stratification is not the same thing as social exclusion. Pre-modern societies, whether in India or in Europe, accepted social exclusion based on caste, creed, and gender in both practice and principle. Discrimination based on race, caste, and gender is incompatible with citizenship; stratification based on income, occupation, and education is not.

I have said that citizenship is a universalizing concept. I must insist, that universality is not the same thing as equality even though the two are frequently confused (see Chapter 10). Universality requires that certain basic facilities and capabilities be placed within the reach of all members of society without consideration of individual merit or individual need; in short, that they be made universally available. It is not concerned, or at least not directly concerned, with the distribution of benefits in society as a whole, say for instance, with disparities of income or esteem between managers and civil servants or between different ranks of civil servants. Under certain circumstances universality may be more effectively secured through measures that increase rather than decrease income differentials at certain levels of the occupational system.

Apart from the opposition of public and private, I have tried to distinguish between public and community, particularly the community of birth based on race, caste, and clan. There is another distinction that I would like to consider at the end, and that is the distinction between public and mass. Civil society in the liberal democratic conception is a society of publics; it is not a mass society. The liberal critique of totalitarian regimes is that under such regimes the public is transformed into a mass. The anxiety about mass society goes beyond the critique of fascism or communism; with some it is a critique of the homogenizing tendency that they see as inherent in the age of technology.

C. Wright Mills (1956: 298–324) had warned against 'the transformation of public into mass' in the United States in a work that received wide attention in the 1950s and 1960s. According to him, this would be the outcome of the emergence of a strong power elite which secured increasing control over the instruments of coercion as well as the instruments of communication. The more cohesive and unified the elite became, the more fragmented and impotent the masses would become. He contrasted the society of publics that had prevailed in the USA in the nineteenth century with the mass society that was emerging in the twentieth.

A crucial distinction between public and mass, according to Mills, lay in the dominant modes of communication characteristic of each. Opinion formation through discussion characterizes a society of publics whereas in a mass society opinion is formed by the media, and 'the publics become mere *media markets*' (Mills 1956: 304, emphasis in original). He argued that control of these markets became increasingly concentrated in the hands of the very persons who also controlled the instruments of coercion. Mills was not alone in pointing to the debilitating effects of the mass media in the operation of the democratic process.

Mills's argument about the transformation of public into mass was strongly coloured by a romantic notion of society and politics in nineteenth-century America. He simply assumed that active and vigorous communities of public had existed in the past and were being undermined in his time. He did not ask what positions women, Blacks, and other excluded sections of society occupied in the communities of public in nineteenth-century America. Modern means of communication no doubt alter the operation of the political process. But the role of the media and of modern technology more generally should not be viewed in only a negative light. Certainly in post-independence India both the print and the electronic media have given hitherto excluded sections of society a better sense of the larger political process and a better chance of participating in it than they had in the past. They have contributed to the enlargement of the public, although the enlarged public of today cannot have the same character as the 'communities of public', real or imagined, that existed in the nineteenth century.

A mass society is the antithesis of a society of publics in so far as the former tends to be homogenized whereas the latter is internally differentiated. But the enlargement of the public through the expansion of citizenship need not lead to the homogenization of society. The effective functioning of a democratic polity requires the presence of appropriate institutions to link citizens to each other and to mediate between citizens and the state. A democratic state and democratic citizenship cannot be sustained in the absence of open and secular institutions that are very different from the communities of birth which were so prominent in the societies of the past.

When the state becomes too powerful it penetrates into the institutions of society and either stultifies them or absorbs them within itself. When institutions lose their autonomy there is little to stand between citizen and state in a society in which the old communities of birth have lost their vitality: this is the transformation of public into mass. This is what happened in the Soviet Union under Stalin, in Germany under Hitler, and in Italy under Mussolini. In the 1950s and 1960s many began to fear that this would happen also in the western democracies with the runaway expansion of technology.

The system of differentiated institutions by which a society of publics is sustained is the outcome of a long and complex historical process. It is an open question how far such institutions can be replicated in different parts of the world under historical conditions that are very different from those under which they first emerged. In countries like India they have to contend for space in the political arena with other social formations anchored in kinship and religion.

There is no reason to believe or to expect that the enlargement of citizenship—and through it of the public—will take the same course in India as in the west. We have seen that the purely quantitative enlargement of citizenship has been dramatic, but this has happened without much meaningful qualitative advance. It would be unwise to dismiss as trivial the creation of a more inclusive citizenry in the last fifty years. But we cannot disregard the deepening tension created by the disjunction between the quantitative increase in citizenship and its lack of qualitative advance.

Compared to the west the pace of political expansion appears to be forced. More and more persons participate not only in elections but also in demonstrations, rallies, stoppages, and closures. When a city is brought to a halt by the call for a *bandh*, it is difficult to decide whether we are dealing with public participation or mass participation. It has now become difficult to ignore the wear and tear caused by these forms of participation to the institutions of civil society that provide substance to democratic citizenship.

There is no doubt that the restricted public that existed at the time of independence has been enlarged in the last fifty years and that this is irreversible. However the process of making an exclusive public more inclusive in a relatively short span of time has been accompanied by extensive mobilization on the basis of caste and community, often in the name of equality and social justice. While this leads to the strengthening of caste and community, at least in the short run, it is doubtful that it contributes much to the qualitative advance of citizenship. If the qualitative advance of citizenship has to surrender to caste and community, it will not augur well for the growth of a political public even when the surrender is made for the sake of substantive equality.

6

Distributive Justice and Institutional Well-being

The Problem

The discussion in this chapter will be on the subject of reservation within a broad and general framework of enquiry. It has exercised the pubic mind for some time, and I am not unaware of the risks in attempting a scholarly treatment of a problem to which so many events have brought such a pressing sense of urgency. It presents a difficult challenge to the sociologist who would like to keep apart value judgements and judgements of reality. But the subject is not only of immediate or passing interest; it raises questions of great importance to social and legal theory that ought to be examined fully and openly, and with the maximum possible detachment. I will try to develop here some of the arguments that were first presented in my Ambedkar lectures delivered in the University of Bombay in March 1980 (Béteille 1981b).

Let me begin with a couple of observations on the public response to reservation. It appears that those opposed to it were taken by surprise by the announcement in early August 1990 that the government would implement the recommendations of the Mandal Commission for reservation in employment. Yet those recommendations had been adopted by Parliament with unanimous acclaim eight years previously, on 11 August 1982. My own conclusion then was the somewhat fatalistic one that reservation as recommended by the Mandal Commission, or something similar, would be adopted sooner or later, since there seemed to be so little opposition to it from either politicians or intellectuals (Béteille

1982). Perhaps those who were uneasy over the recommendations hoped that Parliament would, with the passage of time, forget its own unanimous approval and the whole issue would die down. The issue did not die down, but became a source of intense and widespread dissension following the fateful decision of the V.P. Singh government in 1990.

A second striking feature of the public response in 1990 was that moral passions were raised to a very high pitch. Those opposed to reservation argued that injustice would be done by it to the 'forward' castes or that the rights of meritorious individuals would be sacrificed. On the other side, people argued that reservation would vindicate the rights of backward communities and remedy the injustices suffered by them for centuries if not millennia.

I would like to stress the extensive if not universal use of the language of justice and rights in the public debate on reservation. Those who are opposed to it tend to dwell more on the rights of individuals, whereas those in favour speak more of the rights of castes and communities. Affirmative action or positive discrimination—including numerical quotas—has been a subject of public debate also in the United States. There the language of rights has figured far less prominently than here in arguments for and against reservation of the kind with which we are concerned. In America the proponents of even numerical quotas tend to make their case not in terms of justice but in terms of utility; not from arguments about rights but from arguments about policy.

When I compare the Indian case with the American, I sometimes wonder if we have a stronger sense of justice than the Americans; or if our sense of justice is a radically different one. That is not an easy question to answer, but I would like to keep it in mind as I go along. The Dharmashastras, by which Hindus were governed for many centuries, were animated by a very different sense of justice from the one on which the Indian Constitution is based. The old sense of justice corresponded to a distinctive culture and a distinctive social structure. It is far from clear to what extent it has been displaced by the changes taking place in Indian society and culture today.

The social and cultural changes of the last hundred years have been associated with the emergence and growth of administrative, educational, scientific, medical, financial, and other institutions of a public or semi-public character that are either completely new or so different from their traditional counterparts as to count effectively as new. I would like to devote some attention to these institutions because the hopes and aspirations of many Indians, both supporters and opponents of reservation, turn on their survival and success. They have a certain universal character in the sense that they are a part of the social landscape not only of modern India but of the whole modern world.

Universities, hospitals, laboratories, banks, and secretariats have become an important part of the modernization of India. I introduce the term 'modernization' with some hesitation because it has acquired a somewhat bad odour through the persistent, though in my judgement misguided, exertions of social scientists with a radical vocabulary. But I need not discuss the concept further here, because there does not appear to be any systematic disagreement between supporters and opponents of reservation on the value to be assigned to a hospital, a science laboratory, or a bank. Today, the disagreement is not so much about the value of these modern institutions as about the criteria by which access to positions of respect and responsibility in them should be regulated.

Now, it is a sociological truism that all institutions do not work in the same way; each has its own rules and requirements, its own structure of rights and obligations, and its own internal culture. The structure of rights and obligations that governs a joint family would not be appropriate to a science laboratory; and the culture of a village *panchayat* would not be appropriate to a university.

I am not aware of any satisfactory definition of institutional well-being, and I do not attempt to provide one. It is easy to anticipate the difficulties that such an attempt must encounter. Yet, we have an intuitive sense of the well-being of individuals, and we can, at least for a start, use that sense to guide us when we speak of the well-being of institutions. It appears evident that institutions have conditions of well-being that differ from one type to another. These conditions can hardly be specified with the clarity and precision of a scientific formula. The best that we can do is to exercise our judgement in a sober and dispassionate manner on the basis of accumulated experience. At any rate, it is useful to remind ourselves that institutions cannot be squeezed and stretched at will without serious risk to their continued existence.

I have introduced the subject of justice, and I have made a few observations on institutions. I am now in a position to formulate my central problem in a provisional and tentative way: it is the problem of the compatibility between the requirements of institutional well-being and the claims made by or on behalf of disadvantaged groups in the name of distributive justice. How far can such claims be accommodated without damage to the interior lives of these institutions? I believe that it is disingenuous to pretend that every institution can accommodate without any strain all the claims that are made on it in the name of distributive justice.

Groups and Individuals

The fundamental issue in distributive justice is equality: a more equal or at least a less unequal distribution of 'the benefits and burdens of social co-operation' (Rawls 1972: 4). In that sense distributive justice seeks to go beyond equality in the purely formal sense: equality before the law, the equal protection of laws, or even formal equality of opportunity. Its central concern is, in the language of Rawls, 'to redress the bias of contingencies in the direction of equality' (Ibid.: 100–1). There can be not doubt that the concern for a more equal distribution of benefits and burdens figures in the Indian Constitution, but I should point out that it figures most prominently in the part on Directive Principles of State Policy. I may also point out that some contemporary authors have questioned the very concept of 'distributive justice' (Hayek 1976, vol. 2), although I would like to leave open, at least for the time being, the question as to where any preconceived pattern of distribution is a matter of justice and where it is a matter of utility.

Any attempt to promote distributive justice must begin with a consideration of the existing inequalities in a society. The presence of large social inequalities is a striking feature of contemporary India. There are many different forms of inequality in Indian society, as in other contemporary societies. In our perspective, it is essential to keep in sight both inequalities between individuals and disparities between groups. Disparities between groups have been historically of great significance in Indian society, although they are not unique to it.

The distinction between individuals and groups is important in the present context since the claims for a more just distribution of benefits and burdens on behalf of individuals are not identical with those made on behalf of groups. There are also broader historical and sociological reasons for paying attention to the distinction between the two. I would like to examine a little more closely the place assigned to individuals and to groups in different types of society and in different historical epochs.

Let us begin with the individual. While all societies are made up of individuals in the empirical sense, they do not all assign the same value to him or her as an autonomous moral agent (Dumont 1977a; Béteille 1986). Where a high value is placed on the individual, he is expected to make his own life for himself and to be judged on his own merit, irrespective of the family or community of which he is a member. To be sure, this is only an ideal, but it is a social ideal that has acquired a peculiar force in the modern world.

At least in the western historical experience, egalitarianism and individualism were closely linked in their origin (Béteille 1986). Before the modern age, a different kind of social order prevailed in which the individual was subordinated to the group, and society was cast in a hierarchical mould. The eighteenth and nineteenth centuries witnessed not only large economic and political changes, but the displacement of the old social ideal of a hierarchy of estates by a new one of the equality of individuals as citizens. The new social ideal became anchored in new institutions, particularly in education and employment where equality of opportunity and 'careers open to talent' became the watchwords. Needless to say, these far-reaching changes in the institutional system did not lead at once to the elimination or even the reduction of inequalities in the distribution of income between individuals.

The subordination of the individual to the group is associated with the prevalence of birth over achievement: one's position in society is marked by the group into which one is born, not by what one achieves for oneself. Traditional India has been described as 'the land of the most inviolable organization by birth' (Weber 1958: 3). Here the group prevailed over the individual more completely and more continuously than in any other society known to history. What counted socially was the village community, the joint family, and, above all, caste, but not the individual (Nehru 1961: 247–8). The individual had very little space for movement within society: he could of course fulfill himself outside society by adopting the way of the renouncer.

Whether in pre-revolutionary France or in traditional India—or for that matter in pre-modern China—the subordination of the individual to the group went hand in hand with the hierarchical arrangement of groups. The more rigid the social hierarchy, the more strict the subordination of the individual. If there be any sociological law, it is this: in all hierarchical societies—by which I mean societies that are hierarchical by design and not merely in fact—the individual counts for little and the group for a great deal; there is, so far as I know, no exception to this.

Whatever its other virtues—and it had positive functions in the traditional order—for a thousand years and more, caste has stood for the most rigid social hierarchy and at the same time for the most complete subordination of the individual to the group. However, things have not stood still in India for the last hundred and fifty years. The legitimacy of the traditional social hierarchy was shaken by the legal and economic changes introduced by the British in the nineteenth century. A first hesitant turn was taken in 1850 with the Removal of Caste Disabilities Act; a hundred years later, the Constitution of India not only questioned the legitimacy of caste, but repudiated it altogether.

The social reformers of the nineteenth century who sought to dismantle the edifice of caste did so from a mixture of motives and for a variety of reasons. They found the all-pervasive ranking of groups repugnant and even absurd in the light of the new social ideal of equality; but they also sought freedom for the individual from the restrictions imposed by the group, irrespective of its social rank. Today the situation has taken a different turn because opinion is sharply divided between those who believe that the cause of equality can be advanced under the banner of caste and those who believe that this is impossible.

In the traditional Indian village it was acknowledged that every caste had a just claim to a share—not an equal share, to be sure, but a certain share—of the social product. We may say that this reflected the traditional concept of distributive justice which attended directly to the claims of groups, and only indirectly and by implication to those of its individual members. The claim that the state should distribute the benefits of education and employment equitably between the different castes and communities is a strong one because it raises echoes of a social ideal that had prevailed in India for centuries (Bose 1975).

While it may be true that proposals for caste quotas in education and employment raise echoes of traditional ideas of distributive justice, this does not mean that nothing has changed between then and now. Although all castes could claim shares in the social product, it was clearly understood by all parties in the past that these shares must be unequal. Now the claim is for equal shares or shares proportionate to population. At a deeper level the caste system has changed fundamentally. The moral claims of castes over their individual members have weakened at all levels of society, and especially for the urban middle class where the battle over reservation is being fought. It will be safe to say that no caste today has the moral authority to enforce on its middle class members any of its traditional sanctions. Having freed themselves from the moral authority of their caste, such individuals are now able to use it instrumentally for economic and political advantage.

In the traditional order, the village priest, or the village barber, or the village scavenger had a moral right to claim a share of the social product in the name of caste because each of them was bound by the moral authority of the caste of which he was a member. That moral authority has been, for good or evil, shattered for ever. On what ground can individuals now claim distributive shares for themselves in the name of their caste after having repudiated their moral obligations to it?

Rights and Policies

I would now like to turn to some of the specific arguments that have been made in support of reservations. I have to say, at the risk of appearing unpatriotic, that the best arguments of that kind have been made not in India but in the United States. It is true that the American situation is in many ways different from the Indian, but there too preferential policies in favour of disadvantaged groups defined by race and ethnicity—rather than caste and tribe as in our case—have become a subject of public debate.

To my mind the most forceful and at the same time the most acute argument in support of reverse discrimination—including numerical quotas—has been made by the American lawyer Ronald Dworkin who is Professor of Jurisprudence in Oxford. The current bias of intellectual opinion in the United States is much more in favour of equality of opportunity and much more against discrimination in any form than in India, even though it is the Indian Constitution, and not the American, that has an equal opportunities clause and an anti-discrimination clause in its part on Fundamental Rights. Given that bias of opinion, those who argue for reverse discrimination in the United States have to present strong arguments.

Dworkin first presented his argument for reverse discrimination in connection with the DeFunis case in a paper that received wide attention when it appeared in 1977 in *The New York Review of Books* (Dworkin 1984: 223–39). A white man named Macro DeFunis had applied for admission to the Law School in the University of Washington, but was rejected even though he had done better on college grades and test scores than others belonging to disadvantaged races who were admitted. DeFunis was by conventional academic criteria the better candidate, but he was passed over in order to make room for others, ostensibly on grounds of race. The case led to a sharp division of liberal opinion in the United States. Dworkin supported the decision of the Washington University Law School to reject DeFunis in the interest of a more racially-mixed student body.

Those who are opposed to reservation on the basis of race, caste, or ethnicity come forward, sooner or later, with the argument that it entails a sacrifice of individual merit. Dworkin faced that argument directly by saying that merit did not by itself create the kind of right that the Law School was accused of violating by denying admission to DeFunis. He did not say that merit was irrelevant or unimportant, only that it did not create a right of admission in DeFunis or anyone.

Dworkin maintained that the argument that the Washington University Law School had violated an individual right by denying admission to DeFunis was misconceived, because he did not have such a right in the first place. 'DeFunis plainly has no Constitutional right that the state provide him a legal education of a certain quality' (Ibid.: 225). Dworkin was not saying that the individual had no rights: he was saying that he did not have the kind of right that was being claimed by DeFunis or on his behalf:

DeFunis does not have a right to equal treatment in the assignment of law school places; he does not have a right to a place just because others are given places. Individuals may have a right to equal treatment in elementary education, because someone who is denied elementary education is unlikely to lead a useful life. But legal education is not so vital that everyone has an equal right to it (Ibid.: 227).

Dworkin returned to the same argument a few years later in an essay on the Bakke case where a white applicant had been denied admission to a medical school that had set aside a number of places for members of 'educationally and economically disadvantaged minorities'. He repeated the argument that Bakke had no constitutional right that had been violated by the medical school when it denied him a place in the interest of its affirmative action programme. The programme was a good one because it served a useful policy and, although it might cause disappointment or even hardship to the individual, it did not violate his constitutional rights (Dworkin 1985: 293–303; see also Béteille 1987b).

I am a little uncertain as to how fully these arguments apply in the Indian case. The Indian Constitution, unlike the American, has clear provisions proscribing discrimination and prescribing equality of opportunity in the part on Fundamental Rights. Further, it is the citizen as an individual, rather than any caste or community, who has the right to equal opportunity. It is true that the right is not absolute or unqualified since it has to accommodate special provisions; but that accommodation cannot be so extensive as to render the right fictitious.

Dr Ambedkar had, in the Constituent Assembly, drawn attention to this kind of threat to equality of opportunity. He had said,

Supposing, for instance, reservations were made for a community or a collection of communities, the total of which came to something like 70 per cent of the total posts under the state and only 30 per cent are retained as the unreserved. Could anybody say that the reservation of 30 per cent as open to general competition would be satisfactory from the point of view of giving effect to the first principle, that there should be equality of opportunity? (Constituent Assembly Debates 1989: VII, 701).

Whether or not the individual citizen has, on the ground of 'merit', an unqualified right to admission to a medical college or the civil service, the principle of equality of opportunity is a first principle that we cannot afford to devalue. It cannot but be devalued by the extension of massive caste quotas into every area of public life.

My purpose in drawing attention to the American debate was to make the point that quotas for disadvantaged groups are best viewed as matters not of right but of policy. In the United States, the strongest arguments in support of reverse discrimination are made not on grounds of rights and justice but on those of policy and utility. Dworkin rejects categorically the assumption that 'racial and ethnic groups are entitled to proportionate shares of opportunities', and adds, 'That is a plain mistake; the programmes are not based on the idea that those who are aided are entitled to aid, but only on the strategic hypothesis that helping them is now an effective way of attacking a national problem' (Dworkin 1985: 297; see also Nagel 1977). Among other things, this allows a degree of freedom and flexibility in the formulation and administration of such programmes.

In India, we face a somewhat different situation. A case for reverse discrimination is made persistently, and with increasing intensity, in the language of rights. This at once raises the temperature of the debate and forces people to adopt intransigent positions. Understandably, they find it far more difficult to yield on what they believe, or are led to believe, to be matters of right and justice than they would on matters of utility or policy.

It is difficult to see how the idea that castes and communities have *rights* to proportionate shares in public employment can be made compatible with the working of a modern society committed to economic development and liberal democracy. It is true that caste continues to operate in many spheres of social life; but it does not do so any longer as a matter of right. The continued existence of caste is one thing; its legitimacy is a different thing altogether. The attempt to invest the caste system with legitimacy by claiming that its constituent units have rights and entitlements is bound to be defeated in the end; but in the meantime it can cause enormous harm to society and its institutions.

The persistent use of the language of rights in the public debate for and against reservations is bound to lead to an increase in the consciousness of caste, and in that way to defeat the basic objective of affirmative action which is to reduce and not increase caste consciousness. All parties to the debate say that they wish to dismantle the structure of caste. But caste is not a material edifice that can be physically dismantled and destroyed. It exists above all in the consciousness of people—in their deep sense of division and separation on the one hand and of rank and inequality on the other. How can we exorcise caste from the public mind by deepening the sense in society that castes are entitled to their separate shares as a matter of right?

Undoubtedly, there are vast disparities in Indian society that need to be redressed. For that we require policies that will be useful and effective. Flexibility is of the essence in the design and application of policies to redress disparities that have arisen from many causes and not just caste. The insistence on rights where none exist in either law or morality destroys the very flexibility without which no policy of affirmative action can be useful or effective.

Individuals and Institutions

I take it for granted that policies for the redress of severe social and economic disadvantages are in themselves desirable. Such policies have to aim at different sectors of society and at the widest possible base. An obvious field for the application of preferential policies is that of education where the maximum attention should be devoted to primary and secondary education which develop the base on which the success of higher education depends. Other fields for which preferential policies may be designed include those of childcare, health, and housing.

Policies, unlike rights, are not absolutes; they have to be examined in terms of costs and benefits. We may not always be able to measure these, but that should not prevent us from trying to form clear judgements about them. Both costs and benefits must be taken into account in assessing any policy of affirmative action. Here I shall confine myself to job reservation in public institutions. This is not because it constitutes the most useful or effective application of the principle of redress, but because it helps to bring into focus issues that I consider important and because it has received such wide public attention.

When people think of reservations today, they think first and foremost of employment, and, above all, of salaried employment in the services of the union and state governments and in other public institutions. The conditions of success and failure in securing such employment have become a kind of acid test of the fairness of the system among the supporters as well as the opponents of reservation. This is inevitable in an economy where there is so much unemployment all around and where for every vacancy there are numerous applicants. Salaried employment is a source of security and status to the individual and his family; but it is difficult to judge how far the benefits of public employment can or should spread from the individual to his kith and kin, and to his community.

The middle class, or what some now describe as the service class, looks after its own and tends to reproduce itself from one generation to the next. In every society, a crucial part is played in this process by the family. It is true that the caste system is a serious obstacle to equality of opportunity; but at a deeper level the family system is a far more persistent obstacle to it. I make this point because, although the family system is universally present, it is stronger in some societies than in others. Given the exceptional strength of the family among all social classes in India, all talk about equality of result as an attainable objective has to be taken with a very large pinch of salt. Thus, the first institutional obstacle that the removal of inequality encounters is the family; it is not an easily removable obstacle (see Chapter 7).

There is of course a certain amount of mobility or circulation of individuals between different social strata, despite the persistence and strength of the family. The extent of such mobility varies from one society to another, and social policy has undoubtedly some part to play in increasing mobility by removing obsolete or artificial obstacles to it. In India the tendency of the service class to reproduce itself is in both appearance and reality particularly marked. Firstly, because this class is small relatively to the population as a whole, its unity and continuity appear stronger than in societies where it is relatively large. Second, the dramatic changes in the occupational structure of the advanced industrial societies have led to a net increase of upward over downward mobility (Goldthorpe 1987); in the absence of such changes in India, there has been little, if any, aggregate increase in upward mobility. Thirdly, the residues of a rigidly hierarchical system have acted as obstacles to the free flow of lower-caste individuals into the service class.

There is no denying the fact that individuals from different castes are found in very different proportions in the service class. There are good grounds for feeling that such wide disparities are undesirable, and reasons for believing that they can be corrected, at least to some extent, by useful and effective policy. But we must first understand the reasons why the lower castes are so thinly represented in the higher occupations. There is extensive prejudice against their members, but this applies particularly to the Harijans and Adivasis. There is also a marked decline in the number of qualified candidates as we move down from the higher to the lower levels of the caste hierarchy; here the family system plays a crucial role in socializing children differently and transmitting cultural capital to them unequally. The best course would be to make all-out efforts to expand the pool of qualified candidates at the lowest level; but that would take the kind of patience and care that no government in India has so far shown. A quicker course, whose effects would show immediately in official statistics, would be to alter the proportions directly through the reservation of jobs.

Changing the pattern of employment through extensive reservations in public institutions will affect some individuals favourably, but others adversely. It may be argued, quite plausibly, that even if the gains to some individuals are balanced by the losses to others, there may be a net benefit to society, certain conditions being met, by having a better mix of public servants. Upper caste candidates will face some reduction in their opportunities for employment, but it does not necessarily follow that they can claim that their rights have been violated. There will no doubt be disappointment and discontent, and the state will have to take account of them, but as matters of policy rather than right.

The government has in fact responded with some sympathy and concern for those whose employment opportunities are likely to be reduced on account of reservations. It has offered to create more employment so that reservations do not dramatically reduce the number of jobs available through open competition. I leave it to the experts to determine the capacity of the economy to absorb the additional employment productively. I presume that much will depend on the scale on which these shifts are made and the time span over which they are spread, but that from the viewpoint of employment there is nothing in principle against creating some new jobs for open competition while increasing the number of those in the reserved category.

Any discussion of changes in patterns of employment must give due importance to magnitudes, and it has to be admitted that the magnitudes involved here are relatively small. We are dealing in fact with jobs that have to be counted in tens of thousands or at best in lakhs in a population of one billion persons or around 200 million households. In these circumstances, job reservation can hardly be expected to bring about a significant reduction in social and economic disparities by altering the balance of employment. It is in this sense that Mr Mandal's Commission has characterized them as 'palliatives'.

Let me repeat that I do not wish to make light of the problem of unemployment. That is a problem of the first magnitude in both rural and urbān India, which calls for the most serious attention in its own right. Here I wish to make the simple point that altering the caste composition of the service class, with or without some addition of posts in the services of the union and state governments, cannot possibly be regarded as a viable policy for solving the problem of unemployment in an economy that is predominantly rural, predominantly agricultural, and predominantly outside the organized sector.

A consideration of employment and the opportunities gained and lost by individuals of different castes gives us one view of reservation. We get a different, and in my opinion a more significant, view of it by a consideration of the nature and functioning of institutions. In the first view, we deal with quantities, and the quantities, as we have seen, are not very large in relation to the labour force as a whole. In the second view, the number of individuals who gain or lose is less important than the quality of each of the institutions concerned.

In considering institutions, we have first of all to keep in mind the differences in their nature and functioning. Their size, or the number of persons employed in them, is of less significance. The Supreme Court is an institution of first importance; we do not take the number of jobs available in it as the first consideration in judging its quality and efficacy.

I would like to stress the need to maintain a differentiated approach to institutions in the matter of reservations. That approach is clear in the Constitution which has mandatory provisions for reservations in the Lok Sabha but not in the Supreme Court. I have sometimes heard it said that this is because the Supreme Court has to maintain a level of excellence that we do not ordinarily expect from the Lok Sabha. That is a mistaken idea. The two institutions differ not in the levels of excellence expected of them but in their functions. The Lok Sabha performs representational functions of a kind that the Supreme Court does not.

A certain conception of democracy has come to prevail among large sections of our society, including the intelligentsia, that can only be described as the populist conception. That conception requires that all public institutions, irrespective of nature and function, should involve the representation and participation of the people; it is as if all public institutions should be and act like political councils and committees. What is surprising is not so much the eagerness of the politicians to impose the political model as the general model for public life every-where, as the readiness of the intellectuals to accept it in the name of democracy. I hardly need to say that that is the opposite of my conception of democracy which assigns a central place to institutional auton-omy based on an understanding of and a respect for the differentiated character of institutions.

I take it for granted that courts, hospitals, universities, laboratories, and banks are useful not just to the people to whom they provide employment but for the public at large and for society as a whole. The social utility of a public institution has to be judged not just by the criterion of employment but by a whole range of criteria among which employment need not be the most important. Further, it is neither the purpose nor the function of these institutions to provide representation to the different sections of Indian society. They have to meet other requirements that differ widely from one type of institution to another. It would be unreasonable to expect the High Court of Karnataka to function in the same way as the Indian Institute of Science, or the recruitment of scientists to be made by the same criteria that are used in the recruitment of judges.

It is good not only that institutions should be differentiated from each other, but also, though for a different reason, that each should be as varied in composition as possible. An institution that is all-male or all-Bengali, or has only Hindus or only Brahmans is likely to be less resilient, less sensitive, and less rich in the quality of its life than one with a more mixed composition. It is a fact that, as a result of complex social and historical processes, the Supreme Court did not have until recently any woman member on the bench. It might have been better if we had from the start more women judges, not because women have a right to their proportionate share on the bench but because their presence might have widened the range of experience of its members. However, that cannot become even now an overriding consideration in constituting the Supreme Court bench or any other bench.

What is true of courts of justice is true to a greater or lesser extent of other institutions as well. It is certainly true to a large extent for the university though perhaps not to the same extent for a specialized research institution. A university stands for the meeting of minds, and variety in the social composition of its faculty and student body is definitely an asset in that regard. Where a university has among its members individuals from severely disadvantaged groups, their experiences and perspectives add to the variety and richness of its life. I view this not as a matter of justice or rights, but as one of institutional well-being.

But an institution cannot enhance its well-being by compromising the ends and means specific to it merely for the sake of greater variety. Nor is it true that mere variety of social background is a guarantee of equal variety in the thoughts and feelings of people. There is little reason to believe that those who move into privileged positions from severely disadvantaged backgrounds always remain faithful to the thoughts and feelings of their early environment; in many cases, if not most, they try instead to suppress those thoughts and feelings, to escape from their past in order to adjust more effectively to the demands of their new ambitions. Rapid upward mobility affects people's perceptions and orientations in ways that still remain largely obscure.

It is said that a teacher or a doctor or a lawyer has to deal with problems not only on a technical plane but also on the human plane. But what does it mean for a teacher to deal with his students—or a doctor with his patients—on the human plane? It means that the teacher should be able to put himself in the place of his student—or the doctor in the place of his patient—and view his or her problems with concern and sympathy, and not just technical ability. No university or hospital or court of justice could function as an institution unless its responsible members had some capacity to put themselves in the places of others, without regard for caste, creed, and provenance.

Every college or university department has to deal with students who have special problems that arise from social disadvantages or personal misfortunes of a hundred different kinds. Some teachers deal with such problems more successfully than others. It cannot be said that problems that arise among students from personal misfortune or social disadvantage can be dealt with only by teachers who have themselves experienced identical problems. Nor can it be said that the only problems among students—or patients, or some other category of citizens—that call for treatment with special concern and sympathy are those that arise from the disadvantages of caste. Nothing can be more misleading than to argue that all the problems that we, as members of institutions, have to deal with on the human plane arise from the past excesses of caste, and from those alone.

Institutions of the kind I have in mind have not only to deal with problems on the human plane, they have also to deal with them impersonally. There has to be a balance between the requirements of treating individuals with concern and sympathy, and treating them without fear or favour; but the right balance will be different for different institutions. Institutions devoted to science and scholarship have greater flexibility than purely administrative institutions where conduct is, or ought to be, bound more strictly by impersonal rules. But no modern institution can free itself fully from the demands of the latter. However acute the problems faced by a particular student, the teacher has to apply the same standards in checking his experiments or marking his examination papers that he applies to others. Nothing can be more misconceived than to condone faulty experiments or wrong calculations on 'humanitarian' grounds.

I believe that it is here, in the domain that is, or ought to be, governed by impersonal rules that our modern institutions will face their most severe test. Several years ago I had made a distinction between societies that are governed by rules and those that are governed by persons (Béteille 1968, 1971: 146–59). That was a crude distinction and defective on a number of points. It is nevertheless the case that in our traditional institutions—village, caste, and joint family—personal considerations prevailed to a large extent, although this does not mean that all persons received equal treatment or even equal consideration. Modern institutions are organized differently, reflecting partly a change in scale and partly a shift in normative orientation. Their organization requires the prevalence of impersonal rules over claims based on ascribed social positions such as those of kinship, caste, and community.

The intrusion of ascriptive criteria, or considerations of community, caste, and kinship into institutions that value performance and

achievement vitiates not only their composition but also their functioning. Two factors are very important here: (i) the scale on which
these ascriptive criteria are introduced, and (ii) the legitimacy accorded
to them.

So long as only a few places are kept aside in order to create special
opportunities for severely disadvantaged groups such as the Harijans
and the Adivasis, considerations of caste and community can be kept
under control and not allowed to vitiate the functioning of institutions.
But those very considerations are bound to loom large where half the
places in an institution are set apart for specified castes and communities
and the other half filled by open competition.

The question of legitimacy is also important. It is said that in India,
institutions such as universities, hospitals, and even research laboratories are already riddled with caste. So far at least, people say this not to
praise these institutions but to blame them. But how can we blame
public institutions for being caste-ridden if we declare that castes and
communities are entitled to their 'due share' of positions in them as a
matter of right? I go back to the crucial importance of the distinction
I made earlier between matters of right and matters of policy.

To me the most important argument in support of caste quotas is
not the one about employment but the one that it is only through them
that the interests of backward communities can be protected in public
institutions. This is not a new argument, but one that was first formulated by the British on the basis of their perception of the Indian
national character. British civil servants widely believed—and sometimes said—that Indians could not be trusted to deal justly, or fairly,
or even-handedly with other Indians if they were of a different caste or
community. They believed, perhaps sincerely, that Indians lacked the
character to act without fear or favour, that they had a strong conception of the interests of their caste or community, but none, or only a
weak one, of the public interest. That is a severe judgement, but we
must not flinch from facing it.

Three generations of Indian nationalists sought to disprove the British view of the Indian character, and their spirit animates the eloquent
letter to the President with which Kaka Kalelkar forwarded the Report
of the first Backward Classes Commission (Government of India 1956:
1, i–xxxiii). What could be more ironical than the determination of our
present political leaders to prove, after four decades of independence,
that the British perception of the Indian character was right after all?

The argument that job reservation is essential because we need watchdogs in every public institution to look after the interests of Harijans, Adivasis, backward castes, and minorities needs to be brought out more fully into the open. If the argument is right, or, despite being wrong, is widely believed to be right, our institutions cannot function as they ought to: their well-being will be irreparably damaged. We cannot say what kinds of universities, hospitals, and scientific laboratories we will then have in the future, but they will be very different from the ones that at the time of independence people had hoped for.

It is said that those institutions from which we expect the highest levels of excellence in terms of international standards should be exempted from the rule of reservations so that they are able to attract the very best talent. While that may be so, I do not believe that excellence in that sense is the first consideration in institutional well-being. There are other, more important considerations, such as those of probity, integrity, and trust. They are first considerations because, without them, institutional, as against purely individual, excellence will have very little meaning or content.

Every modern institution has a framework of more of less formal rules that define the rights and obligations of its individual members and specify sanctions to uphold them. But its well-being depends on much more than a framework of formal rules. No hospital or university or bank could operate successfully if its members sought to assert their formal rights or to have their obligations formally specified at every turn. These rights and obligations have to be so internalized as to enable most persons to take them for granted most of the time. There has, thus, to be a fiduciary component, or a component of trust, at the very core of such an institution as of every social institution. It is this fiduciary component that is put seriously in question when people claim that caste biases cannot be corrected without the representation of all major castes or groups of castes in hospitals, laboratories, universities, banks, and secretariats.

Apart from its structure of rights and obligations, an institution has also its own subculture, consisting of a distinctive set of ideas, beliefs, and values. This subculture varies from one type of institution to another, but there are also certain commonalties among modern institutions in general. Whatever the difference from one subtype to another, the subculture of a modern institution—its spirit or ethos—is at the opposite pole from the culture of caste. If it is to function properly, and not necessarily at a high level of excellence, a hospital, a laboratory, or a secretariat must be to some extent insulated from that culture. Here again, it is no argument to say that these institutions are already to some extent infected by caste; it cannot be sound policy to make that infection as deep and extensive as possible.

It is narrow and short-sighted to regard the well-being of institutions as of concern to only those to whom they provide a livelihood; to judge them by their capacity to meet the demands of employment is to do precisely that. An institution such as a university or a hospital or a bank has responsibilities not only to its own members but also to a much wider public. When a public institution suffers decline due to faults in the system of recruitment and rewards, the resulting harm affects not only its internal order but also, and necessarily, its capacity to fulfil its obligations to society as a whole.

India is a large, complex, and changing society that provides ample scope for combining the rhetoric of social justice with the pursuit of private interest. In several crucial spheres, including health and education, both public and private facilities are available. Those who have the resources can and do make use of both, and the members of the service class have shown themselves to be increasingly ambidextrous. Since access to private facilities requires both money and influence, the poor and disadvantaged have to depend on public institutions irrespective of their quality. When influential members of a society cease to make use of a public institution because it is under decline, its further decline becomes inevitable; it then survives only as the refuge of those who cannot turn elsewhere. The neglect of public institutions hits harder the poor and the disadvantaged because for them there is no alternative; therefore, it is not at all obvious that the extension of caste quotas will reduce and not increase inequality overall.

It is not that the intelligentsia are unaware of the corrosive influence of caste on the kinds of institutions I have spoken about. If some of them are nevertheless prepared to see the corrosion spread a little further, they have a number of arguments on their side. An extreme position is that these are basically bourgeois institutions of little intrinsic value, and have to be overhauled to make room for alternative institutions to be constituted on Marxian, or Gandhian, or some other principles. This is too large a subject to enter at this point; and it is difficult to discuss it in the absence of any clear account of what such alternative institutions would look like or how they would function.

Others feel that these institutions are of intrinsic value, and that they should be preserved and improved, but also that they can be made to bear an extra burden, at least for some time, in the interest of greater equality overall. That is not an unreasonable view, and it deserves serious consideration. Much depends on how large the extra burden is likely to be, and how we weigh it against the presumed benefits. Even if we take an optimistic view of those benefits, which I do not, we have to consider the costs at two levels: firstly, the costs to the institutions severally; and, secondly, the cost to society as a whole of concentrating the extra burden so heavily on a few strategic institutions in the belief that the citadels of elitism must yield before the demands of distributive justice.

State and Civil Society

Once the uneven distribution of castes in public institutions comes to be perceived and represented as a problem in distributive justice, institutional well-being takes a back seat. This does not mean that institutions will be consciously or wilfully harmed. But their requirements will be ignored, and the costs to them from ambitious but ill-conceived policies to attain equality and justice will receive little or no attention.

It is in a way natural that after having lived in a hierarchical society for centuries, Indians should now be eager to establish a new pattern of distributive justice here and now. The old ideal has lost its appeal and is being replaced by a new one. But everything does not change when people decide to change their ideal from hierarchy to equality. The passage from a hierarchical society to one based on equality of status and opportunity has been a slow and painful one in the western world, and nowhere has it led—or can it lead—to the elimination of inequality in every form (see Chapter 9).

We in India have barely begun the passage from a hierarchical to an egalitarian society. It is true that we have changed our laws and our Constitution, but many other things remain unchanged. Many of the old material conditions of life remain, and many ideas are still cast in the same hierarchical mould as before. There is widespread poverty, illiteracy, ignorance, superstition, and prejudice. The economic forces that loosened the hierarchical structures of western society in the eighteenth and nineteenth centuries have had little scope for expansion in India, and the impact of education has been limited. Yet we feel that what has failed on so many fronts can somehow be made good by powerful and effective governmental action.

It is a mistake to believe, as many tend to do under frustration or despair, that every desirable state can be brought into existence by the government. In India, paradoxically, the belief in the power and efficacy of government as such has increased with the experience of corruption and inefficiency of every successive government. It is one thing to have a sound policy for education or employment, but quite another to design one that can abolish hierarchy and inequality, or establish equality of result.

It is not true that the natural advance of equality is always helped and never harmed by the increasing penetration of public life by the government. That the government is always for the people because it has declared itself against capitalism, elitism, and patriarchy is a myth that can no longer be used to give any direction to policy. The machinery of government is an independent source of inequality in all societies, and can be particularly oppressive in those that have a predominantly rural population with very low levels of income and education. Undoubtedly, the government can do something to remedy these very conditions, but it cannot do everything; where it tries to do too many things, it expands its own apparatus to the detriment of the public interest.

The fact that some inequalities can be removed or reduced by direct governmental action does not mean that they can all be removed or reduced by it. Here I would like to draw attention to the distinction between (i) the removal of disabilities, and (ii) the equalization of life chances. The two are by no means unrelated; but they are not the same in terms of either priority or feasibility, and they call for different types of strategic action.

Any programme for the advance of equality must give first priority to the removal of the disabilities imposed by law and custom. Landmarks in this direction were Article 17 of the Constitution abolishing untouchability, and the adoption in 1955 of the Untouchability (Offences) Act, amended and renamed in 1976 as the Protection of Civil Rights Act. In the traditional order, disabilities were imposed in their most severe form on the untouchables, but the order as a whole was based on privileges and disabilities that were upheld by both *shastric* and customary law. Hence, the removal of disabilities has to be viewed as the first condition of the change from hierarchy to equality.

Experience has shown that disabilities that have been maintained by law and custom for centuries cannot be effectively removed by a single act of legislation. Bad laws may be annulled by the state; it is far more difficult to legislate effectively against bad customs. It is one thing to legislate equal rights for all citizens but quite another to make those rights secure for those who have been excluded from civil life for generations. There is much scope for affirmative action by the government to give security to the rights made available in principle to all. Although the problem takes a particularly acute form for the Harijans and requires special measures in their case, it is a general one for the vast masses of poor and illiterate persons, to some extent irrespective of caste. It may be useful to have some Harijan officers to keep an eye against violations of the Protection of Civil Rights Act. But reservation of posts beyond a point becomes counter-productive when it creates or reinforces the feeling that the rights of the weak can be protected only by those of their own caste.

The removal of disabilities is not only an urgent task, but, at least in principle, also a feasible one. The question of the equalization of life chances is altogether different. The former may be said to pertain to the legal and the latter to the economic domain, broadly conceived. We know from the experiences of other countries that started before us that legal equality and economic equality do not advance in the same rhythm. The experience of the western countries was that inequality of income was increasing during roughly the same period which experienced a steady advance of legal equality (Kuznets 1955). It is difficult to guarantee that, even with the best economic management, things can be made to turn out differently in India.

Therefore, we must not allow ourselves to be diverted by the declaration that what we should have in India is not just equality of treatment or even equality of opportunity, but equality of result. 'Equality of results', according to Mr Mandal, is 'the real acid test of effective equality' (Government of India 1980: I, 22). It can hardly be said that by imposing caste quotas in government employment we are taking a significant step towards equality of result—or any kind of equality—in a country where substantial numbers of persons remain ill-fed and unlettered. The rhetoric about equality of results does very little good; if taken at face value, it can do much harm to the operation of economic forces and social institutions.

The record of economic management in India since independence has been uneven; it has been better than many would make it out to be, but it has not been one of spectacular or unqualified success. Economic management has to be based on a sober assessment of feasibilities. Where it has failed in India, an important cause of failure has been the pursuit of unattainable objectives. Providing basic facilities for health, childcare, and education are slow and difficult, but feasible ways of bringing about some equalization of life chances. Providing 'good jobs' for all and establishing equality of result are not attainable objectives.

Faith in the capacity of the state to abolish the class system, or the disparities between groups, or to otherwise transform society by direct intervention in its processes has not been equally marked everywhere or in all historical periods. It was particularly marked, not only in India but in many other countries, when the process of decolonization began. There are reasons to believe that that historical period is in some significant respects drawing to a close. In the present age, our consciousness is formed not only by our own particular experience but by the historical experience of the world as a whole. In reviewing our prospects for the future, it is important to take some account of that historical experience.

The Bolshevik revolution not only created a new type of society—a new civilization, as some then called it—but extended the horizon of possibilities in the minds of people in many countries. The Chinese revolution of 1949 was another major step in a new direction. Our own concepts of 'planned democracy' and 'participatory democracy' were strongly marked by these experiences.

Indian ideas about planning and a centrally-regulated economy and society were shaped significantly by the perception of their success in the Soviet Union and other East European countries. I am speaking now not of planning as a merely technical exercise in economic management, but of a whole outlook and philosophy for social and economic change. Many things went wrong with Indian planning; but these were viewed as technical failures that could be corrected by better techniques and larger plans. Our perception of the overall success of planned social change in the USSR remained as a perennial source of assurance that ultimately our plans too would meet with success. The state grew socially more ineffective as it tried to increase its power; but the intelligentsia continued for long to remain in the belief that all this would be corrected and that India too would have, as some other countries seemed to have, a socially effective state.

In the 1990s, a massive current of change swept through the whole of eastern and central Europe, across those very countries that had stood for socialism and the planned society. Some beneficial features were swept away by it along with many that were obsolete, ineffectual, and oppressive. It is still too early to attempt a balance sheet for the new arrangements that are replacing the old ones. But one thing is clear beyond any doubt: in Poland, in Czechoslovakia, in Hungary, in East Germany, and, above all, in the erstwhile Soviet Union, a new consciousness has come into being that makes it impossible to view the relationship between the state and civil society in the old way. We will jeopardize only our own future by insulating ourselves from this new consciousness with the protective armour of old shibboleths and outmoded slogans.

7

The Reproduction
of Inequality

The Problem

'The spirit of the age is in favour of equality', Nehru (1961: 521) wrote on the eve of India's independence, 'though practice denies it almost everywhere.' That was characteristic of Nehru's sense of history and of his desire to keep his thoughts on India in tune with it. He was calling for a change in the existing order of things to make it more consistent with the new spirit. In India, imperialism was still a reality and so was the hierarchy of castes and communities based on immemorial tradition; but these were beginning to appear increasingly anachronistic to many who had caught something of the new spirit of which Nehru spoke.

'Yet', continued Nehru (1961: 521), 'the spirit of the age will triumph'. He was not alone in his enthusiasm for equality, for Tagore and Gandhi, to name only two, had both expressed themselves in its favour. The members of the Constituent Assembly, representing different sections of Indian society, clearly wanted equality to be the basis of the new legal and political order in India. Finally, in the last several decades, the commitment to equality has been repeatedly expressed in public life: politicians, judges, civil servants, lawyers, religious leaders, journalists, scholars, and social workers have all spoken in one voice in its favour. It may safely be said that in India today, everyone is prepared to speak publicly in support of equality, but none in support of hierarchy or inequality.

More than half a century after Nehru wrote, the contradiction between the ideal of equality and the practice of inequality still remains deeply and firmly lodged in Indian society. Why has 'the spirit of the age' failed to triumph? If indeed the commitment to equality has spread and grown stronger in these years, why has it made so little difference to social practice? Where, specifically, do the obstacles to the further advance of equality lie?

We must not minimize the change that takes place when hierarchy is replaced by equality as the social ideal of a nation. The hierarchical conception of society was not unique to the Indian past, but it was carried much further and prevailed much longer there than in the west. This is not to say that equality meant nothing at all to Indians in the past, but rather, that religion, morality, law, and custom combined to severely restrict its scope in the social domain, particularly in the relations between upper and lower castes, and between men and women.

Today, Indians no longer idealize hierarchy; what they, or at least the more articulate among them, idealize is equality. It may well be that some of this is make-believe, or merely for show, or a concession to liberal opinion in the west which enjoys cultural hegemony in the contemporary world. Be that as it may, our Constitution, our laws, and the programmes of all our political parties stress equality clearly and persistently; and they are an ineluctable part of the social reality of contemporary India.

We know that the modern conception of equality as a social ideal first emerged and became established in western countries such as Britain, France, and the United States, and then spread to other parts of the world. The laws and constitutions of the former countries acted as models for others to emulate in their movement towards equality. No less significant than the legal and the constitutional changes in the west are those that have taken place in the rules and conventions of everyday life; if social equality has come to signify so much in the west, it is due in no small measure to these unwritten rules and conventions.

While it is true that equality is a reasonably effective social ideal in western countries, one can find from each of them many examples of inequality in social practice in virtually every domain. Further, although particular forms or instances of inequality may be condemned by some or many, there is general recognition that inequality as such cannot be eradicated from social life, but has to be accommodated or even encouraged up to a point (Jencks 1975; Letwin 1983; Rawls 1972). It is the Indian, and not the western, intelligentsia that is likely to adopt the more intransigent public position on inequality. But how can we expect to eradicate inequality root and branch when countries that started on the road to equality long before us and have advanced much further along it are prepared to live with it in some measure?

There are of course those who could argue that the true exemplars of equality in the contemporary world are not countries like Britain, France, and the United States which have chosen the path of capitalism with its inevitable division into classes, but the USSR and other east European countries which have advanced much further towards equality along the path of socialism. It is true that in the twentieth century, it is socialism and not capitalism that has stood for equality, at least in the countries of Asia, Africa, and Latin America. But it is no longer possible to view the achievements of real socialism in the same light as before. The record has to be reinterpreted, and in part rewritten. Suffice it to say that throughout eastern Europe, including the USSR, there is today wide and open acknowledgement of the need to accommodate a measure of economic inequality if only to moderate the extremes of political inequality.

While assigning to the social ideal of equality the importance it deserves, we must recognize that it is an equivocal ideal. As one of the great sociologists of our time has reminded us, 'In every century it has been defined by negating some form of inequality' (Aron 1968: 3). This only means that it cannot be expected to negate every form of it. In what follows I will show that some forms of inequality are constitutive of certain arrangements in all modern societies, and that inequalities of income, esteem, and authority have to find accommodation within the prevalent ideal of equality. But the matter does not end there, for we must deal not only with the prevalence of inequality but also with its social reproduction. We have to ask not only why social positions should be graded and ranked, but also how it comes about that the same sorts of persons occupy the same sorts of positions from one generation to the next. I shall concentrate on only one sector of Indian society, conceived broadly as the service class, and argue that certain fundamental changes are taking place in the social mechanism of the reproduction of inequality in which the family and not caste now plays the active part. While on the surface present inequalities appear much like past ones, the internal mechanisms of their reproduction are undergoing significant change. I try to shift attention in this chapter from the macro-structure of society to its micro-processes; but those processes can be closely examined only after a general discussion of the structure of inequality.

Professions and Institutions

Modern societies are characterized by the presence of a number of professions whose members perform a variety of specialized functions. These include doctors, lawyers, accountants, engineers, scientists, journalists, and a host of others. Although we can find their counterparts in earlier societies, they are far more numerous today than in any previous historical epoch. Moreover, their social importance far exceeds their numerical strength (Parsons 1968). It has been pointed out that the expansion of these professions was historically linked to the expansion of bourgeois society (Perkin 1989). But their importance today is not confined to any particular type of society; doctors, engineers, scientists, and economists are as important in the Soviet Union as they are in the United States or Great Britain.

In modern India, the professions have come to acquire not only great functional importance but also high social prestige. I hardly need to point to the significant part played by members of the liberal professions in the leadership of the nationalist movement. That apart, it is difficult to visualize an India of the future without doctors, engineers, scientists, journalists, lawyers, and so on. Not only has there been an enormous expansion in these professions since independence but also a more or less continuous demand for their further expansion (Gandhi 1982; Madan 1980).

For all their great and increasing variety, modern professions have certain features in common. Entry into such a profession is typically based on formal qualifications that can in practice be secured by only some and not all members of society. High levels of education, or specialized training, or both are required, and these involve the expenditure at least of time and usually also of money. Among the various professions, some are more exclusive than others, and there are variations from one society to another in the procedures that regulate entry into them.

Doctors, engineers, academics, and other professionals enjoy greater esteem than most other members of society. It is difficult to explain fully why this should be so, and, certainly, an explanation that takes only income into account will be unsatisfactory, for one can argue as well that income differentials are the result of unequal esteem as that they are the cause of it. It is true that many professionals earn very high incomes in capitalist countries such as the United States, but their counterparts in the USSR enjoyed the same sort of esteem, despite their much lower income. Comparative studies have established conclusively the remarkable similarity in the esteem enjoyed by the professions in capitalist and socialist societies. And one can argue without much fear of contradiction that they enjoy very high esteem in India.

Important factors behind the esteem enjoyed by the professions in all modern societies are the high levels of education required for entry into them and their real or presumed association with specialized knowledge and technical ability. Specialized knowledge and technical ability are valued in themselves and not merely for the material returns their possession undoubtedly secures. Perhaps they are especially valued—some might say overvalued—in our society where even literacy and primary education are beyond the reach of many.

In our society, as in any other, while doctors as a whole enjoy high esteem, some among them enjoy higher esteem than others. Professional reputation and success are determined by a complex of factors, including some that are extrinsic to professional requirements. The esteem enjoyed by a doctor is determined partly by his personality, but also by such impersonal factors as qualification, skill, and experience. Very broadly speaking, specialists are more highly esteemed than general practitioners, mainly because they are presumed to be more highly qualified and to possess superior skills.

One might ask whether it is possible or even desirable to have a social order in which all doctors—or all engineers, or all scientists—will be treated as equal. Apart from its effect on efficiency, such a state of affairs will bespeak complete indifference to all distinctions of knowledge, skill, experience, and ability. One must doubt whether a society that is indifferent to the quality of what it professes to value can be regarded as a good society, let alone the question of its being an efficient one.

Where there are wide disparities among doctors, or among members of any other profession, it would be unreasonable to expect equality of treatment towards them. One would expect some inequality of rewards where it is recognized that such disparities exist. The very recognition of such disparities, to the extent that it is a social and not merely an individual fact, entails unequal esteem. Of course, inequality of esteem is difficult to measure, or even agree upon, in every case, so people tend to go by inequality of income which is a general, though by no means always a reliable, index of it.

We must distinguish the acceptance in principle of income differentials between members of a profession from satisfaction with the existing differentials at any given place or time. There is indeed wide public dissatisfaction over the large and sometimes extortionate fees charged by members of the medical, legal, and some other professions in India. These developments are viewed with misgiving by professionals themselves as breaches of professional norms, and there are pressures for the regulation of professional incomes by the state or some other public agency. Such regulation works better in some cases than in others, and generates problems of its own. Moreover, even the strongest advocates of the regulation of professional incomes must stop short of recommending equal incomes for all doctors—or all engineers, or all accountants—when they reflect on the Soviet or the Polish experience.

The older professions such as law, medicine, and accountancy were known as 'independent professions'; lawyers, doctors, accountants, and others practised independently and received fees rather than salaries. This has changed substantially throughout the world, though not to the same extent everywhere and not equally in all professions. Most professionals, and particularly those in the new ones, now work in institutions, and the terms and conditions of their work, including their emoluments, are regulated by the institutions in which they are employed. These institutions vary enormously in nature and type. Some are very large and others are small; some are privately controlled and managed, and others are of a public or semi-public nature.

The increasing bureaucratization of professional activities means that more and more professionals—doctors, accountants, engineers, and so on—have to work in and through administrative hierarchies of various kinds. One has only to glance at a list of engineers in a public works department to get an idea of their hierarchy of ranks. There is a similar hierarchy of ranks among the medical personnel in a large public hospital, and of scientists in a large scientific establishment such as the National Physical Laboratory or the National Chemical Laboratory (Visvanathan 1985).

Bureaucratization reduces the disparities of income to a large extent, as can be seen by comparing doctors in private practice with those in a public hospital. But it introduces a new kind of inequality associated with the rank and authority of office. In private practice, a meagerly-qualified GP may have a very much lower income than a highly-qualified specialist, but he is nobody's subordinate. In a public hospital there are chief and subordinate medical officers, and, although this is partly a matter of age and experience, it is not entirely so. Sometimes the chain of command in a public institution can be quite long, and junior professionals in a scientific establishment typically complain of the arbitrary restrictions imposed on their work by superiors who have lost touch with their discipline.

There is probably a good deal of bureaucratic fat in many public institutions performing specialized functions, and some of this can be cut down to the advantage of both the professionals and the publics they serve. I have so far spoken only indirectly of the bureaucracy and deferred a consideration of its prototype which is the administrative bureaucracy whose *locus classicus* is the secretariat. In view of the central place of the administrative bureaucracy in modern Indian society and culture, I would like to make a few observations on its hierarchical structure.

The classic account of bureaucracy as an ideal type is to be found in the work of Max Weber who also described in detail its historical origin and gradual expansion in all modern societies (Weber 1978). We need not enter into a comprehensive discussion of bureaucracy but will only enumerate some of its principal features. These are: (i) the adherence to impersonal rules, (ii) the concept of the office as a distinct sphere of activity, (iii) the delimitation of areas of competence within the office, and (iv) an established order of super- and subordination of official ranks.

Max Weber stressed the 'rational-legal' character of bureaucracy and its functional efficiency. Later sociologists, while accepting his basic ideas, have also discussed the dysfunctions of bureaucracy, as a result of which we are now more aware of its negative features (Crozier 1964; Merton 1957). These negative features are very conspicuous in contemporary India, and one can certainly argue that a great deal of the hierarchy associated with the Indian bureaucracy is dysfunctional.

Although it had its counterparts in Mughal India, the framework of modern bureaucratic administration was laid by the British in this country with the Indian Civil Service as its 'steel frame'. As an important part of an imperial system, the British Indian bureaucracy acquired and maintained a markedly hierarchical character: the Indian Civil Servants were known as 'the heaven born', and were concerned as much about exercising power as about maintaining an image. The metaphor of caste was frequently used to describe the rigid and ceremonial nature of the official hierarchy in India, and in the south it became common to compare and contrast the 'British bureaucracy' with the 'Brahman oligarchy'.

When India became independent, there were pressures to jettison the ICS because of its association with imperial rule. Both Nehru and

Patel withstood these pressures, for they felt that India needed a strong and capable administration in the interest of stability and progress. They also felt that the administration could be made more sensitive to the needs of the people by being brought into closer contact with them. The most notable change in the administration since independence has been a quantitative one: it has grown enormously in size. Some say that it is now more in tune with the needs of the people, and others that it has become more callous. It has certainly lost some of its ceremonial rigidity and is now more exposed to public criticism. It is difficult to say whether, with all these changes, administration in India has become less or more hierarchical. Clearly, there is much scope for streamlining in the interest of both equity and efficiency, but it is difficult to see how administration can work in a modern society without some super- and subordination among officials.

If the market is the nightmare of egalitarians under capitalism, under socialism it is the bureaucracy. It should by now be abundantly clear that no modern society can succeed in eliminating either; they can be dissolved by the force of ideas only in the world of fantasy. They are realities that shape our lives as much as what has been described as 'the spirit of the age'. We cannot turn away from the real change of orientation in our norms and values in the direction of equality; nor can we ignore or wish out of existence the many social arrangements of which inequality is a constitutive part.

Occupational Ranking and Mobility

The inescapable reality that I have briefly described and that coexists in a kind of dialectical relationship with the spirit of equality, falls within the broad category of social stratification. This is a very broad domain, and I have dwelt mainly on inequalities attached to positions and offices open to all. They are the inequalities characteristic of the modern world, associated with modern institutions, modern professions, and the modern occupational system in general. They are very different form the inequalities of caste, attached to positions not open to all in either practice or principle.

New occupations have grown and expanded enormously in India since independence, and there are now millions of persons in every part of the country who secure their livelihood from them. It is true that many more are still engaged and will probably continue to be engaged in agriculture and other occupations in settings that may be broadly described as 'traditional'. The new occupations are of many different kinds: professional, administrative, managerial, and other non-manual occupations; and skilled, semi-skilled, and unskilled manual ones. These occupations, and particularly the former, are very important, not only because of their numbers but also because of the high value placed on them by all sections of society.

Sociologists have noted the significance of the occupational system in all modern societies (Blau and Duncan 1968; Parsons 1954; Treiman 1977). The individual's position in society—his social identity—his economic standing, his social status, his own self-esteem are all to some extent dependent on his occupation. A large part of his adult life is devoted to it, and much of his early life is a preparation for it. This is not to say that occupation alone shapes a person's social identity; race, religion, and provenance are important in many societies, and gender is an important basis of identity in every society. In India, caste is a very important basis of social identity, although we can no longer assume that it is always more important than occupation in every sector of society.

I turn briefly to two related aspects of modern occupational systems: occupational ranking and occupational mobility. Studies conducted in different parts of the world show a fair measure of consistency in the ranking of occupations in every society; this does not mean that all the individual members of a society rank all occupations in identically the same way, but that there is considerable agreement about their ranks (Svalastoga 1959). Second, despite the displacement of old occupations by new ones due to rapid technological change, the prestige structure of occupations retains a fair degree of stability over time (Hodge et al. 1966). Finally, comparative studies tend to show that, despite historical and cultural variations, similar occupations tend to be similarly ranked across a wide range of contemporary societies in different parts of the world (Treiman 1977).

The differentiation and ranking of occupations go hand in hand with mobility between occupations, both within a lifetime and between generations. Occupational ranking and occupational mobility are two important and closely-related features of all modern societies. While there is no necessary relationship between the span of occupational ranking and the rate of occupational mobility, one can speak meaningfully about upward and downward mobility only within a generally-accepted framework of ranks. It does not appear that many persons would actually wish to see all ranks abolished; for them the requirement of 'practical equality' (Tawney 1964: 106) would be reasonably satisfied if there were relatively free movement across the ranks of the occupational hierarchy.

There is a large body of literature on occupational mobility in the advanced industrial societies (Robinson 1985; Treiman and Robinson 1981), and, although we do not have many systematic studies of the subject in India, a beginning has been made (Pande 1986; Rao 1989). The facts relating to occupational mobility are extremely complex, and there are disagreements about their correct interpretation. Although sociologists have tried to measure and compare rates of mobility, it is difficult to do so in a direct and straightforward manner. One has to distinguish between intra- and intergenerational mobility; between absolute and relative mobility; and between mobility under different rates of occupational change (Goldthorpe 1987).

Despite all the difficulties of accurate measurement and reliable comparison, it is now clear that there is widespread occupational mobility, both intra- and intergenerational, in all advanced industrial societies. Further—and this is of particular importance—in countries such as Britain and the United States, the secular trend in the twentieth century has been towards greater upward than downward mobility (Goldthorpe 1987). This paradox of a net balance of upward mobility is resolved when we take into account changes in the occupational system in these societies, leading to an aggregate displacement of occupations with lower by those with higher prestige. In a very broad way, agricultural occupations have been displaced by non-agricultural ones, and inferior manual occupations by superior non-manual ones.

The relation between occupational mobility and the class structure is a controversial subject on which there is much disagreement (Giddens 1973). Much depends on how one defines classes, and it is possible to define them in such a way as to make changing rates of mobility irrelevant to their structure (Poulantzas 1976). The old definition of classes in terms of distinctions among the 'owners merely of labour power, owners of capital, and landowners' (Marx 1959: 885) cannot take us very far without substantial modification to accommodate the differentiation of occupations. Some sociologists are inclined to the view that, particularly in the United States, the combined effect of high occupational differentiation and extensive occupational mobility has been the obliteration of classes as well-marked features of the social morphology (Blau and Duncan 1968).

It would, however, be premature to maintain that classes have disappeared from advanced industrial societies. The working class still has a clear social identity, although one may wonder about the utility of the old concept of the bourgeoisie. A recent important study has described three broad classes that occupy a prominent place in British social structure, despite occupational differentiation and mobility. These are: (i) the service class, (ii) the intermediate class, and (iii) the working class (Goldthorpe 1987).

The service class, which has been studied in detail in Germany, Britain, and other western countries, has its counterpart in India. Professional, administrative, and managerial occupations are of crucial importance in Indian society, but their sociological study is still in its infancy. In what follows I shall make some general observations on stratification and mobility in contemporary Indian society on the basis of the little that we know about these occupations.

Reproduction of Inequality

When people, in India or elsewhere, say that they are opposed to inequality or to extreme forms of it, they have in mind two distinct things whose mutual relationship is not always clear to them. They might feel that the disparities between the top and the bottom in society as a whole or in its various institutions and organizations are too large; for instance, they might say that in Indian hospitals the disparities of income, authority, and esteem between senior and junior medical personnel, or between them and sweepers, cleaners, and attendants are much larger than in hospitals elsewhere, and that they can and should be reduced. Alternatively, they might point out that access to the medical profession is so severely restricted in India that only some sorts of persons can possibly expect to reach senior positions in a hospital, whereas most others can expect at best to become sweepers, cleaners, and attendants. The first relates to the extent of disparity, and the second to the rate of mobility; it does not follow that where disparities are high, the rates of mobility must always be low.

It is frequently maintained that our public institutions are too hierarchical, that they have too many ranks in them, and that there is too much distance between the top and the bottom. Civil servants themselves often say this about the administrative bureaucracy, and then point out, not without reason, that in India most public institutions tend to model themselves on the administrative bureaucracy. It is difficult to form a clear judgement on this, because public institutions in general and administrative bureaucracies in particular are favourite targets of attack for egalitarians throughout the world. No doubt, public institutions often show larger inequalities in India than elsewhere, but they are also undergoing change. To take one example, the hierarchy of academic ranks has undergone considerable change in the last two decades, so that university departments in India are less hierarchical, at least in their internal organization, than they were in the past and than they are in some western countries (Béteille 1981a, 1990c). But this does not mean that access to academic positions is in practice as open to the different sections of society as it is in those same countries.

There is no society in which access to the service class is in practice equally open to persons from all sections of society: social origin and background play some part in restricting or facilitating such access in all societies. All that we can say is that it is more open in some societies than in others. It would be reasonable to maintain, even without exhaustive enquiry, that in India such access is severely restricted by social origin and background (Navlakha 1989). This is markedly at odds with the strong provisions on equality, including equality of opportunity, in the Constitution of India.

I shall take for granted the fact that positions in society carry unequal rewards in terms of income, esteem, and authority, and also the continued existence of a service class whose members enjoy a high position in society. The question to which I would like to address myself here relates to the reproduction of the service class from one generation to another, and the unequal distribution of life chances among members of society in terms of their access to it. Why is access to the service class almost automatically ensured for some members of society whereas others find it very hard, if not impossible, to enter it, despite the removal of all legal barriers to entry and despite the extensive concern expressed in our society for equality of opportunity?

There are marked disparities of wealth and caste in India, and these two disparities reinforced each other in the traditional order (Béteille 1972). Disparities of wealth are related to the inequalities to which I have referred, though not as closely as one might assume: sons and daughters of landowners do not necessarily have better prospects of entering the professions or the civil service than those of school teachers or section officers. There is also a marked correlation between caste status and occupational position, but the direct influence of caste on the distribution of life chances is changing; one no longer has automatic access to a particular occupation by virtue of one's caste as was largely the case in the past.

In every society some measure of continuity from one generation to the next is maintained through what is described by means of a biological metaphor as social and cultural reproduction. Indeed, what we describe as a society or culture would be incomprehensible without some continuity and reproduction. It is my central argument that the family plays a crucial if not decisive role in the reproduction of social structure, including the structure of inequality. To be sure, the family as an institution is not equally effective everywhere, and it does not act in isolation from other institutions anywhere. But all things considered, it will be safe to say that the family plays a far more active role than caste in reproducing the inequalities associated with the new occupational system. The retreat of caste as an active agent for the reproduction of inequality at the upper levels, and the continuing, if not increasing, importance of the family constitute two of the most striking features of contemporary Indian society.

Since I assign such crucial significance to the active role of the family in reproducing inequalities in the new occupational system in India, I would like to make a few general observations on it. The family is the one social institution that is universally present in all human societies. Nineteenth-century anthropologists commonly believed that it did not exist in the earliest stages of social evolution, and this led some to speculate that it might cease to exist in some future historical period (Engels 1948). These beliefs, at least as far as early societies are concerned, have been proved to be false. However, we must be careful not to repeat the mistake, made by many in the past, that the family has everywhere the same form as in middle-class western society. In fact, it takes a variety of different forms, although one is struck by the regularity with which it takes the form of the nuclear family of parents and unmarried children in the service class in virtually every part of the world (Goode 1970).

Much has been written about the place of the joint or extended family in Indian society. A recent influential study of personality formation among Hindus (Kakar 1978) takes for granted the universal presence of the extended family in all strata of society. This is plainly misleading. Nuclear families outnumber extended ones in many social settings (Narain 1975). It is of course true that the same individual might live in both types of family during different phases of his life. Moreover, grandparents, uncles, aunts, and cousins continue to play an important part in the individual's development, whether from within or outside the family, in all sections of Indian society. Nevertheless, we should not discount the importance of the nuclear family in the service class in large metropolitan cities. In any case, my argument about the displacement of caste by family remains substantially true whether the family is of the extended or the nuclear type.

Without denying variations in morphological form, I shall be more concerned with such questions as the strength, effectiveness, and adaptability of the family in modern societies. Both popular and professional opinion is divided on these questions in the west (Berger and Berger 1983; Morgan 1975). Writing in the mid-1950s, Talcott Parsons had noted the view widely expressed in the preceding years that the family was on its way out in western society and particularly in the United States (Parsons and Bales 1956). Arguing vigorously against that view, he had maintained that a closer look at the evidence would show that the family in America was becoming stronger and not weaker. More recently, the women's movement has reopened the question of the durability of the western family. Changes in gender roles will no doubt have an impact on the family, but there is as yet little evidence to suggest that the family as such is likely to disappear or even to lose its vitality in the foreseeable future.

The family plays a crucial part in the socialization of its children, particularly in the early years (Erikson 1965; Kakar 1978). Although the learning process, broadly conceived, continues throughout life, psychologists have stressed the significance for the child of the first three years of it. The family acts in conjunction with others—kin, neighbours, and so on—in the socialization of the child. The extent to which it shares the responsibility for the socialization of the child with other agencies varies from one society to another, and from one phase of the child's life to the next. It is likely that the family's role in the socialization process, particularly in the early years, has been enlarged in the modern western type of society where the nuclear unit insulates the infant from other kin and neighbours to a greater extent than in other types of society. It is also likely that this happens to some extent in all societies or all social classes where the nuclearization of the family is at work.

Indians of all social classes have a markedly conservative attitude towards both marriage and parenthood. This is in contrast to the relatively more experimental attitude towards domestic arrangements in the west and towards some other social arrangements in India. Among Indians in the upper social strata divorce is rare, and experimental alternatives to marriage even more so. The Indian family severely limits experimentation in the choice of partners by adhering to the practice of arranged marriages. Parents not only select spouses for their children but also play a large part in guiding them towards their careers. The conservative attitude towards marriage and parenthood is able to survive the change from the extended to the nuclear type of family.

The modern Indian family among professionals, civil servants, and others is not a mere replica of the traditional family of the classical texts either in its morphology or in its norms and values. It has its own norms and values. Nor are they identical with those characteristic of the nuclear family in the west. Despite nuclearization, the Indian family remains distinctive in its orientation to marriage, parenthood, and siblingship, and in its involvement in wider kin ties.

In the west, the family surrenders a part of its monopoly over the child when he or she enters school. The experience of school is very important in all societies or social classes where schooling is universal and starts at an early age. The relationship between family and school is a subject in itself, to which I shall advert, though only in passing, a little later; suffice it to say here that the influence of the family on the child continues through school and beyond, although here again there are bound to be variations from one society to another and from one social class to another.

Now, in all modern societies, different families are very differently endowed as to both means and motivations. The atmosphere in which a child grows up in the home of a doctor or a civil servant is very different from the atmosphere in the home of a clerk or a watchman. Children have access to very different kinds and amounts of resources in these homes. It is essential to have a broad view of these resources and not define them narrowly in terms of the economic criteria of wealth and income. In recent years the problem of the reproduction of inequality has been greatly illuminated by the extension of the concept of capital to include cultural and social capital in addition to material capital in the conventional sense (Bourdieu 1984; Bourdieu and Passeron 1977).

To be sure, the unequal distribution of private wealth in the form of land and other material assets is a major constituent of the disparities between families, but there is more to these disparities than that. Apart from its material capital, and to some extent independently of it, each family has a stock of cultural capital, comprising its command over knowledge, skills, tastes, etc., that are a part of its distinctive way of life. It has also its own social capital in the form of networks of relationships, partly acquired from the past and partly constructed through the initiative of its members.

I do not wish to enter into a discussion of the many conceptual difficulties in defining cultural and social capital, and I am concerned here mainly with their variability between families. The attraction of the concept of capital as conventionally used in economic analysis is its amenability to quantitative treatment. Although Pierre Bourdieu (1984: 114), who has played a large part in popularizing the concept, has spoken of different volumes of cultural capital, it is difficult to extract from his work any clear procedure for measuring it; and the same is true for social capital in the sense in which I use it here. Second, although we can think of procedures, at least in principle, for nationalizing, expropriating, or redistributing physical, or material, or economic capital, it is difficult to see how this can be done for cultural or social capital. Only some of the resources of the family can be seen as entitlements that are at least in principle separable from it; others are embedded in its very nature and constitution.

The family forms a very important part of the social environment of the infant, the child, and the adolescent, although it would be absurd to maintain that what a person is in adult life depends entirely on his family environment or his social background. We know very well that many individuals overcome the disadvantages of family and social background; and others move downwards because of failures of one kind or another, sometimes within the family itself. The family has its own internal dynamics, and these are not dependent entirely on its capital, even in the broad sense that we have given to the term. What is remarkable, however, is the extent to which the family, particularly in the service class, does succeed in transmitting its cultural and social capital to its younger members, despite psychological failures of many kinds.

I would like to stress that there is nothing mechanical about the transfer of cultural capital from one generation to another within the family. This transfer is guided by complex social *and* psychological processes whose outcome can never be guaranteed in the individual case. In families that start with substantial social and cultural advantages, there may be major psychological failures that wipe out the advantages of the first generation for the second. Conversely, children from families with slender resources may benefit more than proportionately from an emotionally supportive home environment. The modern educational and occupational systems are highly dynamic, and the personality traits favoured by them are not determined in a straightforward way by social and cultural circumstances.

The family has been and continues to be one of the strongest institutions of Indian society, in all regions, among all communities, and in all social classes. This is not to deny the very great range of variation in family types in India, but only to draw attention to its continued strength as an institution in and through which the individual acquires his capabilities and orientations as a member of society. In what follows, I shall be concerned with the family's role in social reproduction, mainly at the upper levels of the new occupational hierarchy.

Despite the persistence of a basically conservative attitude to marriage and parenthood, some changes are taking place in the Indian family. There is reason to believe that it is undergoing a process of nuclearization, at least in the sense that the small group of parents and unmarried children is acquiring a sharper identity within the wider kin group. Important demographic changes have begun, and are probably quite widespread in the higher occupational strata. The age at marriage is rising for both men and women, and the limitation of family size has become a common strategy. These demographic changes are probably being accompanied by more subtle changes in the relations between spouses, between parents and children, and between siblings. Despite these changes, the Indian family is at this social level much more stable than its counterpart in the west.

The upper-middle class Indian family has shown its strength by the manner in which it has adapted to and retained control over a changing social environment. A very remarkable aspect of this is the manner in which it has shifted its focus of attention away from caste and subcaste and towards school, college, and office. It would be safe to say that in metropolitan cities like Delhi, Bombay, and Calcutta, doctors, engineers, professors, civil servants and others take much less account of their caste and subcaste when planning for the future of their children than of the schools to which they might secure admission for them.

I would like to stress the active role of the family in transmitting to its younger members all the advantages it has at its command. Among doctors, engineers, accountants, civil servants, managers and others, parents do not simply wait for their children to soak up the cultural capital that is a part of the domestic environment. They take an increasingly active part in their education and training. Middle-class parents have become increasingly career conscious, and this consciousness is implanted in their children at a young age. The idea that the child will step automatically or effortlessly into his parent's occupation has ceased to be a secure basis for socialization: a different kind of preparation is now required for his success in the future.

The school has emerged as a major institution for mediating the relationship between the family and the new occupational system, and it also plays a major part in the reproduction of inequality (Coleman 1990; Jencks 1975). Schools are of many different kinds, and they are ranked. As the scholastic agent in Evelyn Waugh's novel (1937: 17) pointed out, ' "We class schools, you see, into four grades: Leading School, First-rate School, Good School, and School". ' ' "Frankly", said Mr. Levy, "School is pretty bad". ' In India, the major distinction is between fee-paying schools that are very expensive and government schools where the charges are nominal. The best schools are not only very expensive but also very difficult to get into, and here the status and 'personality' of the parent counts as much as the aptitude of the child (De Souza 1974).

It is of course well known that schools differ vastly in their quality, and much public animosity is directed against the elitist character of the Indian school system. But those who are most articulate in their criticism of the system take good care to select the best schools for the education of their own children. The moral implications of this contradiction, by no means unique to Indian society, are not always clear. There is no doubt that the Indian school system leaves much to be desired, and a great deal can be done to expand the opportunities for better schooling in the interest of children who are now effectively denied such opportunity because their families are devoid of all resources.

At the same time, the elimination of all disparities between schools does not appear to be a feasible objective. The reduction of disparities will make some contribution to the equalization of life chances, but that contribution may not be as large as one might expect. At the top, the school system is highly competitive and likely to become more so. Middle-class parents have begun to feel increasingly that they cannot leave it entirely to the school to train their children for success in competitive examinations. They take an increasing part in helping their children with their lessons at home; here the cultural capital of the family is extremely important in the development of both skill and motivation. Nor do parents rely entirely on their own abilities to prepare their children for success in examinations. Where they have the means, they engage tutors or send their children to coaching classes. Networks of tutors and coaches have become familiar features of the urban social landscape in contemporary India.

The involvement of parents in the educational progress and career prospects of their children has to some extent altered the atmosphere of the family, at least among those in professional, administrative, and managerial occupations. The rapid expansion of college education among women in these groups is likely to alter it further. Already, women are taking an increasingly active part in the schoolwork of their children; this can be seen from the number of active mothers in what are called 'public schools' in India on occasions such as parent-teacher meetings, prize-giving ceremonies, sports competitions, and so on. Second, change is also coming about in attitudes towards the education of girls; certainly, they continue to be prepared for marriage, but more and more of them are being prepared simultaneously for careers.

Families have variable amounts not only of cultural but also of social capital. The social capital of the family consists of the networks of relations that may be activated for maintaining and furthering the interests of the family as a whole or of its individual members. These networks are made up of many strands. Ties of kinship and marriage are important everywhere. In addition, and particularly in the service class, other ties, developed in school or college, office or profession, and associations of diverse kinds also play an important part (Srinivas and Béteille 1964).

The nature and span of the networks available to Indians vary enormously from one level of society to another. In the traditional order, social networks operated within a more or less fixed framework of village, caste, and lineage, and this still survives to a large extent in the rural areas and at the lower levels of the social hierarchy. But in the urban areas and at the levels with which I am concerned, networks are much more flexible and dynamic; old links are discarded and new ones created to meet the demands, real or perceived, of a changeable environment. This is a social world in which many people are or appear to be on the move; but not many change places or move very far relatively to others.

It is difficult to assess and compare the parts played by family contact and social influence in the successes of individuals from different backgrounds. That they operate extensively and unequally is well known. So far as it concerns the careers of their children, doctors, lawyers, professors, civil servants, and managers have more extensive and more useful contacts than clerks, electricians, plumbers, road menders, and masons. In a society in which family commitments are of such strength, it would be remarkable if children did not benefit from the social contacts of their parents.

The extensive use of the social capital of a family for furthering the prospects of its individual members raises analytical and normative questions whose nature can only be indicated here. It is both extremely important and extremely difficult to keep consistently in view the distinction between the private and the public domains. It would be a mistake to declare unequivocally against the use of social contacts in every case. For instance, they are of crucial importance in securing information essential to career planning, and little can be said against that. Second, in the independent professions and in private enterprise, personal relations are considered to be an important basis of trust, and it is difficult to see how they can be excluded from professional and business activity. The case of public institutions is different, but even here some legitimate ground exists for the use of recommendations based on personal knowledge from responsible members of society. One can easily see that that ground will be repeatedly crossed in a society in which family and kin ties have compelling force and where at the same time independent or private enterprise is displaced by governmental organization.

Family, Class, and Caste

I have described how inequalities are maintained in societies in which careers are, or are believed to be, open to talent. In my account I have drawn attention to the crucial part played by the family in the maintenance of the system. I must emphasize that my purpose was not to explain how inequalities come into existence, but rather to show how existing inequalities are reproduced, not in exactly the same form as before but in recognizably similar forms.

In drawing attention to the crucial part played by the family, it was not my intention to suggest that other institutions, resources, ideas, beliefs, and values play no part in maintaining the system of inequality. However one must make a distinction between patterns and forms that exist as residues from the past in a more or less passive way, and institutions that play an active part in reproducing the structure of inequality. It is the active role of the family in reproducing the structure of unequal life chances, not always clearly perceived, that I have tried to emphasize, for the problem is not simply why inequalities come into being, but why, despite efforts of many kinds, they refuse to disappear.

An important tradition in social theory views the structure of inequality in terms of wealth and property. There are large disparities of wealth and property in Indian society, and these are of great importance in the agrarian system where landownership and landlessness are the two poles between which inequalities are structured (Béteille 1974). Although in the form in which it now exists it is not of very great antiquity, private property in land is today an institution of great strength in rural India. Agrarian reform has altered the distribution of land to some extent, but it has not weakened the institution of property (Herring 1983; Joshi 1975). The two institutions of property and the family are today intimately linked in rural India: what link property had in the past with lineage and subcaste it has largely lost. The meagre success of land reform has repeatedly demonstrated the exceptional strength of the landowning family.

Property and wealth also have a significant place in the system of stratification outside agriculture to which I have mainly devoted my attention. But that system as a whole cannot be understood without taking into account the growth of a new occupational structure. The inequalities in the latter, which enjoys a position of great importance in all modern societies, cannot be easily understood in terms of the traditional definition of capital, and certainly not in terms of one that sharply separates 'capital' and 'labour'. We require a more extended concept of capital, one that incorporates both cultural and social capital in addition to capital in the old sense, but that in turn calls for a considerable change in our analytical strategy. I have in the preceding tried to explore some of the possibilities opened up by such a strategy. My objective was not to deny the great importance of private wealth in the reproduction of inequality, but to draw attention to other resources that are also important in its reproduction.

There remains the structure of caste. No enquiry into inequality can ignore caste which has been widely regarded as the fundamental institution of Hindu, and indeed, Indian society. It has stood as the watchword for the most elaborate, the most rigid, and the most comprehensive system of social hierarchy. It exists as a salient feature of the social morphology in contemporary India, and, although caste is no longer enumerated in the decennial census, a multitude of social surveys and case studies bear witness to its continued existence in all parts of India, not only among Hindus, but among Muslims, Christians, Sikhs, and other religious denominations.

When we say that caste was the fundamental institution of Hinduism, we mean not only that it was a salient feature of Hindu social morphology, but also that it was a central part of religion, morality, and law among the Hindus. It will be impossible to explain the remarkable continuity of the institution of caste, till almost our own time, solely in terms of social morphology, without taking any account of religion, morality, and law. To be sure, there were many changes, and sometimes important ones, in the system till the end of the last century; but through all these changes, and in the long run, both the social morphology and the legal, moral, and religious foundations of caste remained recognizably the same.

Caste not only remains a salient feature of the social morphology, it is still manifestly correlated with every form of social stratification, whether based on wealth, occupation, income, education, or some other criterion. In all public institutions, those in superior positions are likely to be of higher, and those in inferior positions of lower caste. Some take this kind of manifest correlation as proof that caste is at bottom the cause of the ranks that we observe in public life. This is plainly mistaken, for, as we have seen, doctors, scientists, civil servants, and others are ranked in all societies, including those that have had nothing to do with caste. While the ranking of occupations may be somewhat more elaborate and more rigid in our society than in others, the logic of ranking among doctors, scientists, or civil servants is quite different from the hierarchical logic of caste.

The fact that the morphological side of caste still remains salient should not lead us to conclude that the other side of it, having to do with law, morality, and religion, has also remained unchanged. Indeed, it is my argument that profound changes have taken place and are taking place in the religious, legal, and moral foundations of caste, and that these are bound in the long run to alter its social morphology as well.

It cannot be too strongly emphasized that at least among Hindus, the distinctions among castes as well as their ranks were acknowledged, upheld, and reinforced by both *shastric* and customary law for two thousand years (Sivaramayya 1984). Undoubtedly, many changes took place through the centuries in both law and custom, but they were not of the same significance as those that were initiated with the Removal of Caste Disabilities Act in 1850.

The privileges and disabilities of caste were slowly but progressively whittled down between 1850 and 1950 when the Constitution was adopted (Ghurye 1961). The new Constitution repudiated the hierarchical structure of caste, and it is now impossible to use the law to uphold the age-old privileges and disabilities of caste. It is true that custom still takes account of caste distinctions, particularly in the rural areas, but here custom is at variance with the law, whereas in the past it was in harmony with it.

Changes have also taken place in Hindu religion that have a bearing on caste, although it is more difficult to assess the nature and significance of these changes. Scholars are generally agreed that caste was in the past an integral part of the Hindu religion. The fact that this view has been challenged by a large number of Hindu reformers in the last hundred years itself shows that a change of orientation has come about in modern Hinduism. Every important modern reformer of Hinduism, including Vivekananda and Gandhi, has attacked caste or at least the hierarchy of caste, and it will be difficult to find any today who will defend it as an institution.

It is instructive to compare and contrast the attitudes of reformers of Hinduism towards its two most fundamental institutions, caste and the family, in both of which social life was deeply tinged by religion. Now, while many have attacked caste, and some very severely, it will be difficult to find any who have attacked the family as an institution. It is the central argument here that modern Hindus, whether of a secular persuasion or not, are no longer committed to caste, as Hindus were in the past, but that they continue to be committed to the family. This is not to say that the Hindu undivided family is not changing or that it will not change further. It is obvious that many modern Hindus find it possible to visualize their society in the future without the Hindu caste system; it is difficult to say how many of them are able to visualize it without the Hindu family.

It is even in the best of circumstances difficult to demonstrate a change in the moral values of a society, and I will not attempt to do so systematically here. But what we should not forget is that the traditional order of caste had its own morality, centred on a specific sense of duty associated with one's station and stage in life. It is possible that in the rural areas a sense of duty still survives towards the occupation and way of life of one's caste among artisans and cultivators, but that sense of duty has little place in the new occupational order. Modern Indians have at best an ambivalent, if not a negative, attitude towards the morality of caste, and some at least would be surprised to learn that such a thing ever did or could exist.

In the last forty years, whenever caste has come up for public discussion, it has invariably been subjected to censure. How does one account for the continued existence of a social arrangement which everyone is eager to attack and no one is prepared to defend? The recent agitations over the recommendations of the Mandal Commission have brought this out clearly. Those who opposed caste quotas argued that quotas would give a new lease of life to caste whose revival or reinforcement they condemned. But those who supported quotas were no less vocal in their condemnation of caste; they felt that certain measures were needed in the short run to secure more effectively the removal of caste in the long run. It is another matter that the unintended consequences of their actions might be, as their opponents believe they must be, to strengthen and not weaken the identities of caste.

Social institutions such as the family or the school reproduce themselves partly through the conscious actions of individuals who desire their continued existence. But besides these, there are social patterns whose reproduction is the unintended consequence of actions directed to other ends. In the traditional order, caste and subcaste were not only active agents of social placement, they were active agents of social control as well. In the modern occupational system about which I have spoken, if there is still a relationship between caste and social placement, it is a relatively passive one, and caste has ceased to be a significant agent of social control. By contrast, in the same sector, the family is not only an active agent of social control, it is also an active agent of social placement. Further, it continues to be so despite such changes as are coming about in its composition and form.

The doctor in his clinic, the lawyer in his chamber, the civil servant or even the clerk in his office is no longer bound by the moral authority of his caste or subcaste in the way in which the Brahman, the Rajput, the Nai or Dhobi was in the traditional village. The emancipation of the individual from the demands of caste and subcaste has been a complex and long-drawn process that is by no means complete as yet. It has been due partly to conscious action, both individual and collective, and partly to social and economic forces whose consequences no one fully foresaw. The emergence of a new educational and occupational system gave individuals an increasingly secure basis for freeing themselves from the demands of caste and subcaste.

We must avoid hasty conclusions about a development that is complex, uneven, and not free from contradictory tendencies. Even today, the extent to which the individual can repudiate with impunity the demands made on him by his caste or subcaste varies from one sector to another, and from one social stratum to another. We need far more systematic information about the strength and mode of operation of caste sanctions in contemporary India than we have.

Caste sanctions never operated in the same way at all levels of society. It is well known that only some castes had active caste panchayats, whereas others did not (Rowe 1973). Such studies as we have tend to show that caste panchayats are in decline in most parts of the country and at all levels of the hierarchy (Dube 1955: 222; Hutton 1946: 99, 102). However, there are also reports of panchayats becoming activated in response to particular issues thrown up usually by regional or national policies. These and, in particular, caste associations that are activized by the demands and opportunities of modern electoral politics are clearly different in their range and mode of operation from the traditional agencies through which castes and subcastes exercised social control (Kothari 1970). It is not at all clear how far the individual members of a caste or subcaste feel morally or even politically bound by the demands for electoral support made on them by the leaders of their caste associations, or what sanctions such leaders can enforce against those who ignore their demands.

What is clear, however, is that increasing numbers of professionals, civil servants, managers, and others feel free to repudiate such moral claims as may be made on them in the name of the caste to which they happen to belong. Some individuals may feel free to use on occasion their caste connections to further their individual or domestic interests, but this does not generally bind them morally to the demands of their caste; this has now become an instrumental, not to say an amoral, domain of action, used by many and condemned by all. It is in this sense that the middle-class Indian's orientations to caste and to family are quite different. He cannot repudiate his obligations to his family even when he finds them irksome; nothing is easier for him than to repudiate the demands of his caste if he finds them inconvenient.

It will now be clear what I mean when I say that at this level of society caste is no longer an institution in the sense in which the family continues to be one. An institution is not merely a convenient arrangement for individuals to use from time to time in the pursuit of their interests; nor is continuity over time or mere antiquity a test of its effective strength. Above all, an institution must be able to command the loyalties of its individual members who should be prepared to sacrifice their interests, at least to some extent, to secure its well-being and continuity. The plain fact is that modern Indians are prepared to sacrifice many things to protect and promote their family in the narrow or broad sense; they are not prepared to make the same sacrifices for their caste.

I return finally to public-spirited Indians and their frustrations over the persistence of widespread inequality. As I have shown, there are two kinds of response to the latter. The first, which one many call the radical response, is directed against inequality as such, and would wish to see it reduced in every sphere, if not eliminated altogether. The second, which is a more moderate response, is troubled not so much by inequality as such as by its manifest correlation with caste which has somehow come to be viewed as its ultimate cause. It is remarkable how many well-meaning Indians have recently discovered in caste the root of every form of inequality in contemporary India.

It is understandable that those who have formed a commitment to equality should find it difficult to reconcile themselves to so much inequality in their own environment. At the same time, it will be naïve to believe that all these inequalities can be removed at no social cost. Hence it is necessary to attempt some assessment of the costs, no matter how difficult that attempt may be. The difficulty is that there are many different kinds of obstacles to the further advance of equality in the distribution of benefits and burdens, and that they operate at many different levels.

I have argued that it is a mistake to believe that the sole or even the main obstacle to the further advance of equality in social practice today is still caste, however natural that belief may appear. Caste has ceased to play an active part in the reproduction of inequality, at least at the upper levels of the social hierarchy where it is no longer an important agent of either social placement or social control.

The recent attack on caste by egalitarians of both radical and liberal persuasions is misdirected even where it appears well-meaning. Caste should be attacked for its divisive role in electoral politics rather than its active role in the reproduction of inequality which is relatively small and clearly declining. The role of caste in politics is neither small nor declining. Caste is no longer an institution of any great strength among the influential urban intelligentsia; but it is still an instrument of great force in mobilizing political support in the country as a whole. If we remember Nehru's description of the spirit of the age, we will see why all parties that use caste for mobilizing political support say that they are acting in the cause of equality.

Equality, at least at the higher levels of society, can no longer be significantly advanced by attacking caste. Much of the anger that is publicly expressed against the hierarchy of caste—in the newspapers, on television, in conferences—is purposeless if not insincere. Those who are serious about carrying the advance of equality further, particularly in the domain that I have discussed, must direct their attention to the institutions that are the real obstacles in the path of that advance. The two most important ones are the family and the school.

A dispassionate and critical examination of the middle-class family and its role in the reproduction of inequality may turn out to be more disturbing than one might expect. For, if the result of such an examination shows, as I believe it must, that the family is indeed the main obstacle to the further advance of equality, what conclusions for policy can we then draw? Nothing is easier than to get the Government and Opposition together in Parliament to denounce the caste system and ask for its abolition. Who will denounce the Indian family, and ask for that to be abolished? It may not be too fanciful to suggest that both radicals and liberals have found a perfect alibi in caste to draw attention away from those institutions through whose agency inequality is reproduced in the strategic domains of society.

The Indian sociologist engaged in the study of his own society lives much more closely with his family than with his caste. He not only experiences life in his own family but is also more or less actively involved in its changing fortunes; his personal involvement in his own caste is by contrast marginal or atypical. Yet, the sociological literature on caste is voluminous, while that on the family is meagre. The few standard works that we have on the subject refer either to the family as traditionally conceived (Kapadia 1958) or to the rural family (Madan 1988; Shah 1973). The emphasis in these works, with some notable exceptions, is overwhelmingly on family and kinship, family and caste, and family and religion. The point of departure is the Hindu extended family as both social fact and social ideal. Not much can be learnt from them about the interface between the family and the new institutions of society.

We need to give a more central place to the family in the sociology of India, and we need to examine more extensively its distinctively contemporary features, for example, the relations between family and education, family and occupation, and family and social mobility. I have argued elsewhere (Béteille 1990b) that the sociological, as opposed to the Indological, approach must take its orientation from the lived experiences of the present rather than the presumed ideals of the past. There is no better way of finding out what is modern and at the same time Indian in our contemporary society and culture than by examining the family in the kind of context that I have outlined above.

8

The Antinomies of Equality

This chapter is devoted to an examination of the antinomies of equality. My interest in the problem has arisen from my dissatisfaction with the sharpness with which the contrast is often made between two types of society: the hierarchical and the egalitarian, or the aristocratic and the democratic. The contrast between societies is sometimes extended to a contrast between mentalities so that one speaks of *homo hierarchicus* as against *homo equalis*.

There is undoubtedly a difference between the hierarchical and egalitarian principles, and it is true too that societies differ greatly in the extent to which they support the one or the other. At the same time, contrasting whole societies—and indeed whole civilizations—in terms of a single pair of opposites can be misleading. Ideal types have to be used with great caution in contrasting large complexes since the construction of an ideal type necessarily entails a 'one-sided accentuation'. Such accentuation can easily obscure important features and tendencies in a society.

The distinction between hierarchical and egalitarian societies has been used both historically to contrast two different phases in the life of the same society, and sociologically to contrast two different types of society at the same historical moment. Strange though it may sound for a sociologist to say, I have found the first kind of contrast more illuminating than the second, particularly in the understanding of contemporary societies which are marked by so much interpenetration of ideas, beliefs, and values.

The first and most celebrated contrast between hierarchy and equality is the one we owe to Alexis de Tocqueville (1956). It cannot be too strongly emphasized that his contrast between aristocratic and democratic societies was meant to capture a historical transition. For him the exemplary value of the United States lay in the fact that it showed to France—and the rest of the western world—only the image of its own future. There was both a rupture and a continuity between the *ancien régime* of the eighteenth century and the republican regime of the nineteenth. France would not cease to be France in moving from aristocracy to democracy. It is this sense of continuity in change that makes Tocqueville's insight so illuminating for the understanding of contemporary India, even though he wrote in another age and about another place.

The contrast made by Louis Dumont (1966, 1977a) between *homo hierarchicus* and *homo equalis*, though plainly influenced by Tocqueville, is typological rather than historical. The contrast is between India and the west, or, rather, between traditional India and the modern west. Because the focus is so strongly on traditional India, or on 'the past in the present', Dumont pays scant attention to the confusion and disorder among norms and values in India today. But it is the confusion and disorder that is in many ways distinctive of contemporary Indian society and for that reason deserves the most careful attention.

The main concern of this work is with equality rather than hierarchy, and with contemporary rather than traditional India. While writing about equality in contemporary western societies, Dumont was of course fully aware of the presence of stratification in those societies. But for him stratification is quite different from hierarchy since it belongs to the realm of facts and not values (Dumont 1966: 15–7). This relegation of stratification or inequality in western societies to the realm of mere facts is unsatisfactory from the sociological point of view. It simply evades the problem that advocates of equality in those societies have to confront in the face of pervasive and sometimes increasing inequality. Does the promotion of meritocracy reflect the value of equality or its opposite? (See Appendix II).

It will be difficult to say about any large and complex society that it is governed by a single value or set of values, and few sociologists or historians would say so. At the same time, they do not all view in the same light the presence of a plurality of values in the same society. Dumont (1980) would say that, while there may be several values in a society, there is a paramount value which encompasses the other social values; in other words, there is a hierarchical integration of values. As against those who stress the integration of values, hierarchical or otherwise, there are others who stress the conflict of values, viewing society as a field of divergent aims and tendencies.

The emphasis in this chapter as in the book as a whole is on the conflict rather than the integration of values. Whether we choose to emphasize integration or conflict should be a matter of convenience rather than dogma. In the study of a small, homogeneous, and unchanging society, it may be appropriate to stress the integration of values. But Indian society is neither small nor homogeneous, and it is undergoing a major transition. The nature of that transition cannot be grasped if we do not take account of the coexistence and interplay of norms and values of very different kinds.

Beyond the questions specific to the transition in India from one kind of social order to another, this chapter also addresses the more general problem of inequality in egalitarian or democratic societies. Why do inequalities remain in societies that have chosen equality as the governing principle for their constitution, their laws, and their politics? To say that these inequalities are residual does not carry much conviction, particularly for countries such as France and the United States which have been committed to the pursuit of equality for more than two hundred years. And in India, we see new forms of inequality arise even as old forms of it undergo decline.

The argument that inequalities are maintained in egalitarian societies through coercion and domination addresses only part of the question, and not the whole of it. They are also maintained through consent. This consent is given not to inequality as an abstract or formal principle but to the institutional and other arrangements through which society maintains and reproduces itself in both private and public spheres. Whatever people may say or even believe about equality as a general principle, they are socially and even morally committed to specific practices in which different forms of inequality are embedded.

When I speak of the antinomies of equality, what I have in mind are the ambiguities, tensions, and contradictions that we confront as we move from the peripheries of the subject to its core. There is, firstly, the contradiction between social ideal and social practice, particularly manifest in India in many respects, and not just in respect of equality. What is more germane to the present discussion is that there are tensions within the idea of equality itself, as, for instance, between equality of opportunity and distributive equality, or between 'formal' and 'substantive' equality of opportunity.

A discussion of the antinomies of equality requires us to consider, however briefly, the question of norms and values. This is always a difficult thing for a sociologist to do, for his discipline is an empirical rather than a normative one, and his concern is less with value judgements than with matters of fact. To be sure, the sociologist has to deal with more than just the social placement of individuals and groups, the allocation of income and wealth, and the distribution of life chances. But he is concerned with norms and values in the descriptive rather than the prescriptive sense. He observes that norms and values differ between societies and between different phases in the development of the same society. His first task is to describe and analyze those differences methodically and dispassionately without prejudging the merits of one set of norms and values as against another.

In the present discussion I will follow the convention in sociology established by Parsons according to which values refer to 'generalized ends' whereas norms refer to 'regulatory rules' (see Chapter 2; also Béteille 2000a). Values in this sense are embedded in the domain of culture whereas norms have their locus in the legal order. Obviously, there has to be some congruence between values and norms. But even in a relatively stable society there are gaps between the two, and as a society undergoes a major transformation, the gaps begin to widen.

Louis Dumont's work on the social hierarchy in India left a deep impression on students of the subject both in India and outside. It presented a picture in which social morphology, values, and norms were cast in the same hierarchical mould within which they remained for centuries. The hierarchical arrangement of castes was the most conspicuous feature of the social morphology, and it was upheld by values and norms that were tacitly acknowledged not only by superiors but also by inferiors. What stands out in Dumont's account is the unity, the consistency, and the continuity of the social order as a whole.

Paradoxically, at the very time when Dumont was putting forward his account of the traditional order of Indian society, the unity, the consistency, and the continuity of that order was beginning to be seriously undermined. A new Constitution had been adopted in which equality and not hierarchy was given pride of place; a democratic political system based on full adult franchise had been instituted; and the Planning Commission had set to work with new ideas about the distribution of the wealth of the nation.

These major innovations have had varied and sometimes unforeseen consequences. The old divisions of society based on caste and community have changed, but they have not disappeared. Economic inequalities have diminished in some respects but increased in others. New attitudes and sentiments regarding rights and entitlements have come into being, but they have not effaced wholly or even substantially the old ones relating to deference and submission. What I wish to stress is that the inequalities that remain relate not only to income and wealth, but also to attitudes and sentiments.

If we examine how the Constitution and the laws have worked in the last fifty years, we will see how tangled the antinomies of equality are in contemporary India. There is first the mismatch between the norms of equality and the values of deference, respect, obedience, and submissiveness carried over from the traditional hierarchical system. Certainly, it is easier to create new laws than to replace old values by new ones. This is not to say that the new laws amount to nothing but only that their capacity to change the hearts and minds of men must not be overestimated.

The equality provisions in the Constitution of India are strong and far-reaching; they are present in the part on Fundamental Rights and also in the part on Directive Principles of State Policy. The commitment to the norm of equality has been asserted repeatedly in judgements of the highest courts of law. If the attitudes, sentiments, and values prevalent among Indians continue to be on the side of hierarchy, was the creation of such strong and far-reaching provisions for equality in the Constitution an exercise in futility?

First of all, we have to acknowledge that hierarchical values continue to maintain a pervasive presence in India. The evidence presented by Dumont and numerous other anthropologists, both Indian and foreign, makes this abundantly clear. The practice of untouchability, both disguised and open, continues to be reported. The most telling evidence of the depth of the attitudes and sentiments that underlie the practice comes from those studies which show that untouchability is practised not only by the highest castes against the lowest, but also by superior untouchable castes against inferior ones (Moffatt 1979; Deliège 1995). In a hierarchical society it is not enough to change the states of mind of those at the top, for even the very lowly can always find some others whom they regard as lowlier than themselves.

At the same time, attitudes and sentiments do change, and they have been changing in India. For while it is true that old attitudes towards untouchability still survive, it is also true that there are now millions of Indians who find its practice reprehensible; and their number is increasing. Article 19 in the Constitution should not be regarded as a mere exhortation, but as the expression of a new sentiment towards fellow human beings. Similarly, while it is true that women continue to be treated with indignity, increasing numbers of persons, both men and women, regard that treatment to be morally and not just legally wrong.

When sociologists speak of values as 'generalized ends', they take a very great deal for granted. How general are these generalized ends? Sociologists who dwell by preference on the plane of values and norms often fall into the practice of regarding society as a kind of homogeneous medium. But the structure of society has many cleavages, divisions, and fractures. The population of India is made up of different regional, linguistic, and religious groups. There are different classes and strata in it. Even if we ignore the divergence of interests among the different members of society, the values that they may be said to share in common are refracted by the social structure so that they are not perceived or interpreted in the same way by the different classes and communities.

Moreover, societies change and develop, and the movement of knowledge, is an uneven, not to say a disorderly, movement. Even though hierarchical values are on the whole being replaced by egalitarian ones, this is not happening in the same way or to the same extent in all sections of society. Old values may withdraw into a subterranean existence and then emerge again in unforeseen ways.

Not only are there disjunctions between norms and values in a changing society, but in such a society the norms themselves are not all of a piece. When we speak of norms as regulatory rules, we must recognize that the regulatory force of many rules is quite weak. Custom and law may both be regarded as systems of regulatory rules, and, in a changing society, the two often fall out of step with each other. The problem is not simply that it is easier to change laws than to change customs, but that customs do not lose their regulatory force simply because new laws have been created to displace them.

The antinomies of equality, though present universally, manifest themselves in specific ways in contemporary India. These specificities derive from the structure of Indian society and from its history. What I would like to stress here is the continuity of the traditional social structure over a long period of time as well as the historical developments that led to the independence of India in 1947 and the adoption of a republican Constitution in 1950.

The most striking feature of the social structure from ancient until quite recent times was the division of the population into a large number of groups based on language, religion, sect, caste, and tribe. Some degree of diversity one would naturally expect in a country with the size and population of India. But the diversity I am speaking of is a feature not just of the country taken as a whole, but of every region and practically every locality. Even a single village might be divided into as many as twenty or twenty-five distinct castes, sects, and tribes.

Differences between groups, their sections and subsections were maintained through the tolerance, not to say the encouragement, of diversity in material culture, social organization, and religious belief and practice. Subcastes within the same caste or even sub-subcastes within the same subcaste might distinguish themselves from each other in terms of minor differences in craft practice, food habit, kinship terminology, and ritual observance. These distinctions were jealously maintained and reproduced from generation to generation. Even where people lived cheek-by-jowl in the same village, they might maintain these minute distinctions among themselves.

Liberal-minded Indians take pride in the value placed on diversity in the Indian tradition, and point to its positive significance for the growth of a pluralist democracy. Diversity not only prevailed in practice, it was accepted and acknowledged by both law and religion, at least in the great Hindu tradition. It is not enough, however, to say that diversity prevailed or even that it was positively valued. One must also ask how diversity was organized. The plain fact is that within the Hindu tradition, diversity was organized hierarchically and not democratically.

Each sect, caste, and subcaste was allowed to maintain its own way of life, its own customs and even its own religious beliefs and practices, but these were not all equally esteemed. Some practices and the groups that were their characteristic bearers were highly esteemed and honoured, while others were disesteemed or even stigmatized. The ideology of purity and pollution ensured that the diversity was maintained on a more or less strictly hierarchical basis. Nor was it a matter of ideology alone. Where necessary, force was used to prevent the inferior castes from adopting the customs and practices of the superior castes. The tolerance of diversity included the tolerance of untouchability.

Diversity as it was organized in the past was not only at odds with equality, it left very little room for the freedom of individual choice. Although in society as a whole a very wide range of practices was tolerated, the individual was required to conform to the practices of the sect, caste, or community of which he was a member by birth. The subordination of the individual to the group was a pervasive feature of the old social order, although a door was always open for the individual, should he choose to adopt the path of the renouncer. The assertion of collective identities of every kind in contemporary Indian politics bears witness to the continuing presence of a very significant traditional value.

In considering the antinomies of equality, it is impossible to ignore the tensions between the values assigned to the individual and to collectivities such as castes and communities. In a certain view, equality presupposes the autonomy of the individual and hence it can have very little meaning where the individual counts for little because of his subordination to the group. It is also maintained that in India, individuals can never contend with each other on terms of equality unless the disparities between the castes and communities of which they are members by birth are first levelled out. I believe that there is a significant difference between asking for equality between individuals and demanding parity between castes. Some maintain that the organization of society on the basis of caste is an anachronism in the modern world, and others that there is nothing wrong with that organization as such, provided all castes are given equal standing.

I have argued that diversity was valued and respected in the Indian tradition, but that it was organized on a hierarchical basis which is at odds with the spirit of the modern world. Those who value diversity for its own sake are naturally apprehensive about the impact of modernization, and, now of globalization, on India's heritage of diversity. It is undeniable that modernization leads to standardization in a great many fields: dress, marriage practices, and even religious observances. Who could look forward to a bland, uniform, and standardized way of life in which everyone follows more or less the same routine?

Is it possible to have diversity without hierarchy? I believe that it is possible to have it, although the diversity will no longer be of the old kind. It is an error to believe that modernization leads to standardization, and to nothing else. The long-term evolutionary trend has been and will continue to be towards the differentiation of societies and not just towards the standardization of practices (Parsons 1966; Luhmann 1982). Modern societies are on the whole more, and not less, differentiated than the societies of the past.

The differentiation that is continuously at work in every modern society may be seen in many fields, but perhaps nowhere more clearly than in the fields of education and occupation. The occupational differentiation that has taken place since the Industrial Revolution, and particularly in the last hundred years, is unprecedented in human history. It may not be too great an exaggeration to say that modern societies advance mainly through the differentiation of education and occupation.

If we turn to pre-modern societies, we will find that perhaps the most striking example of the differentiation and specialization of occupations was that associated with the caste system in India. There were dozens, if not hundreds, of different crafts and services characterized by minute differences of technique and observance, each associated with a particular caste or subcaste (Bose 1975). But if we make a list of all the occupations practised at any time in the past, such a list will appear very short indeed in comparison with the lists of occupations regularly made by census offices and industrial bureaus in any modern society. Moreover, new items are added to those lists every decade if not every year. It would be impossible to maintain such a pace of occupational differentiation in societies organized on the basis of caste, estate, or guild.

I have chosen to dwell on the occupational system not only on account of its great salience in modern societies but also because it is the pre-eminent site of inequality or stratification in those societies. In all modern occupational systems on which sociologists have done research, the differentiation of occupations has been shown to be intimately linked with the ranking of occupations. The social grading of occupations has become a highly demanding and specialized activity among students of stratification in Britain and the United States (Blau and Duncan 1968; Goldthorpe and Hope 1974). Their studies have shown that the ranking of occupations is no less complex or elaborate than the ranking of castes and subcastes, although the principles of ranking are not the same in the two cases.

It will no doubt be pointed out that in the traditional order of Indian society, the differentiation of castes was not unrelated to the differentiation of occupations. The relationship between caste and occupation was, however, not straightforward. Although the choice of occupation was restricted by caste, the restriction was not absolute. A person might move to an occupation other than the one traditionally associated with his caste, but he did not thereby change his caste. N.K. Bose (1975) showed from the analysis of census data going back to 1901 that large numbers of persons from most castes were in occupations other than the ones associated with their own. It is well known that many Brahmans have had little to do with priestcraft, or the conduct of sacrifice, or the pursuit of learning; yet they demand recognition as Brahmans.

The individual's social identity is made up of many components of which caste is one and occupation is another. But caste and occupation contribute differently to social identity. In modern societies, where education and occupation contribute substantially to social identity, the individual changes that identity, at least to some extent, as he moves from one occupation to another in the course of his own lifetime, or, more commonly, from one generation to the next. It is for this reason that students of social stratification in the west focus as much attention on occupational mobility as on occupational differentiation and ranking. The problem is a difficult one technically, because not only are new occupations continuously emerging in place of old ones, but occupations keep changing from one generation to another. What we have as a result has been aptly described by two of the ablest students of the subject as 'constant flux' (Erikson and Goldthorpe 1992). While there is much movement upwards, downwards, and sideways of the components of the system, the system itself retains a certain continuity over time.

Where caste contributes more to social identity, the identity remains fixed to a greater extent. The individual lives and dies with the social identity he was assigned at birth which is largely the same as that of his forebears. Here individuals are judged socially as high or low according to what they are or are believed to be; where occupation, rather than caste, governs social status, they are judged according to what they do or are expected to do.

Although caste continues to maintain a strong presence in contemporary India, its social significance is undergoing change. It has to contend increasingly with education and occupation as a basis for defining social status, particularly in the expanding urban sector. Today, in a large metropolitan city in India, a man of very superior caste is likely to count for little socially if he has failed to make the grade in the educational and occupational systems. On the other hand, it is possible, though by no means easy, for a person of very inferior caste to rise high in social status through the ladders of education and occupation. There is considerable overlap between the differentiation due to caste and to education and occupation, but they also cut across each other, and increasingly so.

The differentiation of occupations shows certain basic similarities in all modern societies, although sociologists disagree about the degree of similarity. Part of the difference between societies arises from the fact that occupational differentiation combines in quite specific ways with earlier forms of differentiation characteristic of each social and histori-cal setting. Modern societies are complex not only because modern technology is complex and the modern organization of work is com-plex, but also because the modern system of occupational differentia-tion has to combine with pre-existing systems of differentiation based on language, religion, race, caste, ethnicity, and many other factors.

Can we have difference without inequality? Upto a point, and depend-ing on how we conceive of equality. Here I would like to point out that hierarchy is not coterminous with inequality but only a particular expression of it. Inequality is present, in one form or another, in all human societies, but they cannot all for that reason be properly desig-nated as 'hierarchical'. Louis Dumont, who has in recent times made a most significant contribution to the subject, insisted on a strict distinc-tion being maintained between 'hierarchy' and 'stratification' (Du-mont 1961, 1966). He would say that modern western societies are the opposite of being 'hierarchical', but admit at the same time that they are stratified in various ways. For him, hierarchy and its opposite, equality, exist on the plane of values, whereas stratification and, per-haps also, inequality are matters of fact. At the same time, it is difficult to admit that stratification, which is such a pervasive feature of modern western societies, exists only as a matter of fact, without any basis in the values of those societies.

As I have already indicated, Dumont's distinction between *homo hierarchicus* and *homo equalis* echoes the ideas of Alexis de Tocqueville and may, with some simplification, be regarded as a restatement of the nineteenth-century master's contrast between aristrocratic and demo-cratic societies (Tocqueville 1956). But Tocqueville's interest, unlike Dumont's, was mainly a historical one, to examine continuity and change within the same system of civilization. For those whose focus of attention is on the transition taking place in India, Tocqueville's contrast is in some ways more illuminating than Dumont's.

Tocqueville's work reveals the antinomies of equality in a particu-larly vivid way. This may be partly because he was himself torn be-tween the values of hierarchy and equality. He knew that the future lay with democracy although he could not entirely suppress his loyalty to the aristocracy in which his own roots lay. He welcomed the advance of equality as a providential fact, but he could not conceal his many misgivings about it.

Despite his misgivings, Tocqueville believed that at least in the Christian countries in Europe and America, there was a steady advance of equality in every domain: in ideas, beliefs, attitudes, sentiments, values, norms, customs, and laws as well as in the material conditions of existence. But clearly, this was in part a delusion. For, while there was a steady advance in his time of equality on the plane of norms and values, in laws and customs, this was not accompanied by a corresponding increase of economic equality. What evidence we have shows fairly clearly that the early stages of industrial capitalism are characterized by an increase and not a decrease of inequality in the distribution of income and wealth (Kuznets 1955).

Even while the privileges and disabilities based on the old system of estates were being abolished by law to give place to a body of equal citizens, a new educational and occupational system of unimagined potential complexity was coming into being. Tocqueville and his generation saw in this system only the promise of equality: equality of status and of opportunity as expressed in Napoleon's famous slogan of 'careers open to talent'. They did not see in it the seeds of the highly complex systems of social stratification to which future generations of sociologists would have to devote their labours.

When India became independent in 1947, a great deal was expected of the new dispensation. People looked back on the old social order with its hierarchies and its inequities, and felt that they were now free to leave all that behind and to create a new social order based on equality and justice. On the eve of independence, Nehru had pointed to the contradiction between the spirit of the age which was in favour of equality and the social practice that denied it everywhere (Nehru 1961: 521). Generous provisions for equality were written into the Constitution and new ones have been added in the fifty years since it was adopted.

Indians who have their hearts and minds on equality are disappointed by the realities of the world in which they are constrained to live. Why has the spirit of the age not triumphed in the manner and to the extent hoped for by Nehru on the eve of independence? Two things have happened in the last fifty years. The inequalities due to caste and gender have declined, but by no means disappeared; those who had hoped that they would disappear are not prepared even to acknowledge that they have declined. Secondly, new social inequalities rooted in new economic arrangements have come into existence; and those who had hoped that the old forms of inequality would be eliminated are a little surprised to find new forms of it to which they had not had time to give much thought.

Both the trends indicated above—the slow decline in the inequalities due to caste and gender, and the gradual increase in those due to education and occupation—had in fact begun to operate well before the country became independent. Independence brought in a change of pace, but not a revolution. The nationalist movement created a habit of mind which encouraged the attribution of all the ills and inconveniences of our life to the malign working of colonial rule. There are some problems we have come by habit to expect governments to solve that in fact no government, whether national or colonial, can possibly solve. Some aspects of inequality are constitutive of human societies: they are inherent in the very nature of collective life and no government, however beneficent, can conjure them out of existence.

To treat equality as a single and indivisible whole is to adopt an unreasonable attitude to the realities of life in society. I must confess to being baffled by those well-meaning but passionate souls who declare that they find inequality insupportable in no matter what form it exists. Some forms of inequality are no doubt odious and reprehensible; other forms of it are, to my way of thinking, unappealing though inevitable; but there are yet other forms that may be conducive to the well-being and progress of society. Naturally, there will be disagreement about assigning a particular form of inequality to one or another of these three categories. But we cannot even begin a serious discussion if we decide in advance that every form of inequality is to be condemned and equality is to be promoted at any cost.

Modernity does not, indeed cannot, cancel out every kind of inequality. But it does render increasingly odious certain forms of it that had in the past been accepted as a part of the natural scheme of things. Pre-eminent among these are the inequalities due to race, caste, and gender, all tied to attributes acquired by the individual at birth.

By the time independence appeared on the horizon, the inequalities due to caste and gender appeared insupportable to growing sections of the population of the country, and particularly its intelligentsia. The stigma of untouchability, the perpetual tutelage of women, and the many indignities imposed on millions of persons considered to be of inferior birth could no longer be defended in public. This was a modern orientation to society, very different from the traditional one encoded in the Dharmashastra. It did not emerge out of the blue on the day of independence, but had been in the making since the beginning of the nineteenth century. Rammohun Roy was the first in a long line of social reformers who paved the way for the creation of a modern Constitution with strong guarantees of equality among castes, and between men and women.

The Constitution did not change everything; indeed no Constitution can be expected to do so. Many inequalities of caste and gender remain in practice even though repudiated by law. As every anthropologist knows, custom is a very obdurate thing, not easily dislodged by law. The change of heart and mind, so much in evidence in the Constituent Assembly, has not even now reached into every corner of Indian society. There is no denying the fact that Indians remain obstinately preoccupied with status even when they are modern, liberal, and secular. The disparity between the esteem accorded to superior non-manual occupations and the disesteem to which inferior manual and menial ones are condemned, is nowhere as extreme as in contemporary Indian society.

If custom were to repudiate the disabilities suffered by women and by persons of inferior caste, as the law has done to a very great extent, would all persons enjoy the same social standing, irrespective of gender and caste? This is doubtful. Even if the selection process in the educational and occupational systems were made gender-blind and caste-blind, it is unlikely that women and persons of inferior caste would come out on top in proportion to their strength in the population. The selection process can be blind to differences of race, caste, and gender, but it cannot be blind to such differences of ability, aptitude, and qualification as arise from past social experience, or from social experience unconnected with the operation of the educational and the occupational systems.

The Constitution of India in its Preamble offers 'equality of status and of opportunity'. These are both ambiguous terms, admitting divergent interpretations of meaning. Let us consider status first. We may give the term a strictly legal definition, as when speaking of the equal status of all citizens of India in the manner specified in Part II of the Constitution of India as in other modern constitutions. But for the sociologist, as indeed for the ordinary citizen, the term has a much

broader connotation, being governed, over and above its legal definition, by a multiplicity of criteria, including education and occupation.
There is certainly a meaningful sense in which we may say that the
Indians are more status conscious than the Dutch, or that the English
are more status conscious than the Americans. But this broader connotation is replete with ambiguities, even in the writings of sociologists,
as I have pointed out elsewhere (Chapter 2).

We cannot escape the conclusion that, over and above the equality
of *legal* status enjoyed by all citizens, there are numerous differences
and inequalities among the same citizens, depending on who they are
and what they do in a variety of domains. This is true of all modern
societies, and particularly so of contemporary Indian society. Does this
mean that no social significance is to be assigned to the equality of legal
status? It is far from my intention to make that suggestion. We have
to look back a hundred years to recognize the change that has been
brought about in attitudes and sentiments and, to some extent, even in
the actual conditions of life by conferring the status of equal citizenship
on all, irrespective of social position or social antecedent.

Even among those who agree that differences of income, esteem, and
authority—in short, inequalities of status in the broad sense—are inescapable, there may be disagreement about the acceptable limits of inequality—the floor and the ceiling, so to say—and the number of rungs
on the ladder. Moreover, not all egalitarians adopt an extreme position.
Many of them acknowledge the need to have inequalities of status in
the broad sense, provided they are 'attached to positions and offices
open to all' (Rawls 1972: 60). In short, if we can have equality of status
to only a limited extent, we can still have equality of opportunity.

Equality of opportunity plays a significant part in the dynamics of
all modern societies. It answers some of the needs of both equity and
efficiency. It is difficult to see how modern societies can function, far
less advance, without a continuous circulation of skill and talent. Equality of opportunity has been a great ideological force in knocking at the
barriers separating one segment of society from another. In other
words, it has sustained and expanded the operation of social mobility.

The experience of western societies, where the principle of equality
of opportunity was first adopted, has shown that its transformative
powers are not unlimited. Careers are indeed open to talent, but favour-
able social antecedents also help. There has been some mobility, both
intra- and inter-generational; but there has also been much reproduction of inequality. Social mobility and the reproduction of inequality

may be viewed as the two contradictory features of all modern systems of stratification. The balance between the two naturally varies from one case to another. In India, the reproduction of inequality has probably the greater weight, although rates of mobility within the urban middle class may not be significantly lower in India than elsewhere.

In an influential book published in the inter-war period, R.H. Tawney drew attention to the principle of equal opportunities as it operated in Britain under conditions of wide social disparity. He noted that, while the principle was widely acknowledged, the practice was very different from it: 'Rightly interpreted, equality meant, not the absence of violent contrast of income and condition, but equal opportunities of becoming unequal'. Further, 'equality of opportunity is not simply a matter of legal equality. Its existence depends, not merely on the absence of disabilities, but on the presence of abilities' (Tawney 1964: 103). Creating abilities requires comprehensive policy interventions so that equality as a right has to be buttressed by equality as a policy (Béteille 1987c).

Equality of opportunity and its complement, social mobility, are features of societies that favour competition between individuals. But competition cannot be guaranteed to eliminate or even reduce inequalities between individuals; sometimes it increases them. Some have indeed warned that untempered competition can lead in the end only to a callous meritocratic society. It is in this light that Rawls sought to make his case for 'fair equality of opportunity' as a protection against the excesses of untempered competition. So, equality of opportunity is not such a simple idea after all.

I must conclude by drawing attention very briefly to the ambiguity that lies at the very heart of the idea of equality of opportunity. For the idea may refer either to *formal* equality of opportunity or to *substantive* equality of opportunity, and they are not the same. When people find that formal equality of opportunity fails to produce the degree of social mobility they consider desirable, they tend to dismiss it as a means merely for the perpetuation of inequality. They then feel perhaps with Mr B.P. Mandal that equality of opportunity amounts to little, and that 'the real acid test' of society's commitment to equality is equality of result (Government of India 1980: 22).

Substantive equality of opportunity invokes the principle of the level playing field as a basis for fair and not just free competition. Once we appreciate that society is a dynamic system, we will see how intractable the problem of the level playing field is. For the problem is not simply of creating such a field once and for all, but of maintaining it against the natural currents of the competition presupposed by the principle of formal equality of opportunity. This will require social engineering on a scale that no society can sustain for any length of time. There is some kind of a historical precedent in the Soviet Union in the 1920s where the policy of *uravnilovka*, or leveling, was tried out for a while (Lane 1971). But even Stalin was unable to cope with its backlash, and soon denounced *uravnilovka* as a petty bourgeois vice.

Equality of opportunity is perhaps best conceived of as an enabling provision. But in our Constitution, it is a mandatory provision under Article 16. It is true that its application is restricted to matters of public employment. Nevertheless, it is a kind of provision that neither the American nor the French constitution has.

Some might question the wisdom of having a mandatory provision for equality of opportunity in the part on Fundamental Rights. It naturally raises expectations of something more than mere formal equality of opportunity, since that is taken care of by the joint operation of Article 14 which prohibits denial by the state of equality before the law or the equal protection of the laws and Article 15 which prohibits discrimination on grounds of religion, race, caste, sex, or place of birth. What more can a constitution provide? Article 16 has had a vexed career, lending itself to contradictory and inconsistent interpretations by the courts.

Equality is an important value on which no modern society can afford to turn its back. Good laws can protect and promote equality of legal status and formal equality of opportunity. Good policies can create the abilities to enable the disadvantaged to compete on more equal terms with the advantaged. That being said, it must be remembered that there are other important values, such as freedom, individual excellence, amity, mutuality, and many others which cannot be left untouched by the single-minded pursuit of equality at any cost.

9

Hierarchical and Competitive Inequality

In a brief paper first published in 1960 in what was then *The Economic Weekly*, Professor M.N. Srinivas examined the prospects of a 'casteless and classless' society in India (Srinivas 1962: 87–97). The country had attained independence and given itself a republican Constitution barely a decade earlier. A great deal of support was expressed in public for the ideal of equality. But Srinivas issued a salutary warning against taking lightly the hierarchies in the social environment and in the mentality of the people. I would like to re-examine some of the questions raised by him and to carry the argument a little further. Forty years is a long enough time interval in the life of a nation to make the undertaking appear attractive.

Srinivas's approach to the problem, which I shall try to emulate, is that of the sociologist and not the moralist. While broadly in sympathy with the constitutional objective of 'equality of status and of opportunity', he did not devote much time to extolling the virtues of equality as an ideal, but dwelt instead on the many obstacles to its realization in practice.

He noted with approval the many measures adopted by the state for the removal or at least the reduction of inequality through the creation of new rights and new policies. But he drew attention to the pervasive presence of hierarchy and warned against any idea that something so deep-rooted could simply be wished out of existence.

Srinivas had a sharp eye for the contradictions, oppositions, and tensions inherent in his own as in any other human society. He did not by any means wish to belittle the objectives the leaders of the nation had set for themselves at the time of independence. But he called for a clearer understanding of the obstacles with which those objectives would have to contend. He never let himself forget that India was a vast and complex society of great antiquity in which life was lived on many planes. He believed that change was necessary and desirable and that the leaders had an obligation to show the way forward, but that they themselves would lose their way if they did not take account of the habits, practices, and customs deeply rooted in the lives of the ordinary people.

Nor was the educated and forward-looking Indian middle class itself entirely free from the hierarchical habits and practices it wished society as a whole to discard. 'This class may pay lip service to egalitarian ideals', he wrote, 'but that should not blind us to the fact that its attitudes are fundamentally hierarchical' (Srinivas 1962: 96). Ideals were no doubt important in social life, but from the sociological point of view, the study of ideals could never be a substitute for the study of practice. Moreover, the ideals themselves were diverse and, in a changing society, often mutually inconsistent.

While the hierarchical mentality is still widespread among the ordinary people, the Indian intelligentsia tends to be both utopian and fatalistic in its orientation towards equality and inequality. A utopian orientation is one that believes it possible to bring into being any state of affairs that it regards as desirable; a fatalistic orientation takes as inevitable the existing state of affairs, no matter how undesirable. In addressing public gatherings, at conferences, seminars, and workshops, important men and women speak as if all the accumulated inequalities of the past can be made to wither away. The opposite or fatalistic mode is characteristically expressed in private; there people are inclined to lament that nothing changes in India or that, if anything changes, the change is always for the worse. They point to the capitalist class, the bureaucracy and, now of course, the multinationals as the irremovable obstacles to the advance of equality. It is not as if the utopian and the fatalistic orientations are characteristic of two distinct and separate sets of individuals. They coexist in one and the same individual, like the two sides of a coin.

The sociological approach sets itself against the utopian and the fatalistic approaches. It is not an easy approach to follow consistently in an environment permeated by the utopian and the fatalistic modes of thought. The effort of describing and analyzing the different forms of inequality objectively and dispassionately, which is the first task of the sociologist, is often condemned as a disguised attempt to justify it. In my experience, what talented young sociologists fear most today in India is being labelled as conservative or reactionary. As a result, their work as sociologists suffers since description and analysis have to yield to moral exhortation.

The sociological approach is also opposed to the fatalistic because, being comparative and historical, it does not accept any existing form of inequality, no matter how pervasive or well-entrenched, as either inevitable or immutable. Here I would like to make the distinction between regarding inequality itself as inevitable and regarding any specific form of it as inevitable. This distinction is of great importance not only for social theory but also for social policy. One cannot begin to address questions of policy seriously if one commits oneself to the position that inequality as such is an evil and that all forms of its are equally reprehensible.

The advance of equality, where it does take place, does not follow a smooth or uniform course; what we generally witness is a process of uneven development. Important changes were no doubt introduced at the time of independence, but there have been currents as well as counter-currents. Even as old forms of inequality have retreated or become obsolete, new forms of it have emerged and advanced. This has been a continuous process during the last hundred and fifty years, and the adoption of a new Constitution and new social and economic policies in the wake of independence have been important landmarks.

While most progressive intellectuals at the time welcomed the prospect of a 'casteless and classless' society, Srinivas pointed out not only that hierarchy dies hard in India but also that new forms of it were emerging under the very eyes of the egalitarians. He concluded his essay by observing, 'In brief, there are today two types of hierarchy, one which is traditional and the other which is emergent' (Srinivas 1962:95). He did not elaborate on the specific features of the two types of hierarchy, but excluded from consideration 'the "functional hierarchy" which prevails during working hours' (Ibid.: 96), meaning presumably the system of stratification embedded in the modern occupational system to which I will devote attention separately later in the essay.

It is clear that at that time Srinivas's attention was focussed on caste and its great resilience in the face of the changes brought in by the new legal, political, and economic forces. He did not discount the importance of those forces but argued that they not only failed to destroy caste but instead opened up new fields for its operation. For Srinivas, hierarchy meant above all the hierarchy of caste. In the traditional order, the hierarchy operated mainly through the ideas of purity and pollution whose importance he had brought to light in his study of the Coorgs (Srinivas 1952). It was obvious that those ideas were in retreat, and Srinivas was to discuss that retreat in some detail in his Tagore lectures (Srinivas 1966: 118–46). But the retreat of purity and pollution did not bring caste to an end, for it found new ways of operating in the secular domain.

Without gainsaying the resilience of caste and its continuing role in Indian society and politics, it is important to consider on their own terms new forms of inequality that have emerged in Indian society and that operate to some extent independently of caste. There is now a large and expanding middle class—and an industrial working class—in Indian society that can no longer be treated simply as appendages of the caste system. Nor can we afford to treat them as being merely derivative of the inequalities that arise from the functional requirements of modern associations, institutions, and organizations. Those inequalities have become pervasive, but the logic of their operation is different from that of caste.

The modernization of India has not been a painless process and it has not always followed the course it was expected to do fifty years ago; it is all the same a continuing and irreversible process. Modern associations, organizations, and institutions, for all the problems with which they are beset, have grown and diversified; modern markets have reached into rural areas everywhere. Offices, factories, schools, colleges, and universities have grown throughout the country. Caste certainly counts in the estimation of social rank, but there are now many areas of life in which education and occupation count as much if not more.

The Indian middle class is no longer what it was fifty years ago; though occupying an important place in public life, it was then small and socially homogeneous. It has become much larger and socially more diverse. In the past it was dominated by only a handful of upper castes. Many new castes, belonging to the middle or even the lower levels of the traditional hierarchy, have entered the middle class in the last fifty years. Today the Indian middle class is differentiated not only by caste, but also by income, education, and occupation. More and more persons strive to prepare their children for a better education and a better occupation than they have had, even if their caste cannot be changed. Competition and individual mobility have now become pervasive features of Indian society. Caste may have something to do with all this, but it will be unwise to regard it as decisive.

The turnaround in economic policy that began after 1990 created a new interest in the Indian middle class. It has captured the popular imagination and been widely discussed in newspapers and weekly magazines, and on television. Books have also been written on it, but more from a popular than a scholarly point of view; these books either extol the middle class for its economic dynamism (Das 2000) or attack it for its moral deficiency (Varma 1998). But there is little systematic empirical material in this kind of writing and it generally lacks conceptual clarity and analytical rigour. The Indian middle class has not so far received the serious scholarly attention that it deserves from sociologists. Compared to what they have published on caste, Indian sociologists have published very little on the middle class; yet they all belong to that class.

It is in a way natural that so much attention should have been devoted by both Indian and foreign students of Indian society to caste. Caste is distinctive of Indian society if not unique to it. The middle class, as defined by education, occupation, and income, is on the other hand a feature of most if not all modern societies. There is no need to deny the distinctive features of the Indian middle class, but there is no need either to ignore the many features that it has in common with its counterparts in other societies. To those sociologists who believe that theirs is by its very nature a comparative discipline, the middle class provides an attractive field for systematic enquiry; such an enquiry promises opportunities for collaboration between sociologists, demographers, and economists.

I would now like to introduce the distinction between two forms of inequality which may be called 'hierarchical' and 'competitive' inequality. I must insist at the outset that the distinction is conceptual and analytical rather than empirical. There is hardly any society in which either form of inequality is found in its pure state, uncontaminated by any other form of it. Certainly, in contemporary India the two coexist in many areas, and sometimes reinforce each other; but that only makes the need to distinguish between them more urgent. Moreover, the distinction between hierarchical and competitive inequality is of great importance historically and comparatively, for, while they coexist in most societies, they combine differently in different societies.

I must apologize in advance for my somewhat clumsy terminology. 'Hierarchical inequality' sounds like a redundancy, but the phrase is useful because it invokes an idea given currency by Louis Dumont in his influential work on caste (Dumont 1966). Dumont insisted in that work that 'hierarchy' must be distinguished from 'stratification', and I would like to repeat that not all forms of inequality are covered by hierarchy. Nor is the contrast between inequality in general and hierarchy in particular relevant to the understanding only of India. Writing about feudalism in France between the ninth and the twelfth centuries, Marc Bloch said, 'It was an unequal society, rather than a hierarchical one' (Bloch 1962: 443). The hierarchy of estates, about which other European historians wrote, became fully developed only later.

Hierarchical inequality is characteristic of a certain kind of society, based on castes or on estates. Such a society has not only a distinctive morphology, i.e. a distinctive pattern of groups and their arrangement, but also distinctive laws, customs, and practices. There distinctions of status are not only considered right, proper, and desirable—a part of the natural scheme of things as it were—but they permeate every sphere of life, from the domestic to the political. The Indian caste system provides the best example of hierarchical inequality, but other examples of it may be found from Europe or China in past times. In such societies, hierarchical inequality marked the relations not only between castes—or between estates—but also between men and women.

Hierarchical inequality is characteristic of societies with a very different conception of the moral and even the natural order from that prevalent in modern democratic societies. I have elsewhere spoken of harmonic social systems in which inequalities not only exist in fact but are also considered right, proper, and desirable, a part of the natural scheme of things (Béteille 1987a: 54–77). Men and women, and persons belonging to different castes and different communities are assigned different and unequal positions in society as a matter of course. Persons at different ends of the social spectrum are not expected to compete with each other for social recognition and reward.

The hierarchical conception of society attained its most complete, elaborate, and enduring expression in India even though it was not unique to it. One of the most vivid accounts of that conception comes from a study of Europe at the end of the Middle Ages. Three things stand out in Jan Huizinga's account of hierarchical inequality: (i) the elaborateness of the social distinctions maintained between the high- and the low-born; (ii) the acceptance by the common people of their own social insignificance; and (iii) the general belief in the sanctity of the prevalent social hierarchy as being part of a larger, divine scheme of things. Finally, 'The conception of society in the Middle Ages is statistical, not dynamical' (Huizinga 1924: 48).

The hierarchical conception of the world survived in Europe well beyond the Middle Ages. The idea of the Great Chain of Being has had a lasting significance in European Christianity. Its three principles of plentitude, continuity, and gradation treated the social hierarchy as merely a replication of the cosmic hierarchy, beginning with the low- liest of creatures and reaching up to God. Although going back to the Middle Ages and beyond, the idea acquired a new lease of life in Europe in the eighteenth century at precisely that historical juncture when the old social hierarchy was beginning to be threatened by new economic and political forces (Lovejoy 1964: 183–207). What had till then been a part of the common sense of the Christian world would soon come to be seriously questioned.

The common sense of the western world is no longer what it was at the end of the eighteenth century. Changes have taken place continu- ously in legal, political, and economic institutions, and these have slowly eaten into the hierarchical conception of the world. Relations between men and women, between the high- and the low-born, and even between the rich and the poor have altered. New ideas have emerged as to what is due to the individual as a citizen irrespective of his or her social standing. The erosion of the hierarchical conception of the world did not happen all at once or to the same extent in every social field. In many European countries the church continued to ad- here to hierarchy, although that too began to change in the second half of the twentieth century.

Though familiar to students of European history upto the eighteenth or even the nineteenth century, the hierarchical conception of society attained its fullest expression in Indian, and particularly Hindu, society. The Dharmashastra in general and the Manusmriti in particular may be viewed as the charter of a society in which hierarchical practices were upheld by religion, law, and morality. Today the term Manuvad has come to stand for the most oppressive and odious form of social inequality; and yet it was the moral basis of a whole social order.

Although the term 'caste' serves as a metaphor for it, hierarchical inequality extended well beyond caste in the strict sense of the term. It was the form taken by relations not only between upper and lower castes, but also between landlords and tenants, masters and servants, patrons and clients, and, no less important, between men and women. Hierarchical inequality, particularly among the Hindus, was expressed by a distinctive ritual idiom, based on the opposition of purity and pollution, which played a large part in maintaining the segregation of the lowest castes and the many restrictions imposed on women. Though developed in its fullest form among the Hindus, hierarchical inequality, including the idiom of purity and pollution, permeated the whole of Indian society, leaving its impress on Muslims, Sikhs, Christians, and even the relatively isolated tribal communities.

Village, caste, and joint family, which constituted the key institutions of traditional Indian society, were all organized on the basis of hierarchical inequality. Srinivas challenged the conception of the traditional Indian village as a little republic and put in its place the conception of it as a vertical unity. If the different components of the village together constituted a unity, they did not all enjoy equal esteem or equal authority. The economy of land and grain was supplemented by a variety of crafts and services. Occupations were elaborately ranked, and there was little question of the different members of the village competing with each other for the most rewarding ones among them. In an occupational regime in which competition between members of different groups is discouraged if not debarred, the question of equality of opportunity does not generally arise.

In its complete form, the caste system consisted of both a design or an ideal plan of society and a set of relations between social groups, the former represented by *varna* and the latter by *jati*. When Srinivas drew attention to the disjunction between the two, something had already begun to change in the caste system (Srinivas 1962: 63–9; see also Chapter 3). The hierarchical design of *varna* was losing its clarity and authority, and *jatis* were beginning to intensify their competition for power and position. As explained in Chapter 3, when people talk about caste today, they mainly have *jati* in mind, although it must not be forgotten that for centuries the order of *varnas* provided the framework for the social gradation of *jatis*.

Against the vertical unity of the village, Srinivas counterposed the horizontal unity of caste, indicating that the two balanced each other in some sense. The idea of the horizontal unity of caste has to be used with caution. For while members of the same caste are on the same level in opposition to members of superior or inferior castes, there is internal differentiation within the same caste and indeed within the same sub-caste, and this differentiation is generally, if not invariably, accompanied by ideas of superior and inferior rank. As Dumont would argue, hierarchy does not stop short at the boundaries of the caste or even the subcaste, but penetrates and permeates its interior (Dumont 1957, 1966).

Ranking within the caste is expressed as well as regulated by rules of marriage. More important than the principle of endogamy in this respect is the principle of hypergamy. Hypergamy may be obligatory or optional, but the principle is in both cases the same: bride-takers are superior to bride-givers. Hypergamy may be practiced within the same subcaste, between different subcastes of the same caste, or between different castes that are distinctly unequal. Where bride-takers and bride-givers constitute distinct segments, both parties acknowledge that the former are superior to the latter. The principle of hypergamy enjoyed scriptural sanction among the Hindus where, as indicated earlier, it was formulated in the language of *varna* rather than *jati*.

In the scriptures a strict distinction was maintained between hypergamy (or *anuloma*) which was permitted and hypogamy (or *pratiloma*) which was prohibited. It is difficult to say how extensively hypergamy as a rule of marriage between distinct castes or even subcastes was practised in the past. The rule of hypergamy lost much of its force in the twentieth century. There is very little evidence of the systematic practice of obligatory hypergamy; and the distinction between *anuloma* and *pratiloma*, so important to traditional conceptions of hierarchy and marriage alliance, is no longer strictly maintained or even clearly understood. All of this indicates that while castes continue to be unequally ranked, there is decreasing clarity and agreement about their ranks.

Classical ideas regarding *anuloma* and *pratiloma* expressed asymmetry not only between castes but also between men and women. Characteristically, gender disparities were larger among the higher than among the lower castes. An enhancement in the social status of the subcaste or the family meant the imposition of additional restrictions on its women: against post-puberty marriage, against widow remarriage, against divorce and, in general, against free movement outside the domestic sphere. The principle of *anuloma* extended the possibility, at least theoretically, of marriage outside the caste for lower-caste women while the principle of *pratiloma* restricted that possibility for upper-caste women. In the past the burden of polygamy weighed more heavily on upper-caste than on lower-caste women, and a lower-caste woman had a better chance of walking out on her husband than an upper-caste one. All of this is not to deny that the life of a lower-caste woman was one of toil, privation, and hardship.

Men and women were treated unequally in the family law of both Hindus and Muslims, although in somewhat different ways. Traditionally, polygamy was allowed by law for both Hindus and Muslims; the law now prohibits polygamy for Hindus but not for Muslims. In most pre-modern legal systems women were assigned a subordinate legal position. This was exemplified in Roman law by the doctrine of the Perpetual Tutelage of Women. Writing about the doctrine in the middle of the nineteenth century, Sir Henry Maine observed. 'In India, the system survives in absolute completeness, and its operation is so strict that a Hindoo Mother frequently becomes the ward of her own sons' (Maine 1950: 127).

Personal law varied between Hindus and Muslims, and, among Hindus, between patrilineal and matrilineal communities. But within the structure of the family, men exercised authority over women. We get a vivid picture of the differentiation and hierarchy of roles within the extended family in Srinivas's classic account of the Coorg *okka*. 'A woman is not a member of an *okka* in the sense a man is, and the legal rights she enjoys are always inferior to a man's' (Srinivas 1952: 126). Nor is hierarchy in the family a matter of gender alone. 'Enormous emphasis is laid on seniority, and this is visible not only between members of different generations, but also between members of the same generation. The younger member has to behave deferentially towards the older' (Ibid.: 58).

It is true that social relations were structured differently in the matrilineal *taravad* as compared to the patrilineal *okka*. But there too there was a differentiation and hierarchy of roles. Even though in a *taravad* the women continued to live in their own homes after marriage and their husbands came in as visitors, authority lay in the hands of the senior adult men: the brother in place of the husband and the mother's brother in place of the father (Schneider and Gough 1961: 298–404). And generation and age were as important in the one case as in the other.

The hierarchical conception of society was not accepted without question all through Indian history. It was challenged from time to time by socio-religious movements which sought to better the lot of the inferior castes and of women. But these challenges came to be accommodated within the existing order which maintained its basically hierarchical character. In the past the challenge to the social hierarchy generally took the form of religious protest. What began as a religious movement acquired the character of a sect which in turn found a place for itself in the existing hierarchy of castes (Bose 1975). The transformation of sect into caste is a recurrent feature of Indian social history till the nine-teenth century.

A new and more radical conception of equality, which was to have far-reaching consequences for the structure of Indian society, began to emerge in the nineteenth century (Ganguli 1975; Raychaudhuri 1988). The initial impulse for it came from the encounter with western ideas and institutions in the wake of colonial rule. Reflective Indians in the new presidency centres of Calcutta, Bombay, and Madras experienced the freshness and vitality of western culture and recognized that their own civilization, for all its past greatness, had become moribund. But they soon realized that the teachings of Bentham and Mill were one thing, and British colonial practice in India quite another. It may not be too much to say that the nineteenth-century Indian intelligentsia learnt as much about equality from the colonial practice of inequality as from the liberal theory of equality.

The best among the nineteenth-century Indian writers on equality did not rest content with pointing to the contradictions of colonial rule. They were unsparing in their criticism of the contradictions in their own society. In an essay on self-rule and alien-rule, Bankimchandra asked by what right upper-caste Indians complained against the racial discrimination practised by the British when they themselves practised the most odious forms of caste discrimination (Bankimchandra 1961: 241–5). Nor did the inferior condition of women escape the attention of the critics of society. Needless to say, the nineteenth-century critics of the traditional social hierarchy were almost all men and from the higher castes.

The nineteenth century saw the emergence not only of a new con-ception of equality but also of new legal enactments, new economic arrangements and, what is more important, new social institutions. Without the latter, the new conception of equality would have had little practical effect. It is not as if the new legal enactments, the new economic arrangements, and the new social institutions led all at once to the disappearance of hierarchical beliefs and practices. But the continued existence of those beliefs and practices should not lead us to disregard the changes that have taken place and are taking place in Indian society. Many things have in fact changed since the middle of the nineteenth century, although social change rarely follows the course visualized by its initiators.

Many nineteenth-century Indians who championed the cause of equality looked for its roots in their own tradition. Naturally, there was some invention of tradition in the process, and some used their imagination more freely than others. It is difficult to believe that so important and fundamental an idea as that of equality could be wholly unknown to any major civilization. All the same, a new element entered into the nineteenth-century Indian conception of equality. Whereas earlier conceptions of it had been strongly tinged by religion, the new conception of equality was on the whole a secular one. This did not escape the attention of Bankimchandra who wrote an important tract on equality in 1879 which he later withdrew from circulation (Haldar 1977).

A new intelligentsia, with a distinctive attitude towards hierarchy and equality began to emerge in the nineteenth century as part of a new middle class. This was associated with what Srinivas has described as westernization (Srinivas 1966: 46–88). India has had a long and continuous intellectual tradition, but the new intelligentsia was different in its orientation towards the social order from the old literati. This tends to be obscured by the remarkable continuity of membership between the two in terms of family, kinship, and caste. Those who began to question and challenge the traditional hierarchy were, with few exceptions, the descendants of the very persons whose task had been to uphold and justify that hierarchy in the past. The traditional literati in India had been very exclusive in its social composition and the nineteenth-century intelligentsia was not noticeably less so; but a change of orientation was nevertheless beginning to take place.

One must not exaggerate the transformative effect of westernization on Indian society. In the nineteenth century and even into the twentieth, its reach was limited. The rural areas were not affected by it in the same ways as the metropolitan centres. Moreover, as Srinivas pointed out, the same forces that led to the emergence of westernization in certain quarters enlarged the scope of Sanskritization in others. While westernization relaxed the rigours due to caste and gender, Sanskritization reinforced the value placed on traditional symbols of status. It is to Srinivas's credit to have drawn attention to the complex dialectic of

Sanskritization and westernization that began in the middle of the nineteenth century and continues to this day. Both Sanskritization and westernization have implications for social stratification and social mobility, but their implications are somewhat different.

The emergence of a new middle class marks a kind of rupture in the traditional social order. In India its origins derive not so much from an industrial revolution or a democratic revolution as from colonial rule. It was colonial rule that created the modern office, the habitat of the white-collar worker or 'babu', and the modern professions such as law, medicine, engineering, and journalism. It also established the first modern universities, and the law colleges, the medical colleges and the engineering colleges to provide training and certification for entry into the middle class. There are important differences between India and the west, but in both cases the new middle class grew with the growth of a new occupational system and a new educational system.

A middle class, increasingly conscious of its identity and its new role in society, began to take shape in the second half of the nineteenth century. It was confined at first to the presidency capitals of Calcutta, Bombay, and Madras where the first universities as well as the first law and medical colleges were established. In India the emergence of a middle class constituted a bigger break with the past than in the west if only because so much of the initial impulse for its growth came from outside. The demands of life and work in the college, the office, and the professions were very different from those of the traditional institutions, whether among Hindus or among Muslims.

Despite its steady growth since the middle of the nineteenth century, for a hundred years or so the Indian middle class was a small island—or, rather, an archipelago—in the midst of a vast population made up of other classes and strata. Still, its significance in the life of the nation was not inconsiderable. It spearheaded the nationalist movement, and the members of the Constituent Assembly were overwhelmingly from it. It gave shape to and was in turn shaped by the modern institutions of Indian society such as universities, laboratories, libraries, newspapers, hospitals, banks, municipalities, and political parties.

Many of the social restrictions through which the traditional hierarchy was maintained and reproduced are inconsistent with the functional requirements of the kinds of modern institutions to which I have just referred. The whole idiom of purity and pollution, which was the cement as it were of the old social hierarchy, is antithetical to middle-class modes of life and work. It is impossible to organize work in a modern office in conformity with that idiom. Social exclusion on grounds of ritual defilement, if practised consistently, will bring the work of any modern institution—a bank, a laboratory, or a law court—to a standstill. Adjustments and compromises can no doubt be made, but not beyond a point.

As upper-caste Indians entered middle-class occupations, they found the rules by which their forefathers had been governed more and more anachronistic. It is not that people suddenly discovered that the old rules were socially unjust; it is likely that they first found them irksome and then decided that they were unjust. The rules of purity and pollution were enormously important in upholding the traditional hierarchy; when those rules became discredited, the traditional hierarchy could not remain intact. To be sure, invidious social distinctions based on caste and gender are still widely observed; but they no longer have the legitimacy they enjoyed in the past.

The Indian middle class has grown steadily in size in the last fifty years. Although still a minority in the population, it is no longer a miniscule minority. Middle-class occupations have grown and become differentiated. In the nineteenth century these occupations were virtually a monopoly of the upper castes and of men. This has changed substantially. Members of virtually every caste may be found in middle-class occupations and more and more women now work in offices, banks, law courts, hospitals and newspapers in a variety of non-manual occupations. There still are more upper-caste men than lower-caste women in these occupations, but the middle-class working milieu is no longer dominated by traditional considerations of hierarchy.

The continued presence of invidious social distinctions should not lead us to lose sight of the changes taking place in Indian society as a whole. The changes are not all in the same direction and the evidence is not uniform, but the long-term trend has been towards the weakening of hierarchical inequality. I will conclude this section with two examples, one relating to caste and the other to gender. Both are consequences of the weakening of the restrictions of purity and pollution.

The practice of untouchability in its traditional form has declined significantly even though it has not disappeared. Restrictions on movement and on entry into superior occupations have declined and in some places disappeared (Jodhka 2000). What is more important is that Scheduled Caste students as well as teachers are now entering mixed-caste schools in increasing numbers even in the rural areas, and in some parts of the country the practice of untouchability has virtually disappeared from the village school (Shah 2000). This is not to say that the lot of the Scheduled Castes has improved in every respect. There are recurrent outbursts of violence against them. But it is a change when the pervasive practice of untouchability is replaced by the sporadic practice of atrocities (Béteille 2000b).

The position of women is also changing although the change is more visible at the upper than at the lower levels of society. More and more women are entering schools, colleges, and universities, and there are increasing numbers of them in clerical, administrative, and professional employment. There has been a secular trend of increase in the age at marriage for women, and this trend is most conspicuous among the upper castes where pre-puberty marriage was the norm in the past. The change has been driven in no small measure by the compulsions of middle-class life among which the education and employment of women have begun to figure prominently.

The rise and consolidation of the middle class, which is accompanied by the decline of hierarchical inequality, does not bring inequality itself to an end. The middle class brings in its wake its own forms of inequality which are distinct from those characteristic of societies based on caste and estate. Such inequalities have arisen wherever modern societies based on new legal, political, and economic arrangements have displaced the hierarchical societies of the past, and one cannot seriously expect India to be an exception to the general rule. I have described the new type of inequality which accompanies the modernization process as competitive inequality. It is important to keep the analytical distinction between the two clearly in mind, particularly in the case of India where they not only coexist but are closely intertwined.

I shall dwell mainly on the middle class where competition is seen most clearly at work although its operation extends to other classes and strata as well. Because the inequalities due to education, occupation, and income are mixed up with those due to caste and gender, we often fail to notice what is new and what is old in the inequalities that prevail in Indian society today.

The Indian middle class has received wide public attention in the last ten years largely as a result of the shifts introduced into economic policy since 1991. Certainly, the push towards economic liberalization has been conducive to the growth of a certain section of the middle class, just as earlier on the promotion of development planning, the public sector, and the socialistic pattern of society had been conducive to the growth of a somewhat different section of it. In modern India, the middle class has benefited by the growth of the public as well as the private sector.

It is difficult to give a clear estimate of the size of the middle class partly because it is difficult to give an exact definition of it. Estimates of its size range between 100 and 250 million persons. The Indian middle class today is not only very large, it is also highly differentiated internally. It is differentiated, firstly, in terms of language, religion, and caste, and, secondly, in terms of education, occupation, and income. It is unique not so much on account of any peculiarity of the Indian occupational or educational system, but because of the peculiar way in which class is interwoven with caste and community in contemporary India. I will deal in this section mainly with those features of the Indian middle class that are common to middle classes in all modern societies, ignoring for the present the peculiarities that arise from its being embedded in a distinctive structure of castes and communities.

In the earlier sociological literature a distinction was made between the 'old middle class' consisting of own-account workers in agriculture, crafts, and services, and the 'new middle class' made up mainly of salaried, non-manual employees (Mills 1951). The emphasis here will be on education and occupation, and the core of the new middle class in my conception consists of persons in non-manual occupations, both employees and self-employed, with some formal education. A more comprehensive definition of the middle class will have to include persons with small businesses which they operate either as own account workers or as employers; here too, some formal education and non-manual work are what count.

At the time of independence the distinction between the middle class and the class of manual workers was clear. It was not just an economic distinction but also a social one; it would not be too much to say that in the first half of the twentieth century, the two classes inhabited different social worlds even in the industrially-advanced countries, not to speak of India. This has changed to a considerable extent. Technological changes have made the distinction between manual and non-manual work more difficult to maintain. The income gap between skilled manual workers in the organized sector and subordinate non-manual staff has been reduced and sometimes even reversed. Levels of literacy and education have risen steadily among manual workers. The public sector has created a labour aristocracy whose members have adopted many elements of middle-class culture. And white-collar trade unionism has reduced the gap between manual and non-manual employees from the other end. A full discussion of competitive inequality has to take into account the entire range of modern occupations, manual as well as non-manual, but this is beyond the purview of the present exercise.

Modern occupations, whether in the office, the bank, the hospital, the factory, or the workshop, are highly differentiated. This differentiation has been a continuous process, although it has probably been speeded up by the economic changes of the last ten years. Further, it is a worldwide phenomenon, not confined to India, although, as one might expect, it takes different forms under different demographic, economic, and cultural conditions.

It is not that occupational differentiation was absent in pre-capitalist, pre-industrial, or pre-modern societies. Indeed, under the caste system the differentiation of crafts and services was carried further in India than perhaps in any other pre-modern society. But the modern occupational system is enormously more complex than any that has existed in the past. Moreover, occupational differentiation in modern societies is dynamic and not static as in pre-modern ones. In the past new occupations emerged slowly and only over long stretches of time; now they come into being every decade, if not every year. Occupational differentiation in the modern world is driven by two powerful forces: technological innovation and market expansion.

In an economic order in which technological innovation is slow and limited, it is an advantage for occupational skills to be transmitted within the family, from father to son. Occupational specialization then becomes a matter of family and lineage. This principle was used to advantage in the Indian caste system. In course of time family and caste rather than occupation became the basis of social identity. Thus a Kumhar remained a Kumhar even if he practised agriculture and not pottery; likewise a Lohar, a Teli, or a Chamar. But passing occupations down from father to son does not remain an advantage when technological innovation makes occupational skills obsolete from one generation to the next. The detachment of occupational identity from family identity is a source of major social change even though the detachment is rarely complete in any society, leave alone Indian society.

I have given one indication of the dynamic nature of modern occupational systems by referring to the shifting boundaries between manual and non-manual occupations. To say that the distinction between

manual and non-manual occupations is becoming blurred is not to suggest that the process of occupational differentiation is being reversed.
On the contrary, both manual and non-manual occupations are becoming differentiated, and this two-fold differentiation produces a grey area
in which the old distinctions no longer apply. The dynamic nature of
occupational differentiation in modern societies is such that old distinctions are continuously replaced by new ones.

Occupational differentiation is accompanied by occupational ranking. Most students of social stratification in western countries give the
two a central place in their studies, and they are also acquiring increasing importance in India. This is not to say that one's social identity or
one's social rank is in any society determined solely by occupation.
Inherited wealth counts independently of occupation, and it is important in most countries, including India, where the ownership, control,
and use of land are important. Gender is important everywhere as a
basis of social identity and social rank. Caste is important in India just
as race is important in the United States. But occupation (together with
education) has steadily gained ground as a basis of social status in India
in the last hundred years.

Occupation was closely associated with education in the emergence
of a new middle class in India in the second half of the nineteenth
century. For nearly a hundred years, formal education, including some
knowledge of the English language, was virtually a monopoly of the
middle class. This has changed in the last fifty years and many manual
workers, particularly in the organized sector, have had varying amounts
of schooling. But this does not mean that education has ceased to be a
basis of differentiation and ranking. Even in countries like the United
States, Britain, and France, where elementary education is universal,
there are vast differences in the amount and type of schooling available
to members of different sections of society.

Historically, the change from hierarchical to competitive inequality
may be seen most clearly in France, particularly in the new occupational
and educational systems that emerged in the wake of the French revolution. At that time—and later—many saw it as a change from hierarchy
to equality, but that was an illusion. The illusion was in a sense natural.
Till that time people had had experience of only one kind of inequality,
i.e. hierarchical inequality. When the hierarchical order of estates was
being dismantled, it was natural for people to believe that inequality
itself was being laid to rest. A similar illusion was repeated in twentieth-
century Russia when the Bolshevik revolution abolished—though, as it

turns out, only temporarily—inequality based on the private ownership of property.

It seemed a great advance to turn to competition in place of birth and patronage, but competition did not lead to full equality in France or anywhere else. At first the competition was not fully open even in a formal sense. Throughout the nineteenth century women were excluded form competition for places in the *grandes écoles* and the *grands corps*: careers open to talent meant careers for men only. Sons of professional parents did better in the open national competition than sons of peasants and workers, and this is true even today. Still, the opportunities of success through competition opened up new possibilities for talented individuals from even the most disadvantaged sections of society. There was reproduction of inequality but there was also individual mobility.

Formal restrictions on open competition in the educational and occupational systems were progressively removed in the twentieth century. Now women as well as members of disadvantaged races, castes, and communities can compete, and sometimes do compete successfully, for the highest places in those systems. This is a worldwide trend, and from present indications also an irreversible one. But even if all formal restrictions are removed, and the competition made not only free but also fair, some are bound to do well and others badly. Free and fair competition can at best promote social mobility, it cannot eliminate inequality. A competitive system creates its own distinctive forms of inequality which can sometimes be more extreme than in a hierarchical system.

In early nineteenth-century Europe, with memories of the *ancien régime* still fresh in people's minds, the idea of careers open to talent or of reward according to merit must have appeared attractive to those who sought equality. Two hundred years later, when those memories have faded or receded into the background, it does not appear equally attractive. As the contradictions of the meritarian principle become more and more apparent, that principle no longer appears as a panacea for egalitarians. Indeed, for many egalitarians in the west, meritocracy has come to stand not for equality but its opposite (Young 1961; Arrow et al. 2000; see also Appendix II).

In India the memory of the traditional hierarchy is by no means distant or remote. The inequalities of caste, though altered in many respects, are an important part of the present reality. At the same time, new inequalities based on competition in education and employment have also emerged and become widespread. It is difficult to determine how far the two kinds of inequality reinforce each other and how far they cut across.

Should Indians worry about the threat of meritocracy as egalitarians in the west started to do from the 1950s onwards? Or should they promote the principle of merit at the expense of birth and patronage, even if that leads to the creation of a new type of inequality? It is good for sensitive Indians to be concerned about the negative consequences of untempered competition, whether in education or in employment. But it is difficult to see how the role of family, caste, and community can be eliminated or even reduced without promoting free and, as far as possible, fair competition. It is a little unreasonable to wish merit to be rewarded and also to object that the rewards are unequally distributed.

In India there is perhaps less objection to the meritarian principle as such than to the fact that it does not work under Indian conditions where free and fair competition is continually subverted by the demands of kinship, caste, and community. After pointing to the pervasive role of caste in appointments and promotions in the then Mysore state, Srinivas had wistfully concluded some forty years ago: 'No "meritocracy" is going to emerge in this situation' (Srinivas 1962: 89). It is clear that his own sympathy lay with meritocracy rather than caste and community. For Srinivas, as for many intellectuals of his generation, the real challenge in India was to establish equality of opportunity against the resistance of the traditional hierarchical order. If that brought some inequality of result in its train, they were prepared to accept it.

As I have pointed out, the Indian middle class has grown in size. Many of its members have tasted the sweets of success in competition, whether in education or in employment, and their number is increasing. They do not all have the same mistrustful attitude towards meritocracy that liberal intellectuals in the west have developed and some of their Indian counterparts are now developing. We do not have any reliable estimates of rates of individual mobility in the occupational system, either within the middle class or between the working and the middle classes. My guess is that such mobility is not inconsiderable, and it is of course very different from the mobility among castes that Srinivas discussed under the rubric of Sanskritization (Srinivas 1966: 1–45).

It is not as if, in the transition from one type of society to another, everyone prefers the uncertainty of competition to the relative certainty of a stable hierarchical order. Even those in middling positions might prefer the security of a familiar way of life to the risks attendant on seeking a better fortune. Some find the very idea of competition, particularly where it involves competition with one's social inferiors, unappealing. When in the middle of the nineteenth century the Trevleyan-Northcote reform of the civil service replaced recruitment through patronage by recruitment through examinations, not everyone was happy. The old guard in the civil service referred to the new recruits disdainfully as the 'competition wallahs' (Trevelyan 1964). The competition wallahs prevailed in the end, and Indians were soon able to join the 'heaven born' corps of the ICS.

Not all those who seek or achieve success in competition act strictly according to the rules of the competition without using the ties of kinship and caste covertly or even overtly. Upwardly-mobile individuals do not always count the cost to others or to society of their drive for success. The fact that the problem is endemic in contemporary India does not mean that 'snobbery and jobbery' have disappeared from societies with a longer experience of competition in education and employment. Nor will it be true to say that birth and patronage always prevail over ability and aptitude when it comes to social placement in contemporary India. It is almost certain that ability and aptitude play a larger part today than fifty years ago.

A system of competitive inequality which acknowledges the principle of equality of opportunity is not a hierarchical system; it is a stratified system. Every modern society is a stratified society; in moving out of a hierarchical order, we exchange hierarchy not for equality but for stratification. It is difficult not only to create but even to imagine a complex and dynamic society in which all social positions will enjoy equal esteem and command equal authority. The very idea of equality of opportunity would lose its meaning in such a society.

Although all modern societies are stratified, they are not all stratified in the same way or to the same extent. Firstly, societies differ in the distance between the top and the bottom ranks, and in the number of ranks in between. This is true not only of society as a whole but also of its major associations, institutions, and organizations. Secondly, societies differ in the extent to which individuals are able to move between inferior and superior positions. Although social mobility presupposes social stratification, there is no simple, one-to-one relationship between the two. Societies, or social institutions that have many and widely-separated ranks may also have high rates of individual mobility.

As Srinivas foresaw forty years ago, a casteless and classless society has not come into being and does not appear to be within sight. A casteless society is certainly possible as such societies exist in other countries, although, again as Srinivas saw more clearly than most, caste was given a new lease of life by some of the very policies designed to take the sting out of it. As for a classless society, much depends on how we define our terms, for, as Raymond Aron has put it, 'If you define classes with reference to private ownership of the means of production, nothing is easier than to make the former vanish by hoping to suppress the latter' (Aron 1964: 61, my translation). Forty years ago, many Indian intellectuals believed that a classless society, or something very close to it, had been created first in the Soviet Union under Stalin and then in China under Mao. Be that as it may, both caste and stratification on the basis of education, occupation, and income exist as important features of the Indian social reality.

Can social policy do nothing to bring the social reality a little closer to the ideals of equality written into the Constitution? I believe that social policy can do a little but not a very great deal. The little that it can do can easily be jeopardized by grandiose schemes of social transformation that miss the target or backfire. If the wisdom of sociology teaches us anything, it is that social policies have unintended consequences. In the past fifty years we have not been sufficiently watchful of the unintended consequences of social policies and learnt little from our experience with social policies that did not work.

Social policy cannot be effective if it fails or refuses to distinguish between different types of inequality and their distinctive sources of legitimacy. Social stratification based on education and occupation is not only different in its operation from hierarchical inequality based on caste and gender, its legitimacy is derived from a different source. It is both necessary and desirable to eliminate from public institutions the inequalities due to caste and gender, and devising policies to that effect will be well worth the effort; but to attempt to eliminate all forms of inequality from them will be an exercise in futility.

Inequalities due to education, occupation, and income cannot be removed, but they can be regulated. Regulating the inequalities of income may be difficult, but it is not beyond the reach of economic policy. Similarly, a great deal may be done to expand educational opportunities at all levels, although it will be difficult to provide education of the same quality to all members of society and impossible to ensure that they all achieve equal success in their educational careers. Again, while no social policy can eliminate the social ranking of occupations, it should be possible to provide a minimum of security and dignity to all positions, including the lowliest, within the occupational system. But this is not an exercise in policy analysis, leave alone policy prescription; all I have tried to do is to indicate certain distinctions that must be kept in mind while constructing a framework for social policy.

10

Equality and Universality

If we divide public intellectuals in India into those who are egalitarians and those who are not, the egalitarians will vastly outnumber the others. To be sure there are able, well-placed, and successful persons who will say in private that equality goes against nature since the natural talents of individuals are highly unequal; I have shown elsewhere that the argument about natural inequality is generally confused and on the whole mistaken (Béteille 1987a: 7–32). At the same time, whatever the believers in natural inequality may think or say in private, in public they will go along with the general argument in favour of equality or else keep their counsel.

When they speak in public, legislators, judges, vice-chancellors, editors, and the multitude of social activists can be counted upon to speak strongly if not eloquently in support of equality. There is something paradoxical in this because the practice of inequality is widespread if not all-pervasive in Indian society where it may be encountered in all sectors and at all levels. It is difficult to believe that public intellectuals are themselves entirely free from practices that are so widespread in their own society. In my limited experience, where it concerns the equal treatment of others, the conduct of legislators, judges, vice-chancellors, editors, and even social activists is scarcely different from the conduct of other Indians. We are servile towards those deemed to be socially superior and expect servility from those deemed to be socially inferior; yet in public we never tire of advocating equality.

Many lend their voice in support of equality because they feel that that is in keeping with the spirit of the age. In our time the support of equality does not call for any special justification; it is the opposition to it that does so. Democrats, socialists, secularists, nationalists, and humanists, however much they may differ on other matters, all tend to base their respective cases on the premise of equality. In the event, it is not surprising that equality has come to mean all things to all persons. It sometimes happens, as it did in the days of the Great Mandal Agitation, that persons standing at opposite extremes argue with the same intensity that their objective is to secure greater equality.

I believe I have said enough to indicate that I do not count myself among the egalitarians. This does not mean that I support every form of inequality as a desirable or a necessary condition of existence. It also does not mean that I am opposed to equality as being undesirable or unattainable. But it does mean that my support of equality is not unconditional. The pursuit of equality may be desirable or even necessary, but not in all circumstances or at any cost.

The true egalitarian recognizes that our social practice is permeated by inequality, but he maintains that it can and should be brought in line with the principle of equality: the fact that our practice falls short of our ideal cannot be an argument for not having the ideal. Egalitarians will readily concede that there are other values—other ends of life—such as liberty, amity, concord, and so on, but maintain that those values can be harmonized with equality, or else they have to be subordinated to it. Many ingenious arguments have been made about the harmony between equality and liberty, or between equality and efficiency, but I have not found them very convincing and therefore I do not view myself as an egalitarian.

Some authorities believe that different social values can be fully harmonized and others that they cannot. Since I incline towards the second point of view, I would like to quote Sir Isaiah Berlin's classic statement of it:

Equality is one value among many: the degree to which it is compatible with other ends depends on the concrete situation, and cannot be deduced from general laws of any kind; it is neither more or less rational than any other ultimate principle; indeed it is difficult to see what is meant by considering it either rational or non-rational (Berlin 1978: 96).

Berlin was by no means an opponent of equality but he believed that there were other ends that were just as compelling and that sometimes collided with it.

It is not simply that the demands of equality are difficult to harmonize with other cherished values such as liberty or amity. Those demands are themselves diverse and not always easy to reconcile with each other. These are what I call the antinomies of equality (Chapter 8).

If our everyday practice carries so many marks of inequality, part of the reason lies in the contradictions, oppositions, and tensions inherent in the social ideal of equality itself.

Isaiah Berlin was right to point out that the choice of an ultimate end or the primacy assigned to one of those ends over the others cannot, and indeed need not, be justified by rational argument. Today the pursuit of equality has become its own justification. Yet this was not always so, certainly not in our society. Those who wrote the Constitution of India with its many guarantees of equality believed that they were making a break with the past; certainly, Dr Ambedkar, who piloted the document through the Constituent Assembly, did so.

It is this sense of a break with the past that gives its peculiar urgency to the modern Indian's quest for equality. Indian society is not unique in undergoing a break with its hierarchical past. The break with hierarchy in the direction of equality was made in the west in the eighteenth and nineteenth centuries. It is this that Alexis de Tocqueville described as the passage from aristocratic to democratic society although no one will claim that even in the west the passage has been completed. India's adoption of equality in place of hierarchy on the attainment of independence signalled its entry into the modern world.

The passage from hierarchy to equality marked by the Constitution of India appears more dramatic in this country than in the west for two important reasons. Firstly, it is being compressed within a much shorter span of time. Secondly, the social hierarchy in India was more comprehensive and more deep-rooted than in the west or in any other society. The hierarchical conception of society, if not the social hierarchy itself, had a continuity and a legitimacy that is unparalleled in human history. Attempts to question the hierarchy were no doubt made from time to time in the ancient as well as medieval periods, but no sooner did they acquire an organized form than they were co-opted into the system.

The two most pervasive forms of inequality from ancient to modern times were those based on caste and on gender (Sivaramayya 1984). These inequalities which were accepted as a part of the natural scheme of things both appear odious to modern eyes. There was a consensus in the Constituent Assembly to deprive them of the legitimacy they had enjoyed since time immemorial. Many spoke in praise of the Indian tradition but none sought to defend the traditional social hierarchy. Some sought to deny the importance of hierarchy in the past and to argue that true democracy had existed for centuries in India in the form of village republics; they were given short shrift by Dr Ambedkar.

The adoption of a Constitution with plenary provisions did not change everything. Whereas the law today is all for equality, the bias of custom supports many inequalities in the relations between castes and between men and women. Where legislation is completely out of tune with the habits of the heart, its very purpose tends to be defeated. In the last fifty years too much has been attempted through legislative enactments many of which have come to grief on the shoals of established habits and practices.

All this is not to say that only the law has changed and custom has stood still. There is no society in which custom remains at a complete standstill, but changes in custom occur slowly through subterranean movements that are difficult to understand or control. If we look at Europe over the last two to three hundred years we will find innumerable changes in the customs regulating the relations between classes and between men and women; in some matters custom even moved ahead of legislation. In India too custom has changed in the last hundred and fifty years although the change has been of a highly uneven nature. Though many inequalities remain, the social hierarchy today is no longer what it was in the middle of the nineteenth century.

Law and custom have both changed in regard to caste as well as gender. This change is most conspicuous among the rapidly expanding middle classes particularly in the metropolitan cities. Among educated persons in professional, administrative, and managerial occupations many elements in the treatment of women by men or of inferior by superior castes that were a part of everyday life in the past would now be condemned as reprehensible. In public institutions such as universities, hospitals, and banks those who are deemed to be socially inferior no longer have to bear the kinds of social indignities that were a part of their common lot in the past.

Caste practices changed substantially in the course of the twentieth century. Caste movements, of which there has been a great proliferation, have in many cases strengthened caste identity but they have also questioned and undermined the legitimacy of caste hierarchy. The fact that castes have begun to operate, along with other communities of birth, as ethnic groups in the political arena itself signifies a change in the traditional hierarchical order.

Interactions between castes and caste identities themselves were in the past expressed largely through the ritual idiom of purity and pollution. Customs relating to purity and pollution have weakened in all parts of the country, in rural as well as urban areas, and in all classes and communities. Social exclusion on the basis of caste is still practiced but less extensively and less rigorously than in the past, and less among the urban middle classes than among the rural peasantry. Marriages are still arranged largely within the caste if not the subcaste but the rules of commensality have broken down substantially.

The practice of untouchability, which carried the idea of pollution to its furthest limit, has undoubtedly declined. This has happened irrespective of changes in the material conditions of the Scheduled Castes. Even now there are cases where members of these castes are made to undertake defiling tasks against their will because that was the custom in the past, but such cases are becoming less and less common. Residential segregation is less strictly imposed and interdining between members of 'clean' and 'unclean' castes is not uncommon even in the villages. Schools have now become open to members of the Scheduled Castes as both pupils and teachers, and the school is one public arena where even in the villages untouchability is not generally practiced. However, it must also be noted that, while the practice of untouchability has definitely declined, atrocities against the Scheduled Castes appear to have increased (Béteille 2000b).

Changes are also taking place in the position of women although such changes are difficult to measure or evaluate. There have been changes in the legal position of women, and 'the perpetual tutelage of women' which marked the traditional law of the Hindus has been eased, although custom has not moved as far as the law demands. Again, here custom has changed the most in the middle and the upper middle classes where education and professional employment have given women a voice they did not have before.

Inter-caste marriages do take place although they are still uncommon. Perhaps the most striking change in society as a whole is the secular trend of increase in the age at marriage for women. The obsessive concern for the purity of women led to early marriage; and the ideal of pre-puberty marriage reinforced the perpetual tutelage of women. This concern has declined substantially and it is noteworthy that the decline has gone further among the upper strata of society where until a hundred years ago the rules relating to the purity of women were the most zealously observed.

The decline of traditional hierarchical values and of the ritual idiom of purity and pollution in which those values were expressed has been accompanied by the rise and growth of a new middle class. This class is steadily increasing in size, and its social and political influence exceeds its numerical strength. Recruitment to it is through education and employment and not, as in the case of caste, by birth. The middle class has a distinct culture which cannot easily accommodate the segregation of men because their ancestors performed defiling tasks or of women because they are subject to monthly periods. The growth of the middle class will not eliminate caste but it will substantially alter its character and significance.

There can be little doubt about the many changes that have taken place in Indian society from the middle of the nineteenth century to the present. It is no longer a hierarchical society in the strict sense of the term (Dumont 1966; Béteille 1987a: 33–53), although large inequalities still remain. On the plane of legal and political values, hierarchy has been replaced by equality. At the same time, the situation is different on the plane of actual social existence: there one form of inequality based on caste and gender is yielding to another form of it based on education, occupation, and income.

It is essential to underline the distinction between the two forms of inequality because they are very different in their operation and consequence. Caste and gender are fixed at birth and where inequalities are governed mainly by them—or by race—the individual has little or no prospect of attaining a better social position through his or her own effort. Where the individual's standing on the social ladder is governed mainly by education and occupation, advancement through individual effort is always possible, although the scope of such advancement should not be exaggerated. In the first kind of society, which may be designated as hierarchical, individual mobility is disallowed or at least disapproved; in the second kind, which may be called egalitarian, individual mobility, though not always easy, is socially approved.

Indian society is changing from the hierarchical to the egalitarian kind although the change is highly uneven. It is most conspicuous on the constitutional and legal plane where hierarchical norms have been replaced by egalitarian ones. But whereas the law has changed in favour of equality, custom is still largely biased towards hierarchy. Caste bias and gender bias strongly affect the life chances of the individual and restrict the scope of individual mobility. At the same time, the functional requirements of the new educational and occupational systems make the practice of caste discrimination and gender discrimination increasingly anachronistic.

We can understand better the transition that has been taking place in India by viewing it in a comparative perspective. A similar transition took place in the west from the end of the eighteenth century onwards. Because it took place over a much longer stretch of time, we can see in it, in slow motion as it were, some of the processes that are unfolding in India at the present time.

The transition in the west was recorded in the first half of the nineteenth century by Alexis de Tocqueville (1956). The past was represented for him by France during the *ancien régime* and the future by the United States. He believed that the movement from hierarchy to equality—or from aristocratic to democratic society—was providential and irreversible, and that the United States was showing to the rest of the world, or at least the rest of the western world, only the image of its own future.

Born into an aristocratic family, Tocqueville had a fine sense of the inner workings of aristocratic society—its manners, attitudes, and sentiments, its deeply-rooted habits of the heart. In America he encountered a social imagination that was quite different from the aristocratic imagination. There not only was the law in favour of equality but the bias of custom was also in its favour. Tocqueville was struck by the extent to which, barring race and gender, human beings treated each other on an equal footing in public, irrespective of wealth and position. The situation in France was more ambiguous. Whereas the law had changed radically in favour of equality, the old habits of the heart rooted in the aristocratic imagination were still pervasive. But the direction of change was clear: equality in social interchange was to replace disdain on one side and servility on the other.

His fascination with changes in law, custom, and manners led Tocqueville to believe that equality was advancing on every front. But it was not. He had a sharp eye for the kinds of inequality that were characteristic of a society of estates and those certainly were in decline. But a new economic and social order was emerging with its own inequalities whose enormous significance largely escaped Tocqueville. Throughout the nineteenth century the advance of legal equality was accompanied by an increase and not a decrease in the inequality of income.

From the present point of view the most momentous changes throughout the nineteenth century were taking place not in the structure of property but in the occupational system and the educational system closely related to it. In the last two hundred years there has been a continuous differentiation of occupations in the industrially advanced societies. In the twentieth century this differentiation followed broadly the same pattern in the capitalist and the socialist societies, and it may now be seen at work in countries like India as well. Increasingly one's occupation has become the basis of one's social identity, although even in the world's most advanced economy, the United States, race and gender are also of great significance as is caste in India.

The modern occupational system is a highly differentiated one in which the individual occupations run into tens of thousands. The classification and ranking of occupations is a major field of investigation among students of social stratification (Goldthorpe and Hope 1974). There is no 'official' or formal hierarchy of occupations as there was of *varnas* in India or of estates in Europe. 'Officially' all occupations are of equal utility and worth. But in fact all occupations are not equally esteemed nor do they all command equal authority or enjoy equal remuneration. The social ranking of occupations is determined through opinion surveys that involve complex technical procedures. These procedures have been developed and applied in Britain and the United States over the last fifty years, but very little advance has been made in this regard in India.

In all modern societies occupations are socially ranked as superior and inferior even where the social ranking of occupations is contrary to the official ideology. This is very well illustrated by the case of the Soviet Union (and other socialist societies) in the last three quarters of the twentieth century. There labour, and in particular manual labour as the creator of all values, was assigned pre-eminence in the Leninist ideology; nevertheless, non-manual workers or the intelligentsia, and in particular professionals such as scientists, engineers, and doctors enjoyed much higher status than manual workers. In India, middle class ideologues who argue that all occupations are of equal worth and dignity nevertheless choose occupations of only a particular kind as the preferred careers for their children.

The fact that occupations are unequally ranked does not mean that there is no disagreement about the ranking of particular occupations among members of the same society. Such disagreement is inevitable for two reasons. Firstly, new occupations are continuously emerging and displacing old ones; and secondly, the number of occupations has grown so very large that it is impossible for the average member of society to even know the names of more than a small proportion of them. But while there may be disagreement over adjacent occupations, such as typist and telephone operator, there will be general agreement that occupations like judge, ambassador, or scientist are superior to others such as porter, cleaner, or agricultural labourer.

There is a close but complex relationship between occupation and education in all modern societies. In the last two hundred years education has become institutionalized to an extent unknown in human history; more persons of both sexes spend more time, both absolutely and relatively, in school, college, university, and other specialized institutions of education and training than they ever did in the past. The expansion and institutionalization of education has been closely linked with the emergence and growth of the new occupational system. Education provides not only the skills but also the credentials necessary for entry into certain occupations, and one's educational career often foreshadows one's occupational career.

The expansion of education leads to the creation of new opportunities although not all members of society can benefit from those opportunities or benefit from them to the same extent, hence education can also be a source of inequality. This point hardly needs emphasis in a country like India where even elementary education, not to speak of higher education, is outside the reach of large masses of the population. Even in those countries where elementary education has become universal, not everyone can expect to go to the same kind of institution for secondary or higher education. Hence there are clear and distinct inequalities of educational attainment even in countries like Britain, France, and the United States, and these have important implications for the life chances of individuals.

Detailed empirical studies have shown that in Britain the gap in educational attainment between the working class and the service class consisting of professionals, administrators, and managers has not been significantly reduced in the last fifty years despite the substantial expansion of education brought about by the welfare state during that period (Goldthorpe 1996). At the same time, the gap in education between girls and boys has been reduced in each of the major social classes. It will bear repeating that education contributes to social mobility as well as the reproduction of inequality, paradoxical as it may sound.

The way in which high quality education contributes to a successful career may be seen most clearly at the top of the occupational pyramid in France. There a set of elite schools known as the *grandes écoles*, such as the École Polytechnique and the École Normale Supérieure is tightly linked to a set of elite services known as the *grands corps*, such as the Inspection des Finances, the Corps des Mines and the Conseil d'Etat: 'A successful academic career in one of the top grandes écoles leads to a career in one of the grands corps, which then facilitates the choice of a number of other possible careers within and outside state service' (Suleiman 1978: 11). It is with reference to this combination of *grandes écoles* and *grands corps* that Pierre Bourdieu (1996) has spoken of a state nobility.

The French administrative system is reputed to be one of the most efficient in the world and also one of the most elitist. It owes a great deal to the foresight of Napoleon who shaped the *grandes écoles* to give effect to his objective of 'careers open to talent'. Napoleon wanted to turn his back on the social hierarchies of the *ancien régime* and he was determined to select the best in the land through open national competition. That is how the *grandes écoles* still select their entrants. But equality of opportunity means at best that there is equality *before* the competition, not *after* it. Napoleon is not likely to have been disheartened by the discovery that the consequence of his system was a meritocracy.

Equality of opportunity or 'careers open to talent' has promoted equality in one sense but not in every sense. Even as a formal principle, its application was limited in the nineteenth century. It did not apply to women in France where the *concours general* (or general competition) for admission to the *grandes écoles* was open only to men. In the United States race was an additional impediment to free and open competition throughout the nineteenth century and well into the twentieth. But in course of time the impediments of gender and race came to be formally removed as did those of caste.

Despite the removal of formal impediments such as those of race, caste, and gender, the competition for superior positions in both the educational and the occupational systems favours some segments of society over others. Children from families that are well endowed with material, cultural, and social capital will generally do better than others in any system of free and open competition although there will always be openings for the others if they are specially gifted or are favoured by luck. All of this is disturbing to the true egalitarian.

Even a brief reflection on the complex institutional structure of modern societies will show that, the spirit of the age notwithstanding, inequalities of esteem, authority, and income are an integral and perhaps inescapable part of their operation. One cannot think of a scientific profession in which all scientists will enjoy equal esteem or a hospital in which all functionaries will exercise equal authority.

While it is impossible to eliminate inequalities from modern societies which favour free competition and individual achievement, it should be possible to regulate them. Indeed an important concern of social policy in the welfare state has been with the regulation of inequality through progressive taxation and through social security and various other measures of social welfare. They seek not only to keep within limits the distance between the base and the apex of the social pyramid but also to stimulate social mobility. At the same time, social mobility is meaningful only in a society in which social positions are graded in terms of income, esteem, and authority.

It is impossible to root out inequality from society, particularly a dynamic modern society where inequality is both a product of change and a stimulus for it. But is it impossible to eliminate or at least to reduce substantially and continuously poverty, hunger, homelessness, illiteracy and ill-health? It is not possible to eliminate and sometimes even to reduce significantly inequalities of income; but it should be possible to substantially reduce if not to eliminate poverty. It is not possible to ensure equal attainments or even equal facilities in higher education for all; but it should be possible to make elementary education universally available to all. It is not possible to provide every kind of medical treatment on an equal basis for all members of society; but it should be possible to make elementary health care universally available to all.

The observations made above lead us to draw a distinction between equality and universality. This is an important distinction theoretically as well as in matters of policy. Because the idea of equality has acquired such a wide appeal in the contemporary world it tends to be overused. Its use in and out of context opens the way to confusion. When we want universal elementary education we should say that that is what we want instead of declaring that we want equal educational facilities for all.

When we want the elimination of poverty we should say that that is what we want instead of training our guns on economic inequality. A recent reviewer of a book entitled *Inequality Re-examined* has observed:

Now although Sen's official topic is inequality, his motivating interest is poverty, which appears, when it does, at the downward end of the spectrum of advantage, and which is a phenomenon distinct from inequality, since everyone might be equally poor, and since there is (at least) money inequality between millionaires and billionaires (Cohen 1993: 2156).

Attacking inequality and waving the flag of equality have acquired a certain intoxicating power at least in India.

Many modern writers on equality have taken Kant's injunction to 'treat each man as an end in himself and never as a means only' as the starting point of their discussion of the subject. But that is more a prescription for universality than for equality. To say that human beings should be treated as human beings—and not as objects—is to say very little about how authority or esteem or income should be distributed among the members of society. To adopt a distinction proposed by Dworkin (1984: 227), it asks at best for the treatment of human beings as equals, not their equal treatment.

The obligation to treat all men and women as human beings and not as objects has been acknowledged by most of the great religions, although it has not always found a very effective social expression. Even the Hindu Dharmashastra recognized the validity of *sadharanadharma* or *samanyadharma*, i.e. rules governing human beings as such as the substratum of *varnashramadharma* or rules varying according to social station. But in course of time what came to govern everyday life were largely the specific and not the universal codes of conduct.

The principle of universality appeals to the common humanity of all human beings. It reminds us that human beings are owed a certain consideration simply because they are human, because they are capable of suffering pain, loss, and separation and of experiencing and expressing affection, fellow-feeling, and loyalty. It does not mean that the national product, or even the benefits and burdens of society should be equally distributed among all its members without consideration of ability, aptitude, or need. It does not say that valued objects or activities should not be enjoyed by some unless they can also be enjoyed in the same measure by all. The principle of universality cannot wish out of existence the principle of scarcity (Hirsch 1977).

The sociologist will readily concede that social arrangements may be considered from more than one point of view. In a well-known essay on equality, the philosopher Bernard Williams has urged the case for considering them from the human point of view. He insists that the argument that all human beings should be considered from the human point of view is not trivial:

For it is certain that there are political and social arrangements that systematically neglect these characteristics in the case of some groups of men, while being fully aware of them in the case of others; that is to say, they treat certain men as though they did not possess these characteristics, and neglect moral claims that arise from these characteristics and which would be admitted to arise from them (Williams 1964: 112).

To say that all human beings—Blacks, untouchables, women, etc.—are human and have to be treated as such may not appear today to say very much; but it is not to say nothing.

When it was acknowledged in past times, the principle of universality often remained on the plane of moral sentiment. A major step forward is taken when it becomes the basis of a whole legal system.

It is in the modern legal system that we find the principle of universality most clearly acknowledged, although the language used is often the language of equality. When lawyers speak of 'equality before the law' or 'the equal protection of the laws' they have in mind certain rights, capacities, and immunities that should, at least in principle, be universally available to all, irrespective of race, caste, gender, or any other personal quality of body or mind. When, on the other hand, we speak of equality (or equalization) of income, we have in mind inequalities that can be measured and that are perhaps felt to be increasing when they ought to be decreasing. When people say that they are for equality, what they often mean is that they simply want certain basic things to be made universally available to all; but they sometimes also mean that they want every sort of inequality to be eliminated or at least reduced; and the two meanings tend to be frequently confused.

The clearest constitutional expression of the principle of universality is in the concept of citizenship. Citizenship is a modern concept, and a social order based on the rights—and obligations—of citizenship is very different from one based on the privileges and disabilities of estates or of castes. Today in India we are inclined to take citizenship for granted, ignoring its very recent adoption and its infirm social and political base. During the long period of colonial rule Indians were subjects rather than citizens, and before that citizenship in the modern sense could hardly have existed in a world in which discrimination on the basis of community, caste, and gender was the basis of the legal and political order.

An essential component of citizenship in India, as in all modern democracies, is universal adult franchise. The universalization of the franchise, which was spread over two centuries in the west, was achieved at one step with the adoption of the Constitution after independence. Universal adult franchise is not only the basis on which the national parliament and the state assemblies are constituted, it is also the basis for the constitution of all organs of local government, including the village panchayats. The novelty of this principle at the village level should not be lost to sight. It is sometimes said that panchayats are a part of the ancient democratic heritage of India. This is misleading because what was common in the past was the caste panchayat and not the village panchayat in its modern form, the village panchayat of the past being generally the panchayat of the dominant caste of the village.

The idea behind the universalization of the franchise is that each person is to count as one and no person is to count as more than one. This was certainly not the basis on which public affairs were conducted in the traditional Indian village. Even the principle of 'one man, one vote' would appear strange in a caste-based (or an estate-based) society, and the idea of an electoral system based on the equivalence of men and women would appear contrary to the natural scheme of things. The romantic image of village democracy created during the nationalist movement has very little basis in historical or sociological reality, and this was understood by none better than Dr B.R. Ambedkar who played such a significant part in the making of the Indian Constitution.

As a principle, universal citizenship was either absent or inoperative in the medieval world not only in India but also in the west. In France it asserted itself as a fundamental political principle with the revolution of 1789 although its beginnings may be traced back to the preceding century in Britain. In the west the idea of citizenship was no doubt well known in classical antiquity, particularly in Rome, which provided so many images and metaphors to the makers of the French Revolution. But it must not be forgotten that the Roman idea of citizenship was always and in principle one of limited and not universal citizenship from whose ambit large numbers of men, and women in general were excluded. And even that idea of limited citizenship was largely extinguished with the onset of the Middle Ages and the creation of a social order that was hierarchical in both practice and principle.

The idea of universal citizenship did not emerge fully formed in the west at the end of the eighteenth century. It has developed slowly and gradually in the course of the last couple of centuries, and no one will say that it has reached a final form as yet. But compared with other parts of the world, the realization of universality through the growth of citizenship has achieved impressive results in the west.

The quantitative and qualitative expansion of citizenship in Britain from the eighteenth to the middle of the twentieth century was examined in a seminal paper by T.H. Marshall. He traced this development primarily in the language of rights. 'Citizenship is a status bestowed on those who are full members of a community. All those who possess the status are equal with respect to the rights and duties with which the status is endowed' (Marshall 1977: 92). The content of citizenship was enriched by the addition of new rights from one century to the next: civil rights in the eighteenth century, political rights in the nineteenth and social rights in the twentieth century. Marshall saw some kind of culmination of this process in the creation of the welfare state which sought to provide all citizens with the basic amenities of civilized living.

In Marshall's view there has been a fundamental reconstitution of status in British society. Whereas in the past status was viewed primarily in terms of the hierarchy of estates, it has come increasingly to be viewed in terms of the entitlements of citizenship. But even the fullest expansion of the entitlements of citizenship does not and cannot lead to the elimination of the inequalities of class. As Marshall saw it, the rights of citizenship have a bias for equality which keeps in check the tendency towards inequality inherent in the market.

Certainly, the creation of new rights for all citizens contributes to the regulation if not the elimination of invidious social distinctions. This was the objective with which many rights were guaranteed to the citizen in the Constitution of India. A Bill has been prepared to make elementary education a fundamental right. Some time ago it was proposed to create a right to work for all members of society, and more recently a former Prime Minister of India has called for housing to be made a fundamental right.

International agencies too have begun to stress the need for protecting and promoting human rights with increasing urgency. Development itself, which in earlier decades was conceived somewhat narrowly in terms of economic policy, is coming to be defined in terms of rights. The United Nations has initiated a move to treat the right to development as a human right, i.e. a right that should be universally available to all human beings everywhere. This kind of international awareness creates a sense of urgency regarding the universalization of rights, particularly in countries where large sections of the population have for long remained disprivileged and disadvantaged.

At the same time, the mere multiplication of rights is not likely by itself to lead to either equality or universality. Such multiplication soon reaches the point of diminishing returns and then becomes counter-productive. The Constitution of India is a fragile instrument and its fragility has become increasingly apparent since 1975. It is likely to be weakened rather than strengthened by adding more and more rights that remain unenforced and are perhaps unenforceable. Development cannot be carried very far solely on the basis of rights, it also requires resources; and while the United Nations may be very strong on good intentions, its capacity to mobilize and distribute material resources is severely limited.

Universality cannot be made only a matter of right, it has also to be a matter of policy. It is not quite clear that the recent shift from the language of policy to the language of rights in the discourse on development is a step in the right direction. The Constitution of India makes a distinction between matters of right, which are mainly in Part III, and matters of policy, which are in Part IV. This is a wise distinction and to introduce confusion into it will be a disservice to our democratic political order. It is true that many policy directives have been ignored or treated half-heartedly if not casually by the executive government. But it will show little judgment to try to instill a sense of urgency into those directives by turning them into rights, particularly when it is almost certain that those rights will remain largely unenforced.

The attainment of universality on even a very limited scale requires not only the removal of disabilities but also the creation of abilities. Intelligent policy can contribute something to the creation of those abilities, but not without consideration of the resources available to a society. However compelling the demands of universality may be, they cannot disregard the constraints imposed by the scarcity of resources. The presumption that a poor country can create for all its members the same facilities that are universally available in a rich country cannot be a basis for sound policy. The rhetoric of equality among citizens and among nations should not become a drain on the unremitting effort required for formulating and carrying through realistic and sensible policies.

The neglect of elementary education has undoubtedly been the most costly failure of policy in the period since independence. India contains a very large proportion of the illiterate population of the world, despite its considerable material and intellectual resources. It is not that these problems were ever wholly forgotten by the policy makers: what was lacking was not the capacity to formulate the required policies but the will to carry them through. The resources allotted to elementary education were paltry, and even those paltry resources were wastefully used.

More than fifty years after the adoption of the Constitution the literacy rate now shows signs of picking up, even in the most backward regions of the country. If the proposal to make elementary education a fundamental right leads policy makers to put more resources into it and to ensure more effective utilization of those resources, it may well appear peevish to complain against the move. But one thing should be clear: even after elementary education has become universal, inequalities will remain in the quality of what is available to children from the different strata of society. Even at the level of elementary education, universality does not mean equality.

The universalization of elementary education will not lead automatically to the universalization of secondary education, and it certainly will not place higher education within the effective reach of all members of society. In the kind of society envisaged in the Constitution entry into elementary school should not be by competition; it should be open to *all*, irrespective of race, caste, gender, *and* merit or means. Entry into secondary school should also be without consideration of race, caste, and gender, but it is difficult to be categorical as to merit and means, particularly in a poor country. If there are more applicants than places—as may well happen in a poor country—some combination of merit and means will govern the process of selection. In publicly funded schools merit should be the criterion of selection where admission cannot be provided to all; but will it be reasonable to prohibit private schools in which parents who have the means will be able to secure education for their own children even when they are of average or somewhat less than average ability? Should we make it a condition that secondary education should not be available to any except on the basis of merit unless it can be made available to all on identically the same basis?

As we move from lower to higher levels, educational institutions become increasingly differentiated and specialized. Those who have better abilities and better means go to the better secondary schools which equip them better for the competition to take the limited places available in the institutions of higher learning. We cannot say that admission to institutions that provide education for professions such as medicine, engineering, and management should be open to all without consideration of merit or means because no state has the resources to sustain such a policy. Here what can be offered at best is equality of opportunity for those already qualified for admission, and this leads inevitably to inequality of outcome.

I have tried to show with the example of education the limits to which universality can be taken and beyond which inequalities are bound to come into play. These limits are not the same for all societies, being dependent on the resources available to each society, and the ability and willingness to use those resources in the interest of universality. The same argument could have been made by taking healthcare or some other generally desired end as an example. Universality is an important principle, distinct from equality, and to point to the limits of its operation is not to take anything away from its significance in a democratic society.

I have tried to underline the distinction between equality and universality because I believe that sometimes it serves the public interest or at least the interest of the most disadvantaged sections better if inequalities among the better-off sections of society are allowed to increase instead of being artificially reduced. A strongly competitive system of higher education may produce better scientists, better engineers, and better doctors to the general social advantage than a system that discourages competition on the ground that it increases inequality. This is not very different from the position of Rawls who would argue that although the bias of policy should be towards equality, an increase of inequality overall is justified if it benefits the most disadvantaged members of society (Rawls 1972: 75–83). In reality those who are strong advocates of equality for its own sake do not always keep the interests of the most disadvantaged sections of society in mind.

Appendix I

Amartya Sen's Utopia[*]

Ah, but a man's reach should exceed his grasp,
Or what's a Heaven for?

Robert Browning

Amartya Sen's new book on inequality is bound to stir many minds. Whatever he writes is written with great force and precision, and from beginning to end he always remains in control of his argument. He has established a commanding position in the field about which he writes, and all those who are devoted to the cause of equality will be reassured to find that Amartya Sen is on their side.

The present work is in many ways more ambitious than the monograph on economic inequality that he had published some 20 years ago (Sen 1973). Although he had already shown his interest in larger philosophical issues, that book was more narrowly addressed to problems in the measurement of economic inequality. Its argument was presented in a more formal style, and it had too many equations and diagrams to hold the attention of the general reader. This work is presented in a more mature and accommodating style, and, although nobody should regard it as bedside reading, it will undoubtedly have a wider appeal than the earlier one.

The author registers his wider concerns at the very outset by asking: 'equality of what?' He takes pains to emphasize that inequality is not just a matter of income distribution or even of the distribution of

[*] Review of Amartya Sen, *Inequality Re-examined*, Oxford: Clarendon Press, 1992.

material resources in some wider sense of the term. A major driving force behind the sociological study of what is called stratification has been the realization that there are several different, perhaps irreducible, dimensions of inequality, and not just the economic one. The present work is animated by a much deeper awareness of this than one generally encounters in the literature of economics. In the language of its author, inequalities have to be considered not merely within a single space, but within a number of different spaces. A major problem in the study of inequality therefore is to identify these spaces and to analyze how they are related to each other through encompassment, exclusion, or inclusion.

Sen begins with the arresting observation that the presumed opposition between the egalitarian and the libertarian views rests on a category mistake and is therefore a false one. At least in the modern world, all of us, libertarians included, want equality in some sense, though not always in the same sense. If libertarians were opposed to equality consistently and in principle, why would they want, as they invariably do, *equal* liberty for all to the maximum extent possible? To be sure, libertarians may be opposed to the equal distribution of income, but that is not the same thing as being opposed to equality as such. I have said that this is an arresting argument, and, on the whole, it is a persuasive one, although, as we shall see later, there is more than just this to the disagreement between egalitarians and libertarians.

We have to attend to inequality in a variety of spaces if we care seriously about differences among persons. Human beings differ in a multitude of ways, in what they are and what they do, and these differences have an intrinsic value. 'One of the consequences of "human diversity" is that equality in one space tends to go, in fact, with inequality in another' (p. 20). This fact has important ethical implications. For, as Sen puts it, 'The assessment of the claims of equality has to come to terms with the existence of pervasive human diversity' (p. 1). And, again, 'The ethics of equality has to take adequate note of our pervasive diversities that affect the relations between the different spaces' (p. 28).

So, the ethics of equality is no simple matter. It has to accommodate inequality in some respects in order to secure equality in other, more important ones: 'The justification of inequality in some features is made to rest on the equality of some other feature, taken to be more basic in the ethical system' (p. 19). Sen is an egalitarian, not a populist, and it is good that he has made that point clear at the outset, for, at least in India, the line between the two is frequently effaced. We cannot have equality in every space, and very little is to be gained by repeating such catch phrases as 'all men are created equal'. Opting for equality in the real world means making hard choices, and Sen seems to be better prepared now than he was before to accept inequality of income in the interest of equality of something more basic. But he still remains an egalitarian in the strong sense since he is reluctant to accept inequality in any respect unless it secures equality in some more fundamental respect.

It is probably characteristic of the enlargement of the author's intellectual interests in the last 20 years that he engages as much with philosophers as with economists, if not a little more so. The work of Rawls has been a great inspiration to egalitarians throughout the western world, and it is, as Sen generously acknowledges, the single most important influence in the present one. That influence appears to be most marked in the author's desire to build freedom into his very conception of equality. In this discussion of inequality by an economist, we are far from the confining world of Lorenz curves and Gini coefficients.

To locate a work within a certain intellectual tradition is of course not to deny its originality. Sen's capacity to make accurate distinctions is matchless, and the speed with which he moves from one level of distinction to another is breathtaking. Even when he begins with Rawls, he does not stay with him very long. As is well known, Rawls gives a central place in his theory of justice to the distribution of what he calls 'primary goods', among which he includes 'rights and liberties, powers and opportunities, income and wealth' (Rawls 1972: 62). Sen welcomes this move for the effect it has had in 'shifting our concerns from inequalities only in outcomes and achievements to those in opportunities and freedoms' (p. 86). But he feels that the move does not take us far enough, for 'by concentrating on the *means* of freedom rather than the *extent* of freedom, his theory has stopped short of paying adequate attention to freedom as such' (p. 86). Therefore, Sen would maintain, the basal space in which equality has to be secured is the space of freedoms rather than of primary goods.

Sen would argue that in moving from the space of incomes to that of primary goods, and from there again to that of freedoms, we are moving from the periphery towards the core; as we make these moves, the problems of comparing, ordering, and measuring appear to become more and more intractable. He is well aware of these problems, and does not try to sweep them under the carpet. Where it concerns matters of great moment, there are often only partial and not complete solutions, and he has chosen, wisely enough, not to make the best the enemy of the good. This is not a manual of instructions for use in government departments of planning and social welfare, but it has enough in it to set at work the minds of all those who are committed to the pursuit and promotion of equality.

I have not tried to provide a summary of the book, for that would only take away from the power and cogency of its argument. What I have tried to do instead is to give some indication of the richness and variety of the author's concerns. The book, as I have said, is not bedside reading. It compels the attentive reader to reconsider a great number of questions that can no longer be set at rest by conventional answers. I would now like to consider a few specific questions that it raises in my mind, although I would not expect these questions to occupy the same space in every reader's mind. My observations will deal mainly with three things: (i) the inherent properties of social arrangements, particularly institutions and organizations; (ii) the social evaluation of distinctions within institutions; and (iii) the place of power in the maintenance and transformation of organizations.

Sen tells us in the preface that his book attempts the 'evaluation and assessment of social arrangements in general' (p. ix), and the concern with social arrangements is expressed at a number of places, particularly in the earlier part of the book. The author is no narrow economist, nor is he only a philosopher; he is also a distinguished social and political theorist. As such, the book deals with much more than the mathematical patterns formed by distributions in various spaces, and one welcomes the early signal of attention to social arrangements.

However, it is difficult to determine what exactly the author has in mind when he refers to social arrangements. True, this is not a textbook of social stratification, and one should not expect to find in it any extended consideration of the nature and types of social structure or social association. At the same time, it is not easy to understand the case for equality in social arrangements (and the limits to its attainment therein) without some notion of the pre-conditions for the existence and operation of such arrangements. How does a social arrangement of persons—any arrangement, actual or possible—differ from a mere aggregate or assortment of individuals? If a social arrangement differs in some significant way from an aggregate of individuals, does the difference have any implications for inequality?

Where Sen is at his best is in seizing upon the multiplicity of different criteria—or dimensions, or scales, or spaces—in terms of which inequality has to be assessed or evaluated. This would give us a large number and variety of rankings or serial arrangements, and these, taken singly or in combination, may no doubt be regarded as social arrangements in some sense of the term. Surely, this cannot be all that the author has in mind when he speaks of 'the evaluation and assessment of social arrangements in general'.

When the economist deals with inequality in terms of the distribution of income alone, and points out that that itself is a kind of social arrangement, the student of society and its institutions is naturally disappointed. Sen raises our expectations by pointing to the significance of human diversity and dwelling upon the need to take a great many things in addition to income into account. But how are we to conceive of the arrangement of these in relation to each other? Very little is said about the rules of combination that might enable us to proceed from simple, serial arrangements to more complex ones. The problem is not that the outcome would be an incomplete arrangement; would it be a *social* arrangement, recognizable to the members of a society as resembling even partially the ones by which they live?

There is of course a link between human diversity and inequality among persons, and it is this link that the author seems to be most interested in examining. He does not take the view that the more diversity there is, the more inequality there will be, seeking instead to find a way by which human diversity may be so arranged as to minimize inequality in at least those respects that we consider or ought to consider decisive. It is in a way natural to think of inequality in terms of who has how much of what. But it is also possible to think of it as a constitutive feature of a social arrangement independently of the persons occupying various positions in that arrangement. We may equalize a great many things among the individual members of a society but still be left with an arrangement having unequal positions.

Sen would not be himself if he failed to anticipate the kinds of problems raised above, and he does advert to them, though very briefly, in at least two places. Towards the very end of the book, he appears to make some concessions to what he calls the 'operational asymmetry argument', or the argument that 'focuses on the possibility that the need for asymmetric treatment arises from the *social* role of asymmetry (e.g. a few people have to take operational decisions to avoid confusion)' (p. 141). I suppose that the division of labour and all forms of organizational and institutional hierarchy would be put under the rubric of 'operational asymmetry'. This would tend to leave the impression that the elements of such a hierarchy are a little like the pieces of furniture in a room—or the pieces on a chessboard—that can be moved around and rearranged to suit the convenience of the occasion. We might have our own views about the organizational hierarchy in a car factory; but I wonder how many persons would be satisfied with such a view of the institutional hierarchy in, say, Harvard University ('a few people have to take operational decisions to avoid confusion').

Optimism about the possibility of social arrangements freed from the constraints of hierarchy is in fact revealed fairly early in the book in a footnote where the author quotes, it seems to me approvingly, the famous passage from *The German Ideology* which tells of a world in which it is 'possible for me to do one thing today and another tomorrow, to hunt in the morning, fish in the afternoon, rear cattle in the evening, criticize after dinner, just as I have a mind, without ever becoming hunter, fisherman, shepherd or critic' (p. 41, n. 8). These are stirring words, but I wonder if Sen would be prepared to submit them to the same critical scrutiny to which he submits the writings of his less inspired academic colleagues.

It is true that the philosopher has to concern himself with possible and not just actual social arrangements, and perhaps even more with the former than the latter. Sen writes as a philosopher and not as a sociologist, and that distinction has to be kept in mind even though— or, perhaps, especially because—so many sociologists now seem eager to present themselves as philosophers. Philosophers would be unfaithful to their vocation if they failed to dwell upon ideals and to construct ideal social arrangements in their minds, for it is undeniable that no society can exist without an ideal that is in some ways different from the actual. Those who dwell upon ideals tend to be a little impatient about the little constraints of the actual world, and it is then the obligation of the sociologist to bring those constraints to their attention.

Although the book is entitled *Inequality Re-examined*, what its author really sets out to do is to construct a normative theory of equality. The strength of his urge to demonstrate the importance of the norm of equality as the basis of a just society leads him to neglect the obvious fact that inequality too is supported by norms. They are, it is true, not his norms, but they are norms none the less. It is in this sense that the

institutional hierarchy in Harvard University—or any university—is
more than merely a matter of 'operational asymmetry'; it has its own
normative grounding.

At any rate, it is important to note the distinction between norms
in the descriptive and in the prescriptive sense. Sen is interested mainly
in the latter, whereas other social theorists are also interested in the
former. Now, these others would naturally like to know how far a
theory of norms in the prescriptive sense takes into account the norms
in the descriptive sense that exist in every society, making social arrangements a little more than matters merely of operational convenience. The subject bristles with difficulty, for proponents of equality,
while prepared to acknowledge the existence of inequality as a fact, are
often blind to its significance as a norm. But our refusal to recognize
the norms of others does not deprive those norms of their social force.

The author is no doubt right to tell the economists that inequality is
not, in its most fundamental sense, about income distribution. But not
everyone, not even every economist, believed in the first instance that
inequality in 'social arrangements' was at bottom a matter of income
distribution. Some say that inequality is at bottom a matter of social
esteem, i.e. of evaluation of persons and positions in social arrangements.
Income distribution is an extreme example, because here the problem
of evaluation is in a sense so simple that one tends to ignore its very
existence. Everyone knows that a person with an income of Rs 10,000
ranks higher than one with an income of Rs 100—at least in the space
of income distribution—for reasons that are obvious to everyone; no
separate effort at evaluation is required. But this is a limiting case, and
not the typical one. A more typical case would be of the evaluation of
persons in various occupational positions. A neuro-surgeon ranks higher
than a cleaner, but it is not easy to explain exactly why. The common
sense explanation that the former enjoys a higher income than the latter
will not do, for one can wager that the two will continue to be esteemed
unequally even after their incomes are equalized; not in every society
conceivable, but in all those with which most of us are familiar.

One of the persistent concerns of *Inequality Re-examined* is with the
evaluation and assessment of social arrangements from the viewpoint
of equality and inequality. But evaluation is a central concept in the
sociological study of inequality itself. Human beings evaluate each
other and the positions they occupy in social arrangements, largely, if
not wholly, independently of the work of philosophers. Here is one
characteristic of human beings at all times and everywhere that makes

a social arrangement different from an assortment of individuals. The evaluations that are made by the members of a society are extraordinarily complex, but they are not altogether devoid of a structure. Thus, social inequality is not just a matter of the distribution of goods and resources among individuals, but also one of the relations among persons with a component of evaluation built into them.

I personally find it relatively easy to conceive of a social arrangement in which everybody has the same income; whether such an arrangement will last very long or will be very efficient is a different matter. I find it, on the other hand, difficult, if not impossible, to conceive of a *social* arrangement in which all positions, or all persons occupying such positions, enjoy esteem, prestige, or respect in equal measure. As Talcott Parsons had pointed out long ago, equal evaluation of two or more positions in a society is a special case of evaluation and cannot be treated as a demonstration of its irrelevance (Parsons 1953: 93).

Can the equal evaluation of persons and positions be generated through the construction of a social arrangement in which all persons and all positions will be equally esteemed, more or less? No sociologist can really give a categorical answer to this question, and all I can do at this stage is to express a few misgivings. My point can perhaps be made most easily by a consideration of institutions, which I regard as social arrangements of a particular kind where individuals interact with each other on the basis of rights and obligations and which are sustained, at least in part, by common values that are acknowledged if not shared by its members in varying degrees.

For the sake of brevity and convenience, I shall take as my example the kind of institution with which philosophers, economists, and sociologists who write about equality and inequality are familiar from personal experience, namely, the university. Now a university—any university—is an arrangement of differentiated positions that are graded in a number of ways. Some of this is no doubt a matter of convenience, an expression of the kind of 'operational asymmetry' referred to above. At the same time, a university that is unable or unwilling to sort out the better from the worse, the brilliant from the dull among its teachers or its students, and esteem the one more than the other hardly deserves to be acknowledged as one. I must insist that this is not just a question of salary differentials for the teachers or differential grades for the students. It is only when the university is collapsing as an institution, as is now happening in some parts of India, that academic distinction begins to be thought of largely in those terms.

What I wish to stress is that the hierarchical distinctions that are a part of every university as a social arrangement are not matters merely of fact in the narrow sense of the term: they are grounded in the normative structure of the university as an institution. Those who live and work in universities do and must make distinctions, since, generally speaking, they value good physicists more than indifferent ones, outstanding economists more than mediocre ones, and the average geneticist more than the average museologist. Who would like to work in a university in which all economists are equally esteemed, irrespective of quality or performance? And it will not do to say that the poor museologist deserves every bit as much encouragement as the geneticist, for to decide in advance to value all subjects equally would be the death of innovation and progress in academic life.

A consideration of the hierarchy of esteem in a university—or, with appropriate qualifications, in any institution—brings out the complexity of the processes of evaluation on which it rests. The most senior professor is not necessarily the best paid, and the one enjoying the highest esteem personally may not be either the best paid or the most senior. There is the esteem due to the position occupied and that due to personal attainment. It is well known that the criteria by which professionals rank each other are not the same as those by which others rank them. Thus, inequalities on one scale—or in one space—are to some extent balanced by those on another. But to go on from there to suggest that we can construct a social arrangement with so many different scales that all inequalities will disappear through their simultaneous application will be to yield to precisely the kind of empty formula— 'all men are created equal'—that Sen has encouraged us to put aside.

We cannot speak about actual social arrangements—and perhaps even about possible ones—without some attention to the distribution of power, including its unequal distribution. Unequal power, like unequal esteem, is, in my judgment, a far deeper source of inequality than unequal income (Béteille 1977). This is, of course, well appreciated by some economists. Many years ago, J R Hicks had concluded the chapter on income distribution in his textbook of economics, curiously entitled *The Social Framework*, with the following observation:

Inequality of income is the form taken in our society of a more fundamental inequality—the inequality of power. Inequality of power persists in all societies; it is indeed difficult to see how society could be organized without it (Hicks 1942: 190).

I will add a few remarks to Hick's admirably lucid statement of the case. Power, like its counterpart status (in the sense of esteem), is an extremely fluid phenomenon; it exists in many different forms, such as coercion, domination, and manipulation, and it can be thought of as an attribute of either positions or persons. Here, I shall confine myself to the distribution of power in institutions and organizations which, as I have explained, are two of the characteristic forms of social arrangement. Leaving aside the state and its various organs, we have only to think of the organization of a hospital or a research laboratory to recognize the fact that every stable social arrangement organized on any significant scale must accommodate chains of command and obedience.

Of course Sen recognizes that the kind of view expressed above is held by some persons (such as Hicks in the statement quoted, to say nothing of the arch infidel Pareto). He seems to believe, however, that such a view is one among several possible views:

> *In this view*, efficiency of operations would require that *some* people should have more authority or power than others. Asymmetric treatment may be necessary, *in this view*, even if the people who are in authority are no more talented than others are (p. 141, some emphasis added).

But he does not engage with the view he describes, and he does not really explain his own view of the extent to which social arrangements can dispense with inequalities of power.

An alternative view of the distribution of power and authority in social arrangements is of course possible. Granting that the operational conditions of decision making might require that a few persons be given a little extra authority, conditionally and within limits agreed upon by all, one might still maintain that this need not lead to any serious or significant inequality. Such a social arrangement would not be a variant of the organizations on which all large-scale modern societies depend, but an alternative to them; a case for its viability will have to be independently established. Again, while it is true that inequalities of power of different kinds and in different social arrangements do to some extent balance each other (as in the case of esteem or status), a happy outcome in which the net balance of inequality will be zero can never be counted upon or expected to remain stable.

Egalitarians have since the French Revolution pointed to the manifold inequalities in actual social arrangements and contrasted those arrangements with possible ones with equality in a more central place. The present work belongs within that tradition. There are, to be sure, many defects of inequality in our actual social arrangements, and we in India know this only too well, not so much through philosophical reflection as through lived experience. These defects, many feel, ought not to be all present, and our social arrangements ought to be different from what they are. But a difficult question still remains: how, even on the plane of thought, are we to move from 'ought to be' to 'ought to do'?

As we noted, Sen began with a consideration of the presumed disagreement between egalitarians and libertarians, and pointed out that the disagreement has been both misconceived and exaggerated since libertarians, too, are committed to equality in some sense that is fundamental. This is true, but there is a disagreement none the less, and that disagreement is, if one may put it so, about the movement from 'ought to be' to 'ought to do'. Egalitarians and at least some libertarians might both wish to see less inequality than there is, but they would differ profoundly on what one ought to do—or whether one ought to do anything at all—to bring about the preferred social arrangement.

As we have seen, libertarians are not, indeed cannot be, absolutely indifferent to the appeal of equality. Nor are they completely indifferent to inequality, for there is one form of it that is the libertarian's nightmare, namely, inequality in the distribution of power. The libertarian who also values equality differs from the egalitarian *tout court* in his reluctance to intervene in the 'natural processes of social life'. The egalitarian as such has a specific commitment to equality in so far as he is prepared to intervene in order to bring into being his preferred social arrangement even at some cost. Sen has indicated his preference for a certain type of social arrangement, and he has used the resources of his intellect well to justify his preference. But we know that actual social arrangements are different from the one he prefers. He has told us very little about what we ought to do—or what we can do—to bring the preferred social arrangement into being, and at what cost.

To think of social arrangements as matters of operational convenience only is to lose sight of the resistance to alteration that has been offered from within the institutions and organizations of society at all times, everywhere. I am not saying that social arrangements are in principle unalterable, only that I doubt that they can be radically altered solely through the persuasive appeal of cogent ideas. Radical egalitarians I take to be those who are so deeply committed to equality that they do not fear to use power—either the power of the state or the power of the people—to bring it into being. It is here that the libertarian who also values equality parts company with the pure egalitarian, and for a reason that the latter ought to understand and appreciate: the libertarian fears that the power that is used in the cause of equality contains within itself the seeds of new, unknown, and perhaps more sinister forms of inequality. Libertarians are willing to take risks when it comes to making money; they are averse to taking risks when it comes to the use of power. If I were to single out the most serious limitation of the book under review, I would point to the absence in it of a discussion of the inequality of power. This is all the more remarkable as, unlike many others, Sen is not satisfied merely to contemplate the world, he wants also to change it.

Appendix II

Equality and
Individual Achievement[*]

Is there a secular trend leading to the decline of inequality? Does the modern world have a distinctive and singular orientation to equality? It is clear that the progress of equality in the last two hundred years has not been altogether smooth or even; there have been currents as well as counter-currents in each and every society. Now, more than two hundred years after the French Revolution and the industrial revolution, it seems possible to argue not only that the natural tendency of human societies is towards greater equality but also that their natural tendency is towards greater inequality.

This collection of essays put together by Kenneth Arrow and his associates expresses the concern over equality and inequality that has exercised thinking Americans ever since the republic was born. The concern has changed its focus with the passage of time, but it has rarely lost its intensity. Like the three editors, most of the contributors are economists although there are some sociologists as well as a couple of biological scientists. The book provides a wealth of empirical material on income, occupation, and education, and some rigorous and sustained analysis, although it is a pity that Arrow has contented himself with only a brief Introduction and that too written jointly with his two co-editors.

The essays in the collection are written from a broadly egalitarian point of view, and the collection itself was occasioned by what the

* Review of Kenneth Arrow, Samuel Bowles and Steven Durlauf (eds), *Meritocracy and Economic Inequality*. Delhi: Oxford University Press, 2001.

editors believe to be a growing indifference, if not antipathy, to equality in American society. Economic inequality is on the rise and egalitarian policies are out of favour. The picture that emerges from the opinion polls is not altogether clear. Americans believe overwhelmingly in society's obligation to guarantee 'every citizen enough to eat and a place to sleep' (p. ix). But beyond that they do not seem to be very enthusiastic about promoting greater equality in the distribution of benefits and burdens among the members of society.

Most of the essays are directed towards policy: not just policy analysis but also policy prescription. The authors are concerned over what they perceive as shifts in policies aimed at reducing inequalities between individuals and disparities between communities. There are various reasons behind the shifts in policy: confusion over the meaning of fairness, conflicting ideas about the causes of inequality, and disenchantment over the effectiveness of public policy itself.

Shifts in policy are no doubt important, but they have to be distinguished from long-term changes in social values. The editors say, 'A century ago the desirability of at least some redistribution from the rich to the less well off was thought by its advocates to be so transparent that it scarcely required justification' (pp. ix–x). It is doubtful how much those same advocates would have thought about redistribution from Whites to Blacks which is a central concern with the essays in this volume. It is true that affirmative action is no longer in favour in the United States, but that does not necessarily mean that Americans are now less inclined to treat Blacks and Whites—or women and men—on an equal footing than they were thirty years ago, leave alone a hundred years ago. To speak of the 'demise of egalitarianism', as the editors do, is to strike a needlessly dramatic posture.

The United States has had a special place in the social imagination of egalitarians for two hundred years. It has been viewed as the land of opportunity—'the land of the second chance'—where individual ability overcomes every kind of social obstacle. Among students of comparative sociology it has stood for *homo equalis* not only in contrast to India, the classic abode of *homo hierarchicus*, but also in contrast to Europe with its legacy of a feudal past. The abundant empirical material provided in this volume on the United States by American scholars should lead us to look afresh at Louis Dumont's magisterial contrast between *homo hierarchicus* and *homo equalis* (Dumont 1966, 1977a; Béteille 1979).

Today we know a great deal more about the nature and forms of inequality than was known two hundred years ago, yet our knowledge is far from complete. In the early part of the nineteenth century, Alexis de Tocqueville did much to draw attention to the unique significance of equality, as both fact and value, in American society. He maintained that Americans not only enjoyed greater equality in fact but also valued it more highly than Europeans. Himself the scion of an aristocratic family, Tocqueville understood clearly the advantage that America enjoyed in the pursuit of equality from never having had an aristocracy in the European sense. Many of the obstacles that impeded the transition from aristocracy to democracy in Europe simply did not exist in the United States.

Although Tocqueville believed that there was something providential in the advance of equality, at least in the western countries, it is doubtful that he would be regarded as an egalitarian by the standards of the contributors to the present volume. He had his misgivings about an excess of enthusiasm for equality. He feared that that excess might become a threat to liberty. He also worried that the levelling tendencies inherent in the pursuit of equality might make people more tolerant of mediocrity.

Two of Tocqueville's observations are particularly germane to the issues discussed here. Although he believed that the trend towards equality was irreversible, he realized that full equality could never be attained in practice and that at the limit, the small inequalities that remained would appear more odious and intolerable than the larger ones passively tolerated in hierarchical societies: 'Hence the desire of equality always becomes more insatiable in proportion as equality is more complete' (Tocqueville 1956 II: 138). To be sure, the egalitarians of today do not ask for equality of condition, but only equality of opportunity; but it can be easily shown that substantive (as against formal) equality of opportunity is no more attainable in practice than complete equality of condition (Chapter 8).

Tocqueville also saw the enormity of the obstacle to the attainment of equality presented in America by the coexistence of three different races at very unequal levels of development. It is true that his perception of the problem was very different from ours for he believed that the three races were not only unequally placed by society but also unequally endowed by nature. Tocqueville had no illusion about the violence and brutality on which American society was founded, and he did not believe that the abolition of slavery would bring racial discrimination to an end:

On the contrary, the prejudice of race appears to be stronger in the states that have abolished slavery than in those where it still exists; and nowhere is it so intolerant as in those states where servitude has never been known (Tocqueville 1956 I: 359).

Although race prejudice has certainly declined between Tocqueville's time and ours, it has by no means disappeared; and as several of the chapters indicate, the legacy of past prejudice makes the equalization of life chances between Blacks and Whites extremely difficult.

Tocqueville's belief that the natural tendency of western societies was towards equality and that this tendency could be most clearly seen in the United States left a lasting impression on generations of western scholars. The economist Werner Sombart, who was Max Weber's contemporary and associate, published an essay in the early years of the last century in which he asked why there was no socialism in the United States (Sombart 1906). Sombart argued that in the United States workers preferred the path of individual social mobility to that of collective political action as a way to better their conditions. This, he believed, was because individual mobility was far easier in that country than in Europe.

One of the first major empirical studies of social mobility to be undertaken in the United States showed that Sombart was seriously mistaken. That study which compared rates of mobility in a number of industrial countries, concluded that '*the overall pattern of social mobility appears to be much the same in the industrial societies of various Western countries*' (Lipset and Bendix 1967: 12). The authors found their own conclusion 'startling' although it did not lay to rest the idea of American exceptionalism.

The examples of Tocqueville and Sombart show how easy it is to be mistaken in matters relating to equality and inequality. Comparisons of rates of mobility, whether across space or across time, are very difficult to make, and their conclusions are subject to many conditions. As the author of the first essay in this collection, Amartya Sen showed many years ago, even with regard to something so specific as the distribution of income, it is difficult to state categorically that there is greater inequality in one case than in the other (Sen 1973). Yet the general presumption behind the collection as a whole is that economic inequality is now *increasing* in the United States. There have undoubtedly been important shifts in policy in the last 15 to 20 years, but it would be a mistake to believe that long-term trends in inequality are governed solely or even mainly by shifts in economic and social policy.

The volume shows throughout a high level of technical competence in the use of concepts, methods, and data. Yet it suffers from a certain lack of perspective. The studies focus exclusively on American society and on American society in the present. Granted the difficulty of making rigorous comparisons, something may have been gained by looking at other societies, or at least at other societies at a similar stage of economic development. It is not that generalizations are absent, but they are generalizations without comparisons. Economists tend to believe, like physicists, that a single well-conducted experiment is sufficient to reach a generalization; but in the case of economy and society, the single case is never tidy enough to sustain firm and meaningful conclusions on subjects of such deep and wide significance.

The book is divided into four parts, but they are of unequal length and weight. The bulk of the empirical and analytical material is in Part III which comprises more than half the book. It is entitled 'Schooling and Economic Opportunity' and it deals with a range of closely related issues such as cognitive ability, intelligence, education, family background, occupation, and earnings. Because the question of cognitive ability figures so prominently in current debates on the economic returns to education, there is a separate part, Part II, devoted to the genetic aspects of intelligence. Part I, comprising two short pieces, one by Amartya Sen and the other by John Roemer, deals with merit, reward, and opportunity in general and theoretical terms. Part IV is made up of three pieces dealing with policy options. The issue of race figures prominently through Parts II to IV.

Americans do not wish to reward birth, but they do wish to reward intelligence. Unfortunately for Americans—and for egalitarians the world over—birth and intelligence are closely connected, socially and perhaps to some extent also genetically. This is the paradox of equality in America and the cause of much soul searching among American egalitarians. It would be no great exaggeration to say that the modern American obsession with intelligence is like the traditional Hindu obsession with purity; and the fact that intelligence—or merit—cannot be defined any better than purity does not make the obsession less acute. As the redoubtable Arthur Jensen had written some thirty years ago, 'Intelligence, like electricity, is easier to measure than to define' (Jensen 1969: 5); and so, Americans go about measuring intelligence with a vengeance. And as to merit, even those academics who declare that it is 'underdefined' need must spend a fair amount of their time sorting their students and colleagues out 'according to merit'.

Although the value attached to equality in American society should not be discounted, the opposition to egalitarian policies in education is not new. In the late sixties Jensen created a considerable stir by publishing in *Harvard Educational Review* a lengthy paper entitled 'How Much Can We Boost IQ and Scholastic Achievement?' (Jensen 1969). Some liberals found racist undertones in what came to be known as the 'Jensenite heresy'. It was in the context of that debate that the Chicago sociologist James Coleman published a paper also in *Harvard Educational Review* which concluded by describing equality of opportunity as 'a false ideal' (Coleman 1973: 135).

Jensen has been displaced by Herrnstein and Murray, the authors of *The Bell Curve*, published in 1994. The book is an attempt to establish a direct relationship between measured intelligence and social stratification. The argument of *The Bell Curve* is vaguely reminiscent of Michael Young's argument in *The Rise of Meritocracy* (1961); but whereas Young's argument had a satirical edge, Herrnstein and Murray are wholly in earnest. *The Bell Curve* is not a work of great intellectual distinction, but it captured the imagination of many Americans when it was published. It figures prominently in the present volume, and an entire chapter is devoted to a re-examination of its findings.

Put in the form of an aphorism, the message of *The Bell Curve* is that intelligence is destiny. Herrnstein and Murray have put together a wealth of data to argue that performance in the market is governed neither by socioeconomic status nor by amount of schooling but by innate ability as measured by tests of intelligence. Intelligence, according to them, is the principal determinant of social and economic outcomes in the United States. In their own words, 'If a white child of the next generation could be given a choice between being disadvantaged in socio-economic status or disadvantaged in intelligence, there is no question about the right choice' (Herrnstein and Murray 1994: 135). If we add to this the belief that there is a large genetic component in the constitution of intelligence, the implications of the argument for the reproduction of inequality are clear.

Chapter 7 by Sanders Korenman and Christopher Winship provides a thorough reanalysis of *The Bell Curve*. They reveal the many deficiencies of data, method, and analysis in the book. They refer to an earlier work by Jencks et al. (1979) which analyses:

the importance of intelligence, education, family background, and noncognitive abilities in determining various economic outcomes. Jencks et al. conclude that all four sets of factors are important, that no single factor dominates the others, and that their relative importance differs across samples and outcomes (p. 165).

Korenman and Winship are more in agreement with Jensen et al. than with Herrnstein and Murray. In other words, they would not deny an autonomous role to intelligence in determining economic success, but they would not give it the kind of predominance given to it by the authors of *The Bell Curve*.

Although the book is ostensibly about meritocracy, the majority of the papers deal with intelligence rather than merit. Amartya Sen complains that the concept of merit is underdefined, and he is of course right in the context of his own argument. But it may also be argued that merit is not underdefined so much as being too narrowly conceived. It is striking how many of the contributors and the authors they discuss tacitly identify merit with intelligence, and intelligence with test scores. If merit (or intelligence) is defined as the quality which ensures economic success, then those who achieve economic success are bound to have an abundance of that quality. Ultimately, it is American society that decides which individual qualities are socially valued in it. Sen apart, the contributors do not question the structure of values by which American society is governed; their concern is with the qualities and performances of individuals.

One of the reasons why intelligence figures so extensively in discussions by economists, psychologists, and educationists is that it can be easily measured. There are of course many different kinds of tests that focus on abilities of different kinds, and the construction and revision of these tests is a continuing enterprise. Herrnstein and Murray have relied substantially on the widely-used Armed Forces Qualifications Test (AFQT), but others have used other kinds of tests. These tests do not all show the same results, and naturally there is a desire to devise a super test that will give valid results for all populations and all purposes, and identify qualities that govern performance independently of space, time, and circumstance.

In an important paper (chapter 3), James Flynn throws doubt on the possibility of such a super test. He invites us to consider the implications of 'the phenomenon of massive IQ gains over time, that is, the phenomenon of each generation outscoring the previous generation on IQ tests' (p. 36). If one generation outscores another, is it surprising that one society—or one section of a society—outscores another on IQ tests? It is true that things change—and sometimes change radically—from one generation to the next, but it is difficult to believe that basic mental abilities advance so rapidly among human beings.

Some of the gains to IQ across generations, as shown by Flynn, appear spectacular; and such gains are in evidence not just in one country but in several:

Recent IQ gains, those covering the last sixty years, reveal a pattern. They are largest on the tests that are supposed to be the purest measure of intelligence, Raven's and other tests of fluid *g*. The very best data, primarily military tests of comprehensive samples of young men, show Belgium, the Netherlands, and Israel gaining at a rate of twenty points over a generation (thirty years), while Norway, Sweden and Denmark have gained at a rate of about ten points (p. 36).

Similar gains are in evidence for Britain, Australia, and Canada, countries that share broadly the same culture.

There has clearly been an expansion of the knowledge base in the societies just referred to. How far this expansion has contributed to the IQ gains recorded is difficult to tell. But one thing should be clear: when the knowledge base expands, the gains from the expansion may not be equally distributed among individuals. An overall expansion of the knowledge base may in fact lead to a more rather than a less unequal distribution from it. An increase in knowledge does not guarantee a more equal distribution any more than does an increase in wealth.

If there is a natural tendency for inequality to increase, can schooling do something to alter that tendency in the direction of greater equality? Some will say that it cannot do very much, but most of the contributors to this volume believe that it can do a fair amount provided it is organized and funded properly. While many viewpoints are discussed in this volume, a significant omission is that of James Coleman whose *Equality and Achievement in Education* (1990) many would regard as a landmark.

There obviously is some relationship between the extent of schooling and the amount of earning, but the relationship is by no means as clear or as strong as one might expect. The relationship between years of education and average hourly wage appears weak upto the completion of high school and becomes stronger only thereafter:

For example, in 1990 and 1991 high school graduates earned 18 per cent more than high school dropouts with 11 years of schooling. Similarly, those who had completed over one year of college earned 8 percent more than high school graduates (p. 90).

But even here the matter is far from simple; for one might argue that it is only the more intelligent ones who complete high school and go on beyond it, and their higher earnings are due less to more schooling than to superior intelligence. Ashenfelter and Rouse (chapter 5) show that there is indeed a tangible economic return to extended education that operates independently of both measured intelligence and socio-economic status.

One of the limitations of the kind of analysis that Ashenfelter and Rouse undertake is that it deals only with the amount of education and not its kind. Education contributes not only to skill formation but also to the formation of cultural capital, and here the social milieu in which it is acquired may be decisive. Someone who takes an ordinary first degree from Princeton after completing secondary education at Andover is likely to fare better in the job market than someone who has had a more extended study in a series of nondescript institutions.

Even where there is general endorsement of the value of equality, there may be disagreement about what counts for equality. There have been significant changes in this regard in the last two hundred years. Two hundred years ago, Napoleon's slogan of careers open to talent was regarded as a call for equality, but it is now equated with meritocracy which is no longer in favour among egalitarians today. Experience has shown that the simple application of the principle of equality of opportunity does not always lead to a reduction of economic inequality but may in fact lead to an increase of it. Hence the attempt to deconstruct the idea and to look behind formal equality of opportunity for 'fair' or 'real' equality of opportunity. But the quest for real equality of opportunity has so far turned out to be like the quest for the Holy Grail.

Very few egalitarians would like to jettison the principle of equality of opportunity, but they would like to qualify it, redefine it, or combine it with some other principle. Chapter 2, by John Roemer, is devoted to equality of opportunity; it presents a condensed version of the argument presented by him earlier in a brief monograph (Roemer 1998). Roemer's argument is ingenious, but it is not practical. The scheme presented by him is so involuted that it is unlikely to make many converts among Americans who feel that they have had enough of policies designed to promote equality.

Roemer distinguishes between two conceptions of equality of opportunity. The first he calls the 'nondiscrimination or merit principle'; the second, which he himself favours, he calls the 'level-the-playing-field principle'. Roemer's distinction is not altogether new. The jurist Owen Fiss sought to distinguish between the 'anti-discrimination principle' and the 'group-disadvantaging principle' (Fiss 1977); and others have, more simply, pointed to the distinction between 'formal' and 'substantive' equality of opportunity. Roemer is practical enough to recognize that the playing field cannot be levelled completely, and he therefore asks for it to be levelled in the area of education and not employment. In other words, the 'level-the-playing-field principle' is to apply up to the phase of secondary education or even a little beyond that, and the 'nondiscrimination principle' is to take over thereafter.

It is not difficult to see Roemer's dilemma. American society values both equality and the individual, and it is now abundantly clear, as it was not in Tocqueville's time, that the demands of the two are not always in harmony. As an egalitarian, the American wants to ensure that benefits and burdens are not distributed too unequally; but as an individualist, he wants also to ensure that the individual is rewarded for some quality that is his very own, no matter what that quality may be. Roemer would like to eliminate the effects of socio-economic background and even genetic endowment from considerations of distribution. But he cannot eliminate everything. In place of intelligence, or even merit, he would like society to reward effort. But his scheme for isolating the effects of effort is so complicated that it might have served him better to devise an EQ, or effort quotient, to be used in lieu of, or in addition to, IQ in sorting the sheep out from the goats.

Social theory is one thing and social policy is another, and nothing is more difficult than to bring about a satisfactory union of the two. In an important essay on the enforcement of anti-discrimination laws (chapter 11), the Black economist Glenn Loury tries to explain how discrimination in hiring comes about and why policies to counteract it often backfire. Loury's essay is well-balanced, cogent, and clear, and it will provide much food for thought to both supporters and opponents of caste quotas in India.

Lourie points out that there are two main theories to explain how distortions in the hiring process come about in the United States. The first, called 'taste discrimination', we owe to Gary Becker, and the second, called 'statistical discrimination', to Kenneth Arrow. Taste discrimination comes about when some employers with a taste for discrimination against certain groups of workers experience disutility from hiring them, leading to reduced labour-market opportunities for those workers. Statistical discrimination comes about because of disparate statistical generalizations about worker productivity based on incomplete information. Both forms of discrimination reduce incentives for skill formation in the group discriminated against, and the vicious circle becomes closed.

What can be done to correct the distortions that arise, whether from taste discrimination or from statistical discrimination? It is to Loury's credit that he has not only examined the problem carefully but also patiently explained its delicate nature. An aggressive policy of affirmative action may harden the prejudices of employers against the disadvantaged group. More important than that, it may discourage members of the group in question from investing in skill formation by creating the presumption that they will not be tested by the same standards that employers apply to those who do not enjoy the benefit of affirmative action.

In the Unites States, more and more Black economists, lawyers, and sociologists are coming to the conclusion that affirmative action is a double-edged weapon. Loury's conclusion, which he himself presents in italic type, is worth quoting:

Specifically, minorities may underinvest in the skills needed to perform adequately in such positions, relative to the investment rate of majority workers. That is, policies intended to assure equality of achievement may end up producing inequality of skills (p. 315).

In India probably both Roemer and Loury would be condemned by the champions of equality, Roemer for favouring the nondiscrimination (as against the group-disadvantaging) principle in employment, and Loury for placing more emphasis on skill formation than on equality of achievement.

If we go by social and economic policy alone, we might conclude that Indians care more for equality than do Americans. That would be an absurd conclusion. Indians can be more easily persuaded to believe, or half believe, that devising a public policy to square the circle is not beyond their ingenuity. Americans do not like being told by others how they should order their lives, and they have less trust in the efficacy of public policy.

American society values equality but it also values individualism, and the tensions, oppositions, and contradictions between the two values have become increasingly manifest with the passage of time. Individual self-reliance, individual effort, and individual achievement mean much more to Americans than they do to Indians and perhaps more also than they do to Europeans. It was in the United States that individualism first became established as a social value. 'Individualism', Tocqueville wrote, 'is a novel expression, to which a novel idea has given birth' (Tocqueville 1956 II: 98); he had mainly the United States in mind.

The roots of American individualism lie in American history in the eighteenth and nineteenth centuries. The manner in which the land was settled and appropriated created the widespread conviction that the individual could move mountains by his own unaided effort. Spectacular fortunes were made by individuals who appeared to have come out of nowhere. The United States was viewed as the land of opportunity not only by Americans but also by the rest of the world throughout the nineteenth century and beyond; no better evidence for this is needed than the continuing flow of immigrants from Europe and elsewhere. Much has changed in the ground reality in the United States between the nineteenth century and the present, but the belief that individual ability should be respected and individual achievement rewarded remains deeply rooted in the American mind. The American does not turn as easily to the state—or to his community—as does the Indian in trying to build a life for himself.

Tocqueville was right to point out that individualism was contrary to the spirit of aristocracy and congenial to the spirit of democracy. But that does not mean that individualism always goes with equality. Not only does equality mean more than one thing, individualism too has more than one meaning (Béteille 1986). There is the 'ethical individualism' of Kant: 'treat every man as an end in himself and never as a means only'; and there is the 'possessive individualism' of competitive capitalism. Even though they have very different implications for equality, it is difficult to see how 'ethical individualism' could have grown without support and sustenance from 'possessive individualism'.

In conclusion, I would like to say that I have been struck by two features of American social science in this important work: its high seriousness as compared with ours, and also its conspicuous self-sufficiency, not to say insularity. That America is a world unto itself could not be more clearly demonstrated than in these essays. India has had a very rich and varied experience of positive discrimination, and the subject has been studied extensively by both Indian and western, including American, scholars; but one will look in vain for any reference to this work, even in the essays that deal directly with affirmative action.

Much more serious is the complete neglect of the work of British and other European sociologists on education, occupation, and social mobility which are central concerns in these essays. Not only was the idea of meritocracy first articulated in Britain, but British sociologists have made important and significant contributions to the study of social mobility; but it is as if the work of the succession of scholars from David Glass to John Goldthorpe did not exist. Nor is there any reference to the significant work on reproduction in education, society, and culture done in the last thirty years in France by Pierre Bourdieu and his associates. The world has benefited immensely from American social science; it is doubtful how much American social science has benefited from the rest of the world.

References

Ardener, S. (ed.). 1975. *Perceiving Women*. London: Dent.

Ardrey, R. 1966. *The Territorial Imperative*. New York: Delta.

Ariès, P. 1962. *Centuries of Childhood*. New York: Vintage Books.

Aron, R. 1962. *Dix-huit leçons sur la société industrielle*. Paris: Gallimard.

—— 1964. *La lutte de classes*. Paris: Gallimard.

—— 1965. *Democratie et totalitarisme*. Paris: Gallimard.

—— 1968. *Progress and Disillusion*. London: Pall Mall Press.

Arrow, K., S. Bowles and S. Durlauf (eds). 2000. *Meritocracy and Economic Inequality*. Delhi: Oxford University Press.

Bankimchandra. 1961. 'Dharmatattva', In *Bankimrachanabali*, vol. 2, pp. 584–679. Calcutta: Sahitya Samsad.

Bardhan, P. 1984. *Political Economy of Development in India*. Oxford: Basil Blackwell.

Barth, F. 1959. *Political Leadership among Swat Pathans*. London: Athlone Press.

Baxter, P. and B. Sansom (eds). 1972. *Race and Social Difference*. Harmondsworth: Penguin Books.

Bendix, R. and S.M. Lipset (eds). 1966. *Class, Status and Power*. New York: Free Press.

Berger, B. and P.L. Berger. 1983. *The War Over the Family*. New York: Doubleday.

Berlin, I. 1978. *Concepts and Categories*. London: Hogarth Press.

Berreman, G.D. 1960. 'Caste in India and the United States', *American Journal of Sociology* 66: 120–7.

—— 1963. *Hindus of the Himalayas*. Berkeley: University of California Press.

—— 1966. 'Caste in Cross-cultural Perspective', in G. De Vos and H. Wagatsuma (eds), *Japan's Invisible Race*. Berkeley: University of California Press.

Béteille, A. 1964. 'A Note on the Referents of Caste', *European Journal of Sociology* 5: 130–4.

—— 1965. *Caste, Class and Power*. Berkeley: University of California Press.

Béteille, A. 1966. 'Closed and Open Social Stratification in India', *European Journal of Sociology* 7: 224–46.

—— 1968. 'Rules and Persons', *The Times of India*, 4 November.

—— 1969a. *Castes: Old and New*. Bombay: Asia Publishing House.

—— 1969b. 'The Politics of "Non-Antagonistic" Strata', *Contributions to Indian Sociology* (N.S.) 3.1: 17–31.

—— 1971. 'The Social Framework of Agriculture', in L. Lefeber and M. Datta-Chaudhuri (eds), *Regional Development*. The Hague: Mouton (pp. 114–64).

—— 1972. *Inequality and Social Change*. Delhi: Oxford University Press.

—— 1974. *Studies in Agrarian Social Structure*. Delhi: Oxford University Press.

—— 1977. *Inequality among Men*. Oxford: Basil Blackwell.

—— 1979. 'Homo Hierarchicus, Homo Equalis', *Modern Asian Studies* 13(4): 529–48.

—— 1980. *The Idea of Natural Inequality*. London: London School of Economics.

—— 1981a. 'The Indian University', *Minerva* 19(2): 282–310.

—— 1981b. *The Backward Classes and the New Social Order*. Delhi: Oxford University Press.

—— 1982. 'The Indian Road to Equality', *The Times of India*, 28 August.

—— 1985a. *Individualism and the Persistence of Collective Identities*. Colchester: University of Essex.

—— 1985b. *Equality of Opportunity and the Equal Distribution of Benefits*. Pune: Gokhale Institute.

—— 1986. 'Individualism and Equality', *Current Anthropology* 27(2): 121–54.

—— 1987a. *The Idea of Natural Inequality and Other Essays*. Delhi: Oxford University Press.

—— 1987b. 'Equality as a Right and as a Policy', *LSE Quartely* 1(1): 75–98.

—— 1987c. 'On Individualism and Equality: Reply', *Current Anthropology* 28(5): 672–7.

—— 1989. 'Are the Intelligentsia a Ruling Class?', *Economic and Political Weekly* 24(3): 151–5.

—— 1990a. 'Race, Caste and Gender', *Man* (N.S.) 25: 489–504.

—— 1990b. 'Caste and Reservations', *The Hindu*, 20 October.

—— 1990c. 'A Career in a Declining Profession', *Minerva* 28(1): 1–20.

—— 1991. *Society and Politics in India*. London: Athlone Press.

—— 1992. *The Backward Classes in Contemporary India*. Delhi: Oxford University Press.

—— 1998. 'The Conflict of Norms and Values in Contemporary Indian Society', in Peter L. Berger (ed.), *The Limits of Social Cohesion*. Boulder, Colorado: Westview Press, pp. 265–92.

—— 2000a. *Antinomies of Society*. Delhi: Oxford University Press.

—— 2000b. 'The Scheduled Castes', *Journal of the Indian School of Political Economy* XII (3&4): 367–79.

Béteille, A. (ed.). 1969. *Social Inequality*. Harmondsworth: Penguin Books.

Blau, P.M. and O.D. Duncan. 1968. *The American Occupational Structure*. New York: Free Press.

Bloch, M. 1962. *Feudal Society*. London: Routledge and Kegan Paul.

Blunt, E.A.H. 1931. *The Caste System of Northern India*. London: Oxford University Press.

Bose, N.K. 1941. 'The Hindu Method of Tribal Absorption', *Science and Culture* 7: 188–94.

——— 1949a. *Nabin O Prachin*. Calcutta: Bengal Publishers.

——— 1949b. *Hindu Samajer Garan*. Calcutta: Vishvabharati.

——— 1965. 'Calcutta: A Premature Metropolis', *Scientific American* 213(3): 91–102.

——— 1967. *Culture and Society in India*. Bombay: Asia Publishing House.

——— 1975. *The Structure of Hindu Society* (*Hindu Samajer Garan*, 1949, translated from the Bengali with an introduction and notes by A. Béteille). Delhi: Orient Longman.

——— n.d. *Traditions in Indian Architecture*. Calcutta, mimeo.

Bouglé, C. 1971. *Essays on the Caste System*. Cambridge: Cambridge University Press.

Bourdieu, P. 1984. *Distinction*. Cambridge, Mass.: Harvard University Press.

——— 1988. *Homo Academicus*. Stanford: Stanford University Press.

——— 1996. *The State Nobility*. Oxford: Polity Press.

Bourdieu, P. and J.-C. Passeron. 1977. *Reproduction in Education, Society and Culture*. Beverly Hills: Sage.

Carter, S.C. 1991. *Reflections of an Affirmative Action Baby*. New York: Basic Books.

Centre for Social Studies. 1985. *Caste, Caste Conflict and Reservation*. Delhi: Ajanta.

Chaudhuri, N.C. 1979. *Hinduism*. London: Chatto and Windus.

Cohen, G.A. 1993. 'Amarya Sen's Unequal World', *Economic and Political Weekly* 28(40): 2156–60.

Coleman, J.S. 1973. 'Equality of Opportunity and Equality of Results', *Harvard Educational Review* 43(1): 129–37.

——— 1990. *Equality and Achievement in Education*. Boulder: Westview Press.

Constituent Assembly Debates. 1989. *Official Report*. New Delhi: Lok Sabha Secretariat.

Crozier, M. 1964. *The Bureaucratic Phenomenon*. Chicago: University of Chicago Press.

Dahrendorf, R. 1959. *Class and Class Conflict in Industrial Society*. London: Routledge and Kegan Paul.

——— 1968. *Essays in the Theory of Society*, Stanford: Stanford University Press.

Das, G. 2000. *India Unbound*. Delhi: Viking.

Davis, K. and W.E. Moore. 1945. 'Some Principles of Stratification', *American Sociological Review* 10(2): 242–9.

Deliège, R. 1993. *Le système des castes*. Paris: Presses Universitaires de France.

—— 1995. *Les intouchables en Inde*. Paris: Editions Imago.

De Souza, A. 1974. *Indian Public Schools*. New Delhi: Sterling.

Dube, S.C. 1955. *Indian Village*. London: Routledge and Kegan Paul.

Duby, G. 1980. *The Three Orders*. Chicago: University of Chicago Press.

Dumont, L. 1957. *Hierarchy and Marriage Alliance in South Indian Kinship*. London: Royal Anthropological Institute.

—— 1961. 'Caste, Racism and "Stratification"', *Contributions to Indian Sociology* 5: 20–43.

—— 1964. *La civilization indienne et nous*. Paris: Armand Colin.

—— 1966. *Homo hierarchicus*. Paris: Gallimard.

—— 1967. 'Caste: A Phenomenon of Social Structure or an Aspect of Hindu Culture?', in A. de Reuck and J. Knight (eds), *Caste and Race*. London: J. and A. Churchill, pp. 28–38.

—— 1971. *Introduction à deux théories d'anthropologie sociale*. Paris: Mouton.

—— 1977a. *Homo equalis*. Paris: Gallimard.

—— 1977b. *From Mandeville to Marx*. Chicago: University of Chicago Press.

—— 1980. *On Value*. London: The British Academy.

—— 1983. *Essai ssur l'individualisme*. Paris: Seuil.

Durkheim, É. 1915. *The Elementary Forms of the Religious Life*. London: George Allen and Unwin.

—— 1982. *The Division of Labour in Society*. London: Macmillan.

Durkheim, É. and M. Mauss. 1963. *Primitive Classification*. London: Cohen & West.

Dworkin, R. 1984. *Taking Rights Seriously*. London: Duckworth.

—— 1985. *A Matter of Principle*. Cambridge, Mass.: Harvard University Press.

Engels, F. 1948. *The Origins of the Family, Private Property and the State*. Moscow: Progress Publishers.

Enthoven, R.E. 1920–2. *The Tribes and Castes of Bombay*. Bombay: Government Central Press, (3 vols).

Erikson, E. 1965. *Childhood and Society*. London: Hogarth Press.

Erikson, R. and J.H. Goldthorpe. 1992. *The Constant Flux*. Oxford: Clarendon Press.

Evans-Pritchard, E.E. 1940. *The Nuer*. Oxford: Clarendon Press.

—— 1965. *The Position of Women in Primitive Societies, and Other Essays in Social Anthropology*. London: Faber & Faber.

Eysenck, H.J. 1973. *The Inequality of Man*. London: Temple Smith.

Fiss, O.M. 1977. 'Groups and the Equal Protection Clause', in M. Cohen, T. Nagel and T. Scanlon (eds), *Equality and Preferential Treatment*. Princeton: Princeton University Press, pp. 84–154.

Fortes, M. 1945. *The Dynamics of Clanship among the Tallensi.* London: Oxford University Press.

—— 1949. *The Web of Kinship among the Tallensi.* London: Oxford University Press.

—— 1970. *Kinship and the Social Order.* London: Routledge and Kegan Paul.

Foucault, M. 1975. *Surveiller et punir.* Paris: Gallimard.

—— 1980. *Power/Knowledge.* Brighton: Harvester Press.

Frankel, F.R. and M.S.A. Rao (eds). 1989–90. *Dominance and State Power in Modern India.* Delhi: Oxford University Press, 2 vols.

Frazier, E.F. 1957. *Black Bourgeoisie.* New York: Free Press.

Gait, E.A. 1913. *Report on the Census of India.* Calcutta: Government Printing.

Gandhi, J.S. 1982. *Lawyers and Touts.* New Delhi: Hindustan.

Gandhi, M.K. 1962. *Varanashramadharma.* Ahmedabad: Navajivan.

Ganguli B.N. 1975. *Concept of Equality.* Simla: Indian Institute of Advanced Study.

Gellner, E. 1979. 'The Social Roots of Egalitarianism', *Dialectics and Humanism* 4: 27–43.

—— 1981. *Muslim Society.* Cambridge: Cambridge University Press.

Ghurye, G.S. 1950. *Caste and Class in India.* Bombay: Popular.

—— 1961. *Caste, Class and Occupation.* Bombay: Popular.

Giddens, A. 1973. *The Class Structure of Advanced Societies.* London: Hutchinson.

Gluckman, M. 1955. *The Judicial Process among the Barotse of Northern Rhodesia.* Manchester: Manchester University Press.

Goldthorpe, J.H. 1987. *Social Mobility and Class Structure in Modern Britain.* Oxford: Clarendon Press.

—— 1996. 'Class Analysis and the Reorientation of Class Theory', *The British Journal of Sociology* 47(3): 481–505.

—— 2000. *On Sociology.* Oxford: Clarendon Press.

Goldthorpe, J.H. and K. Hope. 1974. *The Social Grading of Occupations.* Oxford: Clarendon Press.

Goode, W.J. 1970. *World Revolution and Family Patterns.* New York: The Free Press.

Goodenough, W.H. 1951. *Property, Kin and Community on Truk.* New Haven: Yale University Press.

Government of India. 1956. *Report of the Backward Classes Commission* (Kalelkar Commission). Delhi: Manager of Publications.

—— 1980. *Report of the Backward Classes Commission* (Mandal Commission). New Delhi: Controller of Publications.

Guhan, S. et al. 1990. 'South India and Reservations: A Reply to André Béteille', *The Hindu*, 27 October.

Haldar, M.K. 1977. *Renaissance and Reaction in Nineteenth Century Bengal.* Calcutta: Minerva Associates.

Hayek, F.A. 1960. *The Constitution of Liberty.* London: Routledge and Kegan Paul.

—— 1976. *Law, Legislation and Liberty.* Chicago: University of Chicago Press, 3 vols.

Heller, C.S. (ed.). 1969. *Structured Social Inequality.* London: Macmillan.

Herring, R.J. 1983. *Land to the Tiller.* New Haven: Yale University Press.

Herrnstein, R.J. and C. Murray. 1994. *The Bell Curve.* New York: Free Press.

Hicks, J.R. 1942. *The Social Framework.* Oxford: Clarendon Press.

Hirsch, F. 1977. *Social Limits to Growth.* London: Routledge and Kegan Paul.

Hirschman, A.O. 1977. *The Passions and the Interests.* Princeton: Princeton University Press.

Hobbes, T. 1973. *Leviathan.* London: Dent.

Hodge, R.W., P.M. Siegel and P.H. Rossi. 1966. 'Occupational Prestige in the United States: 1925–63', in R. Bendix and S.M. Lipset (eds), *Class, Status and Power.* Glencoe: The Free Press, pp. 322–34.

Hsu, F.L.K. 1963. *Clan, Caste and Club.* Princeton: Van Nostrand.

Huizinga, J. 1924. *The Waning of the Middle Ages.* London: Edwin Arnold.

Hutton, J.H. 1946. *Caste in India.* Cambridge: Cambridge University Press.

Ibbetson, D. 1916. *Panjab Castes.* Lahore: Government Press.

Irschick, E.F. 1969. *Politics and Social Conflict in South India.* Berkeley: University of California Press.

Jencks, C. 1975. *Inequality.* Harmondsworth: Penguin Books.

Jencks, C. et al. 1979. *Who Gets Ahead?* New York: Basic Books.

Jensen, A.R. 1969. 'How Much Can We Boost IQ and Scholastic Achievement?', *Harvard Educational Review* 39(1): 1–123.

Jodhka, S.S. 2000. ' "Prejudice" without "Pollution?" ', *Journal of the Indian School of Political Economy* XII (3&4): 381–403.

Joseph, K. and J. Sumption. 1979. *Equality.* London: John Murray.

Joshi, P.C. 1975. *Land Reforms in India.* Bombay: Allied Publishers.

Kakar, S. 1978. *The Inner World.* Delhi: Oxford University Press.

Kane, P.V. 1974. *History of Dharmasastra.* Poona: Bhandarkar Oriental Institute, 2nd edn. vol. 2, part 1.

Kannan, C.T. 1963. *Intercaste and Inter-community Marriage in India.* Bombay: Allied Publishers.

Kapadia, K.M. 1958. *Marriage and Family in India.* Bombay: Oxford University Press.

Karve, I. 1968. *Hindu Society: An Interpretation.* Poona: Deshmukh Prakashan.

Kolakowski, L. 1982. *Religion.* London: Fontana.

Kothari, R. (ed.). 1970. *Caste in Indian Politics.* Delhi: Orient Longman.

Kuznets, S. 1955. 'Economic Growth and Income Inequality', *American Economic Review* 45(1): 257–87.

Lane, D. 1971. *The End of Inequality?* Harmondsworth: Penguin Books.

Larson, G.J. and R.S. Bhattacharya (eds). 1987. *Encyclopedia of Indian Philosophy: Samkhya*. Princeton: Princeton University Press.

Laslett, P. 1977. *Family Life and Illicit Love in Earlier Generations*. Cambridge: Cambridge University Press.

Laslett, P. (ed.). 1972. *Household and Family in Past Times*. Cambridge: Cambridge University Press.

Leach E.R. (ed.). 1960. *Aspects of Caste in South India, Ceylon and North–West Pakistan*. Cambridge: Cambridge University Press.

Leacock, E. 1978. 'Women's Status in Egalitarian Society', *Current Anthropology* 19(2): 247–75.

Letwin, W. (ed.). 1983. *Against Equality*. London: Macmillan.

Lévi-Strauss, C. 1966. *The Savage Mind*. London: Weidenfeld & Nicolson.

Lingat, R. 1973. *The Classical Law of India*. Berkeley: University of California Press.

Linton, R. 1936. *The Study of Man*. New York: Appleton Century.

Lipset, S.M. and R. Bendix. 1967. *Social Mobility in Industrial Society*. Berkeley: University of California Press.

Lockwood, D. 1958. *The Blackcoated Worker*. London: Allen and Unwin.

—— 1992. *Solidarity and Schism*. Oxford: Clarendon Press.

—— 1996. 'Comment on Béteille', *The British Journal of Sociology* 47(3): 527–9.

Lovejoy, A.O. 1964. *The Great Chain of Being*. Cambridge, Mass.: Harvard University Press.

Lowie, R.H. 1960. *Primitive Society*. London: Routledge and Kegan Paul.

Lucas, J.R. 1965. 'Against Equality', *Philosophy* 40(154): 296–307.

Luhmann, N. 1982. *The Differentiation of Society*. New York: Columbia University Press.

MacCormack, C. and M. Strathern (eds). 1980. *Nature, Culture and Gender*. Cambridge: Cambridge University Press.

Macpherson, C.B. 1962. *The Political Theory of Possessive Individualism*. Oxford: Clarendon Press.

Madan, T.N. 1980. *Doctors and Society*. Delhi: Vikas

—— 1988. *Family and Kinship*. Delhi: Oxford University Press.

Maine, H.S. 1950. *Ancient Law*. London: Oxford University Press.

Manu. 1964. *The Law of Manu* (trans. G. Buhler). Delhi: Motilal Banarasidas.

Marriott, M. 1959. 'Interactional and Attributional Theories of Caste Ranking', *Man in India* 39(2): 92–107.

—— 1968. 'Caste Ranking and Food Transactions', in M. Singer and B.S. Cohn (eds). *Structure and Change in Indian Society*, Chicago: Aldine, pp. 133–71.

Marriott, M. (ed.). 1990. *India through Hindu Categories*. New Delhi: Sage.

Marriott, M. and R.B. Inden. 1974. 'Caste Systems', *Encyclopedia Britannica* (Macropedia) 3: 982–91.

Marshall, T.H. 1977. *Class, Citizenship and Social Development*. Chicago: University of Chicago Press.

Marx, K. 1954. *Capital*, vol. 1. Moscow: Progress Publishers.

—— 1959. *Capital*, vol. 3. Moscow: Progress Publishers.

Marx, K. and F. Engels. 1968. *The German Ideology*. Moscow: Progress Publishers.

Mayer, A.C. 1960. *Caste and Kinship in Central India*. London: Routledge and Kegan Paul.

Mead, M. 1963. *Sex and Temperament in Three Primitive Societies*. New York: Morrow.

Merton, R.K. 1957. *Social Theory and Social Structure*. Glencoe: The Free Press.

Mills, C.W. 1951. *White Collar*. New York: Oxford University Press.

—— 1956. *The Power Elite*. New York: Oxford University Press.

Moffatt, M. 1979. *An Untouchable Community in South India*. Princeton: Princeton University Press.

Molund, S. 1991. 'Sociology as Critical Understanding: An Interview with André Béteille', *Antropologiska Studier* 48: 31–47.

Montagu, Ashley. 1974. *Man's Most Dangerous Myth*. London: Oxford University Press.

Morgan, D.H.J. 1975. *Social Theory and the Family*. London: Routledge and Kegan Paul.

Morgan, L.H. 1964. *Ancient Society*. Cambridge, Mass.: Harvard University (Belknap) Press.

Myrdal, G. 1944. *An American Dilemma*. New York: Harper.

Nagel, T. 1977. 'Equal Treatment and Compensatory Discrimination', in M. Cohen, T. Nagel and T. Scanlon (eds), *Equality and Preferential Treatment*. Princeton: Princeton University Press, pp. 3–18.

Naipaul, V.S. 1964. *An Area of Darkness*. London: André Deutsch.

Nakane, Chie. 1975. 'Fieldwork in India', in A. Béteille and T.N. Madan (eds), *Encounter and Experience*. Delhi: Vikas, pp. 3–26.

Nandy, A. 1980. *At the Edge of Psychology*. Delhi: Oxford University Press.

Narain, D. (ed.). 1975. *Explorations in the Family and Other Essays*. Bombay: Thacker.

Navlakha, S. 1989. *Elites and Social Change*. New Delhi: Sage.

Nehru, J. 1961. *The Discovery of India*. Bombay: Asia Publishing House.

Nozick, R. 1980. *Anarchy, State and Utopia*. Oxford: Blackwell.

O'Malley, L.S.S. 1932. *Indian Caste Customs*. Cambridge: Cambridge University Press.

Padgaonkar, D. 1993. 'In Conversation with M.N. Srinivas', *Sunday Times of India*, 12 December.

Pande, S. 1986. *Trends of Occupational Mobility among Migrants*. Jaipur: Rawat.

Parsons, T. 1953. 'A Revised Analytical Approach to the Theory of Social Stratification', in R. Bendix and S.M. Lipset (eds), *Class, Status and Power*. Glenoce, IL: Free Press.

—— 1954. *Essays in Sociological Theory*, New York: The Free Press.

Parsons, T. 1965. 'Full Citizenship for the Negro American?', *Daedalus* 94(4): 1009–54.

—— 1966. *Societies*. Engelwood Cliffs, N.J.: Prentice-Hall.

—— 1968. 'Professions', in D.L. Sils (ed.), *International Encyclopedia of the Social Sciences*, vol. 12, New York: Macmillan, pp. 536–47.

Parsons, T. and R.F. Bales. 1956. *Family*. London: Routledge and Kegan Paul.

Perkin, H. 1989. *The Rise of Professional Society*. London: Routledge.

Pigou, A.C. (ed.). 1956. *Memorials of Alfred Marshall*. New York: Kelley and Millman.

Poulantzas, N. 1976. *Les Classes sociales dans le capitalisme aujourd'hui*. Paris: Seuil.

Radcliffe-Brown, A.R. 1952. 'Foreword', in M.N. Srinivas, *Religion and Society among the Coorgs of South India*. Oxford: Clarendon Press.

Rao, A.V.P.R. 1989. *Urbanization, Occupational Mobility and Integration*. Delhi: Deep and Deep.

Rawls, J. 1972. *A Theory of Justice*. London: Oxford University Press.

Ray, N. 1945. *Bangali Hindur Barnabhed*. Calcutta: Vishvabharati Granthalaya.

Raychaudhuri, T. 1988. *Europe Reconsidered*. Delhi: Oxford University Press.

Redfield, R. 1956. *Peasant Society and Culture*. Chicago: University of Chicago Press.

Rege, M.P. 1984. *Concepts of Justice and Equality in the Indian Tradition*. Pune: Gokhale Institute.

—— 1988. 'Dharma: Man, Society and Polity', *New Quest* 69: 133–40.

Reuck, A. de and J. Knight (eds). 1968. *Caste and Race*. London: J. & A. Churchill.

Risley, H.H. 1892. *The Tribes and Castes of Bengal*. Calcutta: Bengal Secretariat Press.

—— 1969. *The People of India*. New Delhi: Oriental Books.

Rivers, W.H.R. 1924. *Social Organization*. London: Kegan Paul.

Robinson, R.V. (ed.). 1985. *Research in Social Stratification and Mobility*, vol. 5. Greenwich, Conn.: Jai Press.

Roemer, J.E. 1998. *Equality of Opportunity*. Cambridge, Mass.: Harvard University Press.

Rousseau, J.-J. 1938. *The Social Contract and Discourses*. London: J.M. Dent.

Rowe, W.L. 1973. 'Caste, Kinship and Association in Urban India', in A. Southall (ed.), *Urban Anthropology*. New York: Oxford University Press.

Rudra, A. 1989. 'The Intelligentsia as a Ruling Class', *Economic and Political Weekly* 24(3): 142–50.

Runciman, W.G. 1966. *Relative Deprivation and Social Justice*. London: Routledge and Kegan Paul.

Sahlins, M.D. 1968. *Tribesmen*. Englewood Cliffs: Prentice Hall.

Schneider, D.M. 1968. *American Kinship*. Englewood Cliffs: Prentice Hall.

Schneider, D.M. and K. Gough (eds). 1961. *Matrilineal Kinship*. Berkeley: University of California Press.

Sen, A. 1973. *On Economic Inequality*. Oxford: Blackwell.

—— 1992. *Inequality Re-examined*. Oxford: Clarendon Press.

Senart, É. 1930. *Caste in India*. London: Methuen.

Shah, A.M. 1973. *The Household Dimension of the Family in India*. Delhi: Orient Longman.

Shah, G. 2000. 'Hope and Despair', *Journal of the Indian School of Political Economy* XII(3 & 4): 459–72.

Shils, E.A. 1972. *The Intellectuals and the Powers*. Chicago: Chicago University Press.

—— 1975. *Center and Periphery*. Chicago: Chicago University Press.

—— 1981. *Tradition*. Chicago: Chicago University Press.

Sivaramayya, B. 1984. *Inequalities and the Law*. Lucknow: Eastern Book Company.

Smelser, N.J. 1962. *Theory of Collective Behaviour*. New York: Free Press.

Sombart, W. 1906. *Warum Gibt es in den Vereinigen Staaten keinen Sozialismus?* Tuebingen: J.C.B. Mohr.

Srinivas, M.N. 1952. *Religion and Society among the Coorgs of South India*. Oxford: Clarendon Press.

—— 1962. *Caste in Modern India and Other Essays*. Bombay: Asia Publishing House.

—— 1966. *Social Change in Modern India*. Berkeley: University of California Press.

—— 1968. 'Mobility in the Caste System', in M. Singer and B.S. Cohn (eds), *Structure and Change in Indian Society*. Chicago: Aldine, pp. 189–200.

Srinivas, M.N. and A. Béteille. 1964. 'Networks in Indian Social Structure', *Man* 64(212): 165–8.

Suleiman, E.N. 1978. *Elites in French Society*. Princeton: Princeton University Press.

Svalastoga, K. 1959. *Prestige, Class and Mobility*. Copenhagen: Glyndendal.

Tapper, R. (ed.). 1983. *The Conflict of Tribe and State in Iran and Afghanistan*. London: Croom Helm.

Tawney, R.H. 1964. *Equality*. London: Unwin Books.

Thurston, E. 1909. *Castes and Tribes of Southern India*. Madras: Government Press, 7 vols.

Tocqueville, A. de. 1956. *Democracy in America*. New York: Alfred Knopf, 2 vols.

Treiman, D.J. 1977. *Occupational Prestige in Contemporary Perspective*. New York: Academic University Press.

Treiman, D.J. and R.V. Robinson (eds). 1981. *Research in Social Stratification and Mobility*, vol. 1. Greenwich, Conn.: Jai Press.

Trevelyan, G.O. 1964. *The Competition Wallah*. London: Macmillan.

Varma, P.K. 1998. *The Great Indian Middle Class*. Delhi: Viking.

Visvanathan, S. 1985. *Organizing for Science*. Delhi: Oxford University Press.

Warner, W.L. 1941. 'Introduction', in A. Davis, B.B. Gardner and M.R. Gardner, *Deep South*. Chicago: University of Chicago Press.

Warner, W.L. and P.S. Lunt. 1941. *The Social Life of a Modern Community*. New Haven: Yale University Press.

Waugh, E. 1937. *Decline and Fall*. Harmondsworth: Penguin Books.

Weber, M. 1958. *The Religion of India*. New York: Free Press.

—— 1978. *Economy and Society*. Berkeley: University of California Press, 2 vols.

West, C. 1993. *Race Matters*. Boston: Beacon Press.

Whitehead, A.N. 1959. *Symbolism*. New York: Capricorn Books.

Williams, B. 1964. 'The Idea of Equality', in P. Laslett and W.G. Runciman (eds), *Philosophy, Politics and Society* (2nd series). Oxford: Basil Blackwell, pp. 110–31.

Wolf, E.R. 1982. *Europe and the People Without History*. Berkeley: University of California Press.

Woodburn, J. 1982. 'Egalitarian Societies', *Man* (N.S.) 17: 431–51.

Young, M. 1961. *The Rise of Meritocracy*. London: Thames and Hudson.

Zaehner, R.C. (ed.). 1969. *The Bhagvad Gita*. London: Oxford University Press.

Name Index

Subject Index